Anonymous

Acts of the General Assembly of the state of Virginia,

Passed at called session, 1863: in the eighty-eighth year of the Commonwealth

Anonymous

Acts of the General Assembly of the state of Virginia,
Passed at called session, 1863: in the eighty-eighth year of the Commonwealth

ISBN/EAN: 9783337811013

Printed in Europe, USA, Canada, Australia, Japan

Cover: Foto ©ninafisch / pixelio.de

More available books at **www.hansebooks.com**

ACTS

OF THE

GENERAL ASSEMBLY

OF THE

STATE OF VIRGINIA,

PASSED AT CALLED SESSION, 1863,

IN THE

EIGHTY-EIGHTH YEAR OF THE COMMONWEALTH.

RICHMOND:
WILLIAM F. RITCHIE, PUBLIC PRINTER.
1863.

PUBLIC OR GENERAL ACTS.

CHAP. 1.—An ACT amending and re-enacting the 109th section of an act entitled an act imposing Taxes for the Support of Government, passed March 28th, 1863.

Passed September 14, 1863.

1. Be it enacted by the general assembly, that the one hundred and ninth section of an act entitled an act imposing taxes for the support of government, passed March twenty-eighth, eighteen hundred and sixty-three, shall be and the same is hereby amended and re-enacted so as to read as follows: Act of 1863 amended

"§ 109. Be it enacted by the general assembly, that the Confederate States treasury notes shall hereafter be receivable by sheriffs and other collecting officers in payment of taxes and other public dues to this state." What notes receivable in payment of taxes

2. This act shall be in force from its passage. Commencement

CHAP. 2.—An ACT authorizing the payment of Fees of Commissioners of the Revenue.

Passed October 31, 1863.

1. Be it enacted by the general assembly, that if fees for issuing a license to which a commissioner of the revenue is entitled, shall be included in the tax on the license, and paid into the treasury, it shall be lawful for the auditor of public accounts to pay to the commissioner the amount of fees to which he is entitled; to be paid by warrant upon the treasury, out of any money therein not otherwise appropriated. Fees of commissioners, how paid

2. This act shall be in force from its passage. Commencement

CHAP. 3.—An ACT declaring what Contracts shall be payable in Currency.

Passed October 14, 1863.

1. Be it enacted by the general assembly, that every contract made on or after the twentieth day of October eighteen hundred and sixty-three, for the payment of money, shall be deemed to be for the payment of the sum expressed or implied, in the currency which at the time the contract becomes payable, shall be receivable in payments to this state, unless this intendment shall be expressly excluded. What contracts payable in currency

2. This act shall be in force from its passage, and until the expiration of six months after a treaty of peace between the Confederate States and the United States. Commencement and duration

CHAP. 4.—An ACT to suppress the further issuing of Small Notes as a Currency by the Counties, Cities and Towns of this Commonwealth.

Passed September 22, 1863.

1. Be it enacted by the general assembly, that from and after the passage of this act, it shall not be lawful for any county, city or town within this commonwealth to issue, or put in circulation as a currency, any note, scrip or certificate; and all the acts and parts of County, city or town not to issue small notes

acts heretofore enacted authorizing such issues, are hereby repealed: **Proviso** provided, however, that this act shall not be so construed as to prevent the circulation of all such notes as may have been issued by such county, city or town previous to the passage of this act, and not redeemed; but when once redeemed, the said note, scrip or certificate shall not again be put in circulation: and provided further, that this act shall not be so construed as to prevent the several counties, cities and towns of this commonwealth from issuing any bond or bonds, under and by virtue of the laws authorizing such issues, and now in force.

Commencement 2. This act shall be in force from its passage.

CHAP. 5.—An ACT making an Appropriation to pay certain Expenses of Government.

Passed September 26, 1863.

Appropriation 1. Be it enacted by the general assembly, that in addition to the money appropriated by the act entitled an act appropriating the public revenue for the fiscal year eighteen hundred and sixty-two and three, passed March twenty-eighth, eighteen hundred and sixty-three, there be appropriated the following sums, to wit:

General assembly To pay the per diem, mileage and other expenses of the general assembly, incurred in the September session eighteen hundred and sixty-three, sixty thousand dollars.

Convicts To pay for subsistence and other supplies for the support of convicts and transports in the penitentiary, thirty thousand dollars.

Officers and privates To pay officers and privates, for rations, clothing and other allowances to the public guard, and ordnance sergeant at the military institute, including temporary quarters, thirty thousand dollars.

Lieut. E. S. Gay To pay Lieutenant E. S. Gay, the amount of a judgment in his favor, rendered by the circuit court of the city of Richmond, five hundred and eighty-four dollars and forty cents.

Slaves condemned To pay for slaves condemned and executed, or reprieved for sale and transportation, fifteen thousand dollars.

Claims allowed by auditing board To pay claims allowed, or which may be allowed by the auditing board, and when required by the act passed March twenty-eighth, eighteen hundred and sixty-three, to be reported by them to the general assembly for an appropriation by law, an amount not exceeding five thousand dollars.

Commencement 2. This act shall be in force from its passage.

CHAP. 6.—An ACT to amend and re-enact the 1st and 3d sections of an act passed March 13th, 1863, entitled an act to amend and re-enact an act further to provide for the Public Defence, passed October 3d, 1862.

Passed October 10, 1863.

Act of 1863 amended Be it enacted by the general assembly, that the first and third sections of the act passed March thirteenth, eighteen hundred and sixty-three, entitled an act to amend and re-enact an act further to provide for the public defence, passed October third, eighteen hundred and sixty-two, be amended and re-enacted so as to read as follows:

Duty of governor "§ 1. Be it enacted by the general assembly, that it shall be the duty of the governor of this commonwealth, and he is hereby authorized and required, whenever thereto requested by the president of **Slaves, how called out** the Confederate States, to call into the service of the Confederate States, for labor on fortifications and other works for the public defence within this state, from time to time, for a period not exceeding sixty days, a number of male slaves between the ages of eighteen and **Limitation as to number** fifty-five years, not exceeding ten thousand at any one time, and not **Per centage in counties** exceeding in any county, city or town one-fifth of the number of male slaves therein between the ages specified; to be apportioned by the governor. Such requisition shall be apportioned ratably among all the slaveholders in the several counties, cities and towns on which the requisition shall be made, so as to charge each slaveholder with the same proportion of his male slaves between the ages specified, capable of performing ordinary labor, to be judged of by the court, which may be demanded from his county, city or town: provided, however, that the governor, in his discretion, may exempt, wholly or partially, from the operation of this act, such counties as may have lost so large a portion of their slaves, in consequence of their escape to the public enemy, as will materially affect the agricultural products of such counties: and provided further, that it shall be the duty of the governor to exempt from the operation of this act, both in regard to any requisitions now being made, and those which may hereafter be made, any county which has had its slaves, subject to requisition under this act, reduced one-fourth, in consequence of their escape to the public enemy; of which loss he shall judge upon the certificate of the county court, and such other evidence and information as he may deem proper. And the governor may exempt such other counties as, from their geographical position or contiguity to the public enemy, he may deem expedient. And in any county, city or town partially exempted under this act, any person who may satisfy its county or corporation court, or any person appointed by the governor for that purpose, that he or she has lost one-third part of his or her slaves liable to work on the public works, by said slaves going over to the enemy, shall be exempted from the operations of this act. The sum of twenty dollars per month for each slave shall be paid by the Confederate States to the person entitled to his services, and soldiers' rations, medicines and medical attendance furnished, and the value of all such slaves as may die during their term of service, or thereafter, from injuries received, or of diseases contracted in such service, or not be returned to their owners, shall be paid by the Confederate States to the owners of such slaves; and full compensation shall be made for all injuries received whilst in the service of the Confederate States: provided, that the Confederate States shall not be liable for any slave not returned by reason of fraud and collusion on the part of his owner or agent; or if his death should be caused by the act of God, or by disease of such slave existing when received by the confederate authorities; and in all cases the burden of proof shall be on the authorities of the Confederate States, to discharge the latter from liability to the former. Hired slaves shall be regarded as the slaves of their temporary owners, in apportioning for the purposes of this act; but when hired slaves shall be held by persons owning other slaves, it shall not be lawful for the temporary owner to select one or more of the hired slaves to be sent to the public works; but in every such case, the slave or slaves to be sent, shall be ascertained by lot, in which each of said slaves shall be drawn for by the court: provided further, that slaves removed from counties overrun by the public enemy, and in possession of the owner, shall not be liable to this act, except in cases where such owner has more than three slaves subject to requisition. And in cases where, by reason of sickness or by other calamity, a slaveholder shall have but one male slave liable to the provisions of this act, who is able to render the service required by this act, it shall be competent for the governor, in his discretion, to exempt said slaveholder from the impressment or draft."

How apportioned · *Proviso as to certain counties* · *When other counties may be exempted* · *When party has lost one-third of slaves* · *Compensation* · *Responsibility of confederate government* · *When not responsible* · *Hired slaves*

"§ 3. It shall be the duty of the several county and corporation courts, after being duly convened as aforesaid, and not less than five justices being present, to ascertain, by the assistance of the commissioners of the revenue of their respective counties and corporations, or otherwise, the entire number of male slaves therein between the ages specified, subject to requisition under this act; and after ascertaining the same, to apportion the requisition aforesaid, without delay,

Duty of county courts · *Commissioners of revenue* · *Requisitions, how apportioned*

among all the holders of such slaves, so as to charge each slaveholder, as near as may be, with the same proportion of his male slaves between the ages of eighteen and fifty-five, capable of performing ordinary labor, as may be demanded from his county, city or town, throwing into classes, when necessary, the holders of but one or a few slaves, and of fractions of slaves, and ascertaining, by lot, or agreement between the parties, or otherwise, the slave or slaves to be sent to the public works from such classes, and giving, as far as practicable, relief to those upon whom the lot or draft may have fallen under any preceding requisition: provided, that in no case of a soldier in service, or a widow having a son therein, or whose husband has died in such service, owning or hiring but one male slave, shall such slave be subject to requisition under this act. But no slaveholder shall be exempted by reason of having slaves in the employment of the state or confederate government."

Classes, when made

Proviso as to soldiers

Commencement

2. This act shall be in force from its passage.

CHAP. 7.—An ACT to authorize the Governor to call out Forces for the Public Defence.

Passed September 28, 1863.

Volunteers, how called out

1. Be it enacted by the general assembly, that the governor of this commonwealth be and he is hereby authorized to call into the service of the state, for a period not exceeding sixty days at any one time, as many volunteers as may be necessary to repel invasion and protect the citizens of the state, whenever in his opinion the emergency may demand it, and to organize, arm and equip the same with as little delay as possible. No company shall be organized under this act with less than thirty men; and companies of less than fifty men shall have a captain, one first lieutenant and one second lieutenant. In other respects the present militia law shall be observed, so far as the governor deems it applicable: provided, that this act shall not be so construed as to call into the field, without their consent, companies organized under an act entitled an act to organize a home guard, passed the fourteenth May eighteen hundred and sixty-two.

Companies

Proviso as to home guard

Existing organizations to be armed

2. He shall preserve and arm existing organizations, except those for home defence and local service, as far as practicable, and shall apply to the secretary of war for such arms, ammunition and camp equipage as may be necessary.

Act, how published

3. He shall promulgate this act by special messengers and otherwise, at his discretion.

Commencement

4. This act shall be in force from its passage.

CHAP. 8.—An ACT amending and re-enacting the 6th and 11th sections of an act passed March 30th, 1863, entitled an act to provide for the Production and Distribution of Salt.

Passed September 18, 1863.

Act of 1863 amended

1. Be it enacted by the general assembly of Virginia, that the sixth and eleventh sections of the act passed March thirtieth, eighteen hundred and sixty-three, entitled an act to provide for the production and distribution of salt, be amended and re-enacted so as to read as follows:

Control of transportation

"§ 6. The superintendent, under the control of the board of supervisors, shall have control of transportation on the several rail roads in the commonwealth, for the conveyance of supplies to the salt works, and for the distribution of salt throughout the state, with power, if necessary, to impress the same. He shall make distribution among the several counties, cities and towns, from day to day,

Salt, how sold and delivered

or from time to time, and in quantities proportioned to their whole populations respectively, including refugees sojourning therein, as may be directed by the said board of supervisors: provided the superintendent, under the direction of the board of supervisors, shall distribute salt with reference to cattle and other stock requiring salt, after distributing twenty pounds to each person." Refugees

"§ 11. The salt so manufactured shall be sold at cost for cash, and be distributed to the different counties, cities and towns, through duly accredited agents, to be appointed by the county and corporation courts respectively; or where said courts cannot meet because of the presence or proximity of the public enemy, by the board of supervisors, on the recommendation of any three or more justices of said county, or of the senator or delegate or delegates representing such county in the general assembly: and in order to do so, it shall be the duty of the board of supervisors from time to time to ascertain as near as may be the actual cost of production and distribution, and fix the price accordingly, so as to cover such entire cost." Salt, how distributed Price

2. This act shall be in force from its passage. Commencement

CHAP. 9.—An ACT to amend and re-enact the 11th section of the act for the Production and Distribution of Salt, passed March 30th, 1863, as amended by the act passed September 18th, 1863.

Passed October 30, 1863.

1. Be it enacted by the general assembly, that the eleventh section of the act passed March thirtieth, eighteen hundred and sixty-three, entitled an act to provide for the production and distribution of salt, as amended by the act passed September eighteenth, eighteen hundred and sixty-three, entitled an act amending and re-enacting the sixth and eleventh sections of an act passed March thirtieth, eighteen hundred and sixty-three, entitled an act to provide for the production and distribution of salt, be and the same is hereby amended and re-enacted so as to read as follows: Act of 1863 amended

"§ 11. The salt so manufactured shall be sold at cost for cash, and be distributed to the different counties, cities and towns, through duly accredited agents to be appointed by the county and corporation courts respectively; or when said courts cannot meet because of the presence or proximity of the public enemy, by the board of supervisors, on the recommendation of any three or more justices of said county, or of the senator and delegate or delegates representing such county in the general assembly: and in order to do so, it shall be the duty of the board of supervisors from time to time to ascertain as near as may be the actual cost of production and distribution, and fix the price accordingly, so as to cover such entire cost. But no agent of any county or corporation hereafter appointed, shall be entitled to act as such until he shall have given bond, with sufficient sureties, in the penalty of not less than ten thousand nor more than thirty thousand dollars, conditioned for the faithful distribution of the salt received by him, among the people of his county or corporation. Said bonds shall be taken by the said courts when the appointments are made by them, and in all other cases, by the board of supervisors: and such agents shall distribute to refugees, and to persons temporarily sojourning in their counties, cities and towns, as well as to permanent citizens thereof: provided, however, that the said courts and the said board shall respectively have power to revoke any appointment of agent heretofore or hereafter made by them, whenever they deem it proper to do so, and shall in like manner appoint another agent in place of the one so removed." Salt, how sold and delivered Price, how fixed Salt to be distributed to refugees Proviso

2. This act shall be in force from its passage. Commencement

CHAP. 10.—An ACT making an appropriation for the Purchase of Salt
Passed October 29, 1863.

Amount appropriated

1. Be it enacted by the general assembly, that in order to carry into full effect a contract made by and between Robert A. Coghill, chairman of senate committee, and James V. Brooke, chairman of house committee, of the one part, and Stuart, Buchanan & Co. and Charles Scott & Co. of the other part, said contract bearing date the twenty-seventh day of October eighteen hundred and sixty-three, and ratified by the general assembly by joint resolution passed the twenty-ninth day of October eighteen hundred and sixty-three, there is appropriated the sum of eighty thousand dollars; which sum is placed at the disposal of the board of supervisors of salt, by them to be disbursed in payment of the salt contracted for in said contract.

Commencement

2. This act shall be in force from its passage.

CHAP. 11.—An ACT to amend the 1st, 2d, 3d, 4th, 5th, 13th, 14th and 16th sections of chapter 14; the 14th section of chapter 21; the 27th section of chapter 23, and the 10th section of chapter 66 of the Code of Virginia (edition of 1860), so as to increase the Salaries of certain Officers of the Government.
Passed October 13, 1863.

Code amended

1. Be it enacted by the general assembly, that the first, second, third, fourth, fifth, thirteenth, fourteenth and sixteenth sections of chapter fourteen of the Code of Virginia (edition of eighteen hundred and sixty) be and the same are hereby amended and re-enacted so as to read as follows:

"§ 1. The several officers herein after mentioned shall receive annually from the public treasury the following sums, that is to say:

In the executive department.

Salaries in executive department

"The governor the sum of five thousand dollars; the secretary of the commonwealth, four thousand dollars; the assistant clerk, the sum of seventeen hundred and fifty dollars, and the copying clerk, fifteen hundred dollars.

In the office of the auditor of public accounts.

Salaries in office of auditor of public accounts

"§ 2. The auditor of public accounts shall receive the sum of four thousand dollars; the clerk of accounts, two thousand five hundred dollars; the first clerk, seventeen hundred and fifty dollars, and the second, third and fourth clerks, each the sum of fifteen hundred dollars.

In the second auditor's office.

In second auditor's office

"§ 3. The second auditor shall receive the sum of thirty-five hundred dollars; the first clerk, the sum of seventeen hundred and fifty dollars, and the second, third and fourth clerks, each the sum of fifteen hundred dollars.

In the treasurer's office.

In treasurer's office

"§ 4. The treasurer shall receive the sum of thirty-five hundred dollars; the first clerk, the sum of seventeen hundred and fifty dollars; the second clerk, fifteen hundred dollars; and the third clerk, to be denominated clerk of the banking department, an increase from the treasury to make his salary fifteen hundred dollars.

Clerk of banking department

In the land office.

Register's office

"§ 5. The register of the land office shall receive the sum of thirty-five hundred dollars; the first clerk, the sum of seventeen hundred and fifty dollars, and the second clerk, the sum of fifteen hundred dollars."

Clerk of senate,

"§ 13. The clerk of the senate, who is hereby required to prepare an index to the journal of the senate and the documents printed by its order, shall receive an annual salary of twenty-two hundred and fifty dollars; the clerk of the house of delegates, who is hereby required to keep the rolls, to prepare an index to the journal of the house of delegates and the documents, to prepare tables of the places of holding separate elections and of the terms of the courts, as required by the sixteenth chapter, shall receive an annual salary of twenty-five hundred dollars. The further sum of fifty dollars per week during the session of the general assembly shall be allowed to the clerk of the senate, and the same sum to the clerk of the house of delegates, to enable each of said clerks to employ one assistant. Hereafter, at the expiration of each annual session of the general assembly, it shall be the duty of the clerk of the house of delegates to prepare for publication a sketch or synopsis of the several acts and joint resolutions passed during the session. For the services hereby required, the said clerk shall receive fifty dollars.

duties and salaries

Clerk house of delegates, duties and salary

Assistant clerks senate and house of delegates

Sketch of acts, when to be prepared

"§ 14. The sergeant at arms of the senate and the sergeant at arms of the house of delegates shall each receive the sum of fifty dollars per week during the session of the general assembly. Each of said sergeants shall be allowed for taking any person into custody, by the order of the house, two dollars; for every day he detains such person in custody, two dollars; and for the travel of himself or a messenger to take any person into custody by such order, eight cents per mile going, and the same returning. The doorkeepers of both houses shall receive the sum of fifty dollars each week during the session of the general assembly. The clerks of the several standing committees in each house shall be allowed for their services forty dollars per week until discharged; that is to say: In the senate, the clerk of the committee on roads and internal navigation; the clerk of the committees on general laws and of confederate relations; the clerk of the committees for courts of justice and of finance; and the clerk of the committees on public institutions, of privileges and elections and on banks. And in the house of delegates, the clerk of the committees for courts of justice and of schools and colleges; the clerk of the committees of propositions and of claims; the clerk of the committee on finance; the clerk of the committees of privileges and elections and on agriculture and manufactures; the clerk of the committees on banks and on military affairs; and the clerk of the committee of roads and internal navigation. The said clerks shall be appointed by the clerk of the senate and the clerk of the house of delegates respectively, and shall perform the duties of clerks of any other committees in their respective houses, and any similar service that may be required of them, without additional compensation."

Sergeant at arms

Doorkeepers

Clerks of committees

How appointed

Duties

The sixteenth section of chapter fourteen of the Code, as amended by the act passed March twenty-eighth, eighteen hundred and sixty-three, entitled an act to amend and re-enact the sixteenth and eighteenth sections of the fourteenth chapter of the Code of Virginia, so as to increase the salaries of certain officers of the penitentiary, is hereby further amended and re-enacted so as to read as follows:

Code amended

"§ 16. The superintendent of the penitentiary shall receive the sum of two thousand five hundred dollars; the first assistant keeper, one thousand dollars; the second, third, fourth, fifth, sixth and seventh assistant keepers, each nine hundred dollars. Moreover, each of said assistant keepers shall be allowed one hundred dollars worth of the manufactures of the penitentiary, at the prices fixed by the directors, every year in which the labor and manufactures thereof shall amount to the sum of thirty-two thousand dollars. The surgeon of the penitentiary and public guard shall receive the sum of one thousand dollars."

Superintendent and officers of penitentiary, their salary

Surgeon

2. The fourteenth section of chapter twenty-one of the Code of Virginia (edition of eighteen hundred and sixty) is hereby amended and re-enacted so as to read as follows:

Code amended

Superintendent of public buildings

"§ 14. The superintendent of public buildings shall receive annually out of the treasury a salary of eight hundred dollars, payable as other salaries are paid. He shall also receive annually out of the treasury a reasonable sum, to be appropriated thereto, not to exceed eight hundred dollars, payable monthly out of the civil contingent fund, to enable him to pay the servants and assistants he may have to employ."

Code amended

Act of 1862 amended

3. The twenty-seventh section of chapter twenty-three of the Code of Virginia (edition of eighteen hundred and sixty), as amended by an act passed February twenty-first, eighteen hundred and sixty-two, entitled an act to amend section twenty-seven of chapter twenty-four of the Code (new edition), providing for a clerk in the adjutant general's office, is hereby further amended and re-enacted so as to read as follows:

Adjutant general's office

"§ 27. The adjutant general shall receive for his services thirty-five hundred dollars, payable as other salaries are paid. He shall appoint one clerk in his office, who shall receive a salary of seventeen hundred and fifty dollars, to be paid as other salaries are paid. He shall reside at or near, and shall keep his office at the seat of government; but when the public service shall render it expedient, the governor may direct him to remove with his office to any other place within the state."

Code amended

4. The tenth section of chapter sixty-six of the Code of Virginia (edition of eighteen hundred and sixty) is hereby amended and re-enacted so as to read as follows:

Secretary may be appointed

"§ 10. The board of public works shall have power to appoint a secretary, whose salary shall be annually twenty-two hundred and fifty dollars. He shall keep a record of the official acts of the board, and shall discharge such other duties as may be prescribed by the board. The proceedings of each day shall be signed by the person presiding on that day. The said proceedings shall be at all times open to inspection."

When computation of salaries to commence

5. The salary of each of the officers mentioned in the preceding sections of this act shall commence on, and be computed from the first day of April eighteen hundred and sixty-three: provided, that this section shall not be construed to apply to persons not now in office.

Limitation as to fees
Exception

6. No officer whose salary is hereby increased, except the clerk of the senate and the clerk of the house of delegates, shall receive from the treasury any other compensation for services hereafter rendered, by virtue of his office aforesaid, than the salary aforesaid; and the fees and other perquisites hereafter accruing and now allowed by law to any such officer, shall be paid by him into the public treasury.

Commencement

7. This act shall be in force from its passage, and shall continue in force for twelve months after the ratification of a treaty of peace between the United States and the Confederate States of America.

CHAP. 12.—An ACT to amend and re-enact the 14th section of chapter 14 of the Code of Virginia, as amended and re-enacted by an act entitled an act to amend the 1st. 2d, 3d, 4th, 5th, 13th, 14th and 16th sections of chapter 14; the 14th section of chapter 21; the 27th section of chapter 23, and the 10th section of chapter 66 of the Code of Virginia (edition of 1860), so as to increase the salaries of certain Officers of the Government, passed October 13th, 1863.

Passed October 26, 1863.

Act of 1863 amended

1. Be it enacted by the general assembly, that the fourteenth section of chapter fourteen of the Code of Virginia, as amended and re-enacted by the first section of an act entitled an act to amend the first, second, third, fourth, fifth, thirteenth, fourteenth and sixteenth sections of chapter fourteen; the fourteenth section of chapter twenty-one; the twenty-seventh section of chapter twenty-three, and the

tenth section of chapter sixty-six of the Code of Virginia (edition of eighteen hundred and sixty), so as to increase the salaries of certain officers of the government, passed October thirteenth, eighteen hundred and sixty-three, be amended and re-enacted so as to read as follows:

"§ 14. The sergeant at arms of the senate and the sergeant at arms of the house of delegates shall each receive the sum of fifty dollars per week during the session of the general assembly. Each of said sergeants shall be allowed for taking any person into custody by the order of the house, two dollars; for every day he detains such person in custody, two dollars; and for the travel of himself or a messenger to take any person into custody by such order, eight cents per mile going and the same returning. The doorkeepers of both houses shall receive the sum of fifty dollars each week, during the session of the general assembly. The clerks of the several standing committees in each house shall be allowed for their services fifty dollars per week until discharged; that is to say: In the senate, the clerk of the committee of roads and internal navigation; the clerk of the committees on general laws and of confederate relations; the clerk of the committees for courts of justice and finance; and the clerk of the committees on public institutions, of privileges and elections and on banks. And in the house of delegates, the clerk of the committees for courts of justice and of schools and colleges; the clerk of the committees of propositions and of claims; the clerk of the committee on finance; the clerk of the committees of privileges and elections and on agriculture and manufactures; the clerk of the committees on banks and on military affairs, and the clerk of the committees of roads and internal navigation and on the penitentiary. The said clerks shall be appointed by the clerk of the senate and the clerk of the house of delegates respectively, and shall perform the duties of clerks of any other committees in their respective houses, and any similar service that may be required of them, without additional compensation."

Pay of sergeant at arms and doorkeepers

Clerks of committees

How appointed

Their duties

2. This act shall be in force from its passage.

Commencement

CHAP. 13.—An ACT amending and re-enacting the 1st and 3d sections of chapter 10 of the Code of Virginia (edition of 1860), so as to extend the time within which a person intending to contest the election of another as Senator or Delegate, may give notice.

Passed October 30, 1863.

1. Be it enacted by the general assembly, that the first and third sections of chapter ten of the Code of Virginia (edition of eighteen hundred and sixty) be amended and re-enacted so as to read as follows:

Code amended

"§ 1. Any person intending to contest the election of another, as senator or delegate to the general assembly, shall, within twenty days after the day on which the result of the election shall be ascertained, declared and certified, as provided by law, give to the other notice thereof in writing, and a list of the votes he will dispute, with his objections to each, and of the votes improperly rejected, for which he will contend. If he object to the legality of the election, or eligibility of the person elected, the notice shall set forth the objections; and the person whose election is contested shall, within twenty days after receiving such notice, deliver to his adversary a like list of votes which he will dispute, with his objections, and of the votes improperly rejected, which he will claim, and notice of his objections, if any he has, to the eligibility of the contesting party. Each party shall append to the list of votes he intends to dispute or claim, an oath to the following effect: 'I do swear, that I have reason to believe the persons whose names are above mentioned, are

When notice may be given

List of votes

Objections

Eligibility

not legally qualified (or are qualified, as the case may be) to vote in the county of . (or corporation or district of).'"

In special elections

"§ 3. Where, however, such contest arises upon a special election to fill a vacancy, held at any other time than the general election day, the notice, with specifications as above, shall be given by the contesting party within ten days after the day on which the result of the election shall be ascertained, declared and certified, as provided by law; and by the party whose right is contested, within five

Depositions

days after receiving such notice; and they shall respectively begin to take depositions within ten days, and finish them within twenty days after the result of the election is declared and certified as aforesaid, unless further time shall be allowed by a resolution of the house in which the contest exists, or unless the legislature shall adjourn before the time aforesaid shall have expired; in which case the parties may continue to take depositions until within thirty days of the next meeting of the general assembly."

Commencement

2. This act shall be in force from its passage.

Chap. 14.—An ACT to suppress Gaming.

Passed October 16, 1863.

Code amended

1. Be it enacted by the general assembly, that the first, second and fourth sections of chapter one hundred and ninety-eight of the Code of Virginia (edition of eighteen hundred and sixty) be amended and re-enacted so as to read as follows:

Penalty for unlawful gaming Infamous offence

"§ 1. A free person who shall keep or exhibit a gaming table, commonly called A B C, or E O table, or faro bank, or table of like kind, under any denomination, whether the game or table be played with cards, or any evasive substitute for cards, dice, or otherwise, or who shall be a partner, or concerned in interest, or employed or engaged in any manner in the keeping or exhibiting such table or bank, or who shall permit the keeping or exhibition of such table or bank in any room or apartment of his house or premises, shall, upon conviction thereof, be deemed to be guilty of an infamous offence, in the meaning of the constitution of this state, and shall be confined in jail not less than two nor more than twelve months, and be fined not less than one hundred dollars nor more than one thousand dollars,

Whipping

and may, at the discretion of the court, be subjected to stripes on his

Property forfeited

bare back, not exceeding thirty-nine; and all the right, title and interest, legal or equitable, of such person in any real property, including the lot and premises thereto attached, in or upon which such gaming may be carried on, shall be absolutely forfeited to and vested in the

When property may be seized

commonwealth. Any such table or faro bank, and all money found thereon, or other property staked or exhibited to allure persons to bet at such table, and all household or other personal property used or employed in such gaming house, may be seized by order of a court, or under warrant of a justice, mayor of a city or town, or

Amount to person making seizure

judge in vacation; and the money so seized, after deducting therefrom one-half for the person or persons making the seizure, shall be forfeited, as provided in the twenty-fourth section of chapter fifty-one of the Code (edition of eighteen hundred and sixty), in respect to the forfeiture declared by that chapter: provided, that twenty per centum of the entire value of the property forfeited shall, in each case of conviction, be payable to the commonwealth's attorney who prosecuted the case.

Penalty for renting houses for gambling Hiring slaves

"§ 2. Be it further enacted, that any person who shall knowingly rent to any person any real property for such unlawful gaming, with intention to allow the use of the same for the purpose aforesaid, or any person who shall knowingly hire any slave to any such person, with intention to allow such slave to be employed in any service con-

Fines

nected with such gaming, shall be fined not less than one hundred dollars nor more than one thousand dollars; and upon conviction, all their right, title and interest, legal or equitable, in any such real estate, and their right to such slave, shall be absolutely forfeited to and vest in the commonwealth." Property, when forfeited

"§ 4. If a free person bet or play at any such table or bank as is mentioned in the first section, or if at any ordinary, race field or other public place, he play at any game except bowles, chess, backgammon, draughts, or a licensed game, or bet on the sides of those who play, he shall be fined not less than one hundred dollars nor more than one thousand dollars, and shall, if required by the court, give security for his good behavior for one year, or in default thereof, may be imprisoned not more than three months."

2. Be it further enacted, that any free negro who shall knowingly be engaged as a servant, and employed as such in any house or other place kept for such unlawful gaming, shall, upon conviction, be declared to be a slave for life, and sold into slavery. The trial and proceedings against such negro shall be the same, as far as applicable, as that prescribed by law for selling free negroes into slavery. Free negro, when to be sold

3. It shall be the duty of the court in which a conviction may be made, to order any property forfeited under this act to be sold for cash, and after paying all the expenses attending such sale, order one-half of the net proceeds to be paid to the informer, if there shall be an informer, and the residue to be paid into the treasury. Duty of court as to forfeited property

4. If only an equitable right or title to real estate shall be forfeited under this act, the purchaser shall be substituted by suit in equity to all the rights and remedies of the person convicted, in respect to such real estate. How, as to equitable title In all cases in which the person convicted is seized of the title in fee simple, or possessed of a less estate than the freehold in the real estate so sold, the court shall, upon payment of the purchase money into the treasury, order a conveyance to be made to the purchaser. Conveyance, how made

5. No conviction shall be had under this act, upon the testimony of any informer, without other or corroborative evidence, unless such informer shall disclaim any right to the proceeds of any forfeiture under this act. Corroborative evidence

6. It shall be the duty of every justice of the peace, or mayor of a city, who has probable cause to suspect that any house is kept for the purpose of exhibiting any game prohibited by this act, to issue his warrant, directed according to law, for the search and examination of the premises; When search and examination of suspected premises and if upon such search and examination it shall appear that such house is kept for the purpose of exhibiting and carrying on such unlawful gaming, or if it shall appear upon proof that such gaming has been exhibited and carried on, at any time within ten days previous to such search and examination, within such house, Proceedings after search it shall be the duty of the officer to seize and take possession of all property liable to forfeiture under this act, and to hold the same subject to the orders of the justice or mayor issuing the warrant. When officer to seize property And it shall be the duty of the justice or mayor to order the same to be held safely, to abide the orders of the court in which the prosecution may be had, except that gaming tables and money so seized may be disposed of as herein provided. Order as to safekeeping

7. It shall be the duty of the attorney for the commonwealth to file with the indictment or information a description in writing of the property liable to forfeiture; and upon conviction, the court shall immediately cause a rule to be served upon the owner to show cause against the forfeiture; and upon the return of the rule, the court shall proceed, without other pleadings, to determine the question of forfeiture. Duty of attorney for commonwealth

8. This act shall be in force from its passage. Commencement

CHAP. 15.—An ACT to amend and re-enact an act passed March 11th, 1863, entitled an act to amend the 39th section of chapter 184 of the Code of Virginia (edition of 1860) so as to increase the Compensation of Clerks and Sheriffs for Public Services.

Passed October 30, 1863.

Code amended

1. Be it enacted by the general assembly, that the act passed March the eleventh, eighteen hundred and sixty-three, entitled an act to amend the thirty-ninth section of chapter one hundred and eighty-four of the Code of Virginia (edition of eighteen hundred and sixty) be amended and re-enacted so as to read as follows:

Amount to clerks, &c

"§ 39. There shall be chargeable in every county or corporation such sum as the court thereof may, for services to the public of the county, city or town, allow its clerk and the sheriff or sergeant attending it, not exceeding for one year four hundred dollars to its clerk, and seventy-five dollars to its sheriff or sergeant; and the corporation courts of Richmond and Petersburg may make such allowance as they may deem proper to their respective clerks and sergeants, for services for which no other compensation is made by law."

Exception as to Petersburg and Richmond

Commencement

2. This act shall be in force from its passage.

CHAP. 16.—An ACT to amend and re-enact the 17th section of the 61st chapter of the Code of Virginia, giving priority of Transportation for Food to Consumers.

Passed October 31, 1863.

Code amended

1. Be it enacted by the general assembly, that the seventeenth section of chapter sixty-one of the Code of Virginia (edition of eighteen hundred and sixty) be amended and re-enacted so as to read as follows:

When rail road company to transport

"§ 17. So soon as any portion of a rail road may be ready for transportation, the rail road company may, by its officers and agents, or by contractors, transport persons and property on the same; for which purpose, there shall be kept in good order such locomotives, cars and other things as may be proper. The company shall have the exclusive right of transportation on its road, and shall, upon the payment or tender of the lawful rates of freight or toll, transport to, and deliver at any depot, or other regular stopping place indicated by the owner, such articles as shall be delivered or offered at any depot or other receiving place, in proper condition to be transported. The property of all persons shall, as far as practicable, be transported in the order of time in which it shall be delivered or offered, and the freight or tolls paid or tendered: provided, that it shall be the duty of every such company, during the present war, under regulations to be prescribed or approved by the board of public works, to give priority of transportation to articles intended for food, in the hands of, or purchased by consumers, or in the hands of, or purchased by cities, counties and corporations, and designed for gratuitous distribution, or for sale at prices not exceeding the cost and charges: and provided further, that the articles embraced by the preceding proviso shall not be subject to express freight, but shall be transported at the rates prescribed for such articles when carried as ordinary freight."

Order of time of transportation

Priority of transportation

Express freight not to be charged

Commencement

2. This act shall be in force from its passage.

CHAP. 17.—An ACT to amend and re-enact section 11 of chapter 208 of the Code of Virginia.

Passed October 30, 1863.

Code amended

1. Be it enacted by the general assembly, that the eleventh section of chapter two hundred and eight of the Code of Virginia be amended and re-enacted so as to read as follows:

"§ 11. When in a criminal case the jury are kept together beyond the day on which they are impanneled, the court shall direct its officer to furnish them with suitable board and lodging while so confined. The expenses thereof, not exceeding three dollars per day for each juror, shall be paid out of the treasury, when allowed by the court." Board of jurors

2. This act shall be in force from its passage. Commencement

CHAP. 18.—An ACT to amend and re-enact the 4th, 5th and 56th sections of the 87th chapter of the Code of Virginia.

Passed October 10, 1863.

1. Be it enacted by the general assembly, that the fourth, fifth and fifty-sixth sections of chapter eighty-seven of the Code of Virginia be amended and re-enacted so as to read as follows: Code amended

"§ 4. For each hogshead of tobacco received, inspected, stored or delivered out at any such warehouse, rent shall be paid to the inspectors at the following rates, to wit: Three dollars, if the warehouse be in, and two dollars and fifty cents, if it be not in Richmond, Petersburg, Alexandria, Lynchburg, Farmville, Danville or Clarkesville; which rent shall be for the exclusive use of the proprietors of the warehouse, if it be built of brick or stone, with fire proof covering; but if not so built, fifty cents out of every such three dollars or two dollars and fifty cents, shall be for the state. Rates of rent What for state

"§ 5. There shall also be paid to the inspectors at any warehouse, for the use of the proprietor, for all tobacco lying therein more than twelve months, at the rate of thirty cents per month for each hogshead, for each month from and after the passage of this act." Rates of charges for tobacco

"§ 56. If any tobacco stored in any warehouse belonging to the state be damaged by fire at any time while remaining in said warehouse, the owner may in like manner recover the amount of his damages; but if said tobacco should be so damaged after remaining in the warehouse more than a year, then the damage so recovered shall not exceed in amount the value of the tobacco at the time when the same was received for inspection." When value recovered in case of damage by fire Proviso

2. This act shall be in force from its passage, and until six months after the ratification of a treaty of peace between the Confederate States and the United States. Commencement

---

CHAP. 19.—An ACT to amend and re-enact the 9th section of the 57th chapter of the Code of Virginia (edition of 1860).

Passed October 29, 1863.

1. Be it enacted by the general assembly, that section nine, chapter fifty-seven of the Code of Virginia (edition of eighteen hundred and sixty) be amended and re-enacted so as to read as follows: Code amended

"§ 9. To constitute a meeting of stockholders other than the annual meeting of stockholders of a bank of circulation, there must be present those who can give a majority of all the votes which could be given by all the stockholders. If a sufficient number fail to attend at the time and place for a meeting, those who do attend may adjourn from time to time until a meeting shall be regularly constituted. The annual meeting of the stockholders of a bank of circulation may be held by any number that may be present. A meeting of stockholders may adjourn from time to time until its business is completed: provided, that if during the existing war with the United States a majority of all the votes cannot be present as aforesaid, because stockholders are within the lines of the public enemy, such meeting may be held, if there shall be present those who can give a majority of all the votes which could be given by stockholders other than the commonwealth." How meeting of stockholders constituted When to adjourn Proviso

2. This act shall be in force from its passage. Commencement

CHAP. 20.—An ACT to amend the act passed February 13th, 1862, entitled an act to amend section 14 of chapter 163 of the Code, in relation to the Removal of the Records and Papers of Courts.

Passed October 1, 1863.

Code and Act of 1862 amended

1. Be it enacted by the general assembly, that the fourteenth section of chapter one hundred and sixty-three of the Code of Virginia, as amended by the act passed February thirteenth, eighteen hundred and sixty-two, entitled an act to amend section fourteen of chapter one hundred and sixty-three of the Code, in relation to the removal of the records and papers of courts, be amended and re-enacted so as to read as follows:

Records not to be removed

When may be removed

What in case of death of clerk

"§ 14. None of the records or papers of a court shall be removed by the clerk, nor allowed by the court to be removed out of the county or corporation wherein the clerk's office is kept, except on an occasion of invasion or insurrection, actual or threatened, where, in the opinion of the court, or in a very sudden case, of the clerk, the same will be endangered: after which, they are to be returned as soon as the danger ceases; and except in such other cases as are specially provided by law. And in the event of the death of the clerk of the circuit or county court, or of both courts, before such return, it shall be the duty of the surviving clerk of either of said courts, or the clerk pro tempore of either, to take charge of said records and papers, and retain them, subject to all the responsibilities of the former custodian. Any clerk violating this section, shall forfeit six hundred dollars."

Commencement

2. This act shall be in force from its passage.

CHAP. 21.—An ACT amending and re-enacting section 9, chapter 160 of the Code of Virginia (edition of 1860).

Passed October 21, 1863.

Code amended

1. Be it enacted by the general assembly, that section nine of chapter one hundred and sixty of the Code of Virginia (edition of eighteen hundred and sixty) be amended and re-enacted so as to read as follows:

Section 9 of chapter 160 amended

When appellate jurisdiction exercised

"§ 9. The sessions and terms of the supreme court of appeals, and the powers and duties of the court at each place of session, shall continue according to the laws in force at or since the adoption of the constitution, except that the court, at one place of session, may also, if it see fit, appoint and take bond from the clerk of the court at the other place; and except likewise that the appellate jurisdiction of said court in any criminal case, or in any case of habeas corpus, may be exercised at either place of session, no matter in what county or corporation the circuit court may have been held which rendered the judgment in such case; and a criminal case, or a case of habeas corpus, pending in said court at one place, may at any time, by its order, be transferred to the other, and be there heard and determined."

Commencement

2. This act shall be in force from its passage.

CHAP. 22.—An ACT authorizing Special Terms of the Circuit Courts to be held to carry into effect the provisions of the law to prevent the unlawful distillation of Whiskey or other Spirituous or Malt Liquors.

Passed September 30, 1863.

Special terms, how held

1. Be it enacted by the general assembly, that if the judge of any circuit court of the state shall deem it necessary to hold a special term in any county in his circuit, to carry into effect the provisions of the law to prevent the unlawful distillation of whiskey, or other spirituous or malt liquors, out of grain, potatoes, sugar, molasses, sugar cane, molasses cane or sorghum, it shall be lawful for him to

appoint a special term of the court, and to issue his warrant for holding the same, as is prescribed by the twenty-ninth section of chapter one hundred and fifty-eight of the Code of eighteen hundred and sixty; at which term the court may exercise the like jurisdiction as might be exercised under the said laws at a regular term of the said court. Warrant, when issued

2. The mode of proceeding upon presentments, indictments or informations charging offences against the said laws, may be as is now prescribed by law in such cases, or as prescribed by section twenty-third of chapter two hundred and seven of the Code of eighteen hundred and sixty, as to the offences therein referred to, as the court may deem best. Mode of procedure

3. This act shall be in force from its passage. Commencement

CHAP. 23.—An ACT amending the Road Law of the Commonwealth.

Passed October 3, 1863.

1. Be it enacted by the general assembly of Virginia, that the twenty-eighth section of the fifty-second chapter of the Code of Virginia be amended and re-enacted so as to read as follows: Section 28 of chapter 52 of Code amended

"§ 28. Every person appointed under either of the two preceding sections, shall, either in person or by a sufficient substitute, when required by the proper surveyor, attend with proper tools, and work the road on such days as the surveyor may direct. For every day on which there may be a failure, not less than two dollars nor more than four dollars, as a magistrate may determine, shall be paid to the surveyor within twenty days thereafter, by the person in default, if a person of full age; or if he be an infant, by his parent or guardian; or if he be a servant or slave, by his overseer, if he be under one; otherwise, by his master. If the money be not paid, it shall be recoverable by the surveyor, with costs, before a justice. Any money received by a surveyor under this section, after the payment of costs, shall be applied to the improvement of the road of which he is surveyor: provided, that the county court of any county, the magistrates being duly summoned for the purpose, may have power to direct the surveyor not to call for hands to labor upon any road, whenever the number of hands liable to such call may be so reduced in number as that their employment in work upon such road will cause serious injury to the agricultural operations of the people living in the vicinity of said road: and provided further, that any order so made by the said court, shall be a bar to any proceedings against such surveyor for a failure to keep his road in the condition required by law." When persons to work on roads; Penalties for failure; Proviso

2. This act shall be in force from its passage. Commencement

CHAP. 24.—An ACT to provide for the Trial of Friendly Suits in Chancery for Partition, &c., arising in Counties in the possession of the enemy, or threatened with invasion.

Passed October 29, 1863.

1. Be it enacted by the general assembly, that whenever any county or corporation in this state shall be in the possession of the enemy, or shall be threatened with invasion, or whenever the existing state of war shall make it difficult or unsafe for the jurisdiction of the courts to be exercised therein, all suits in chancery arising in said counties or corporations for partition, or for the sale and division of property, or any other proceedings in chancery, in which the rights of the parties are not controverted, may be instituted and proceeded in to a final decree in the circuit court of a county in an adjoining circuit not so situated: provided, that copies of all decrees entered in such causes shall be certified to the clerk of the circuit court of the When friendly suits in chancery may be tried in another county; When copies to be certified

county or corporation in which such cause would have been instituted and tried but for the passage of this act.

Commencement

2. This act shall be in force from its passage.

CHAP. 25.—An ACT to authorize the Transfer of Causes from the Circuit Court for the City of Williamsburg and County of James City to other Circuit Courts.

Passed October 23, 1863.

When cause may be removed

1. Be it enacted by the general assembly, that any cause now depending and undetermined in the circuit court for the city of Williamsburg and county of James City, which cannot be held by reason of the presence or proximity of the public enemy to the place where such court is now required by law to be held, may, during the continuance of the present war, by and with the consent of the parties thereto, or, where such consent cannot be obtained, after notice of ten days, personally served by the plaintiff upon the defendant, or by defendant upon the plaintiff, or by publication of notice in some newspaper published in the city of Richmond, once a week for four weeks successively, be transferred to, and docketed in the circuit court of the city of Richmond, or such other circuit court as may be agreed upon between the parties; or in the absence of such agreement, in the nearest circuit court of the judicial district that may be capable of transacting its business.

Notice, how given

Suit, how proceeded in

2. And be it further enacted, that any cause which may be transferred to, and docketed in any court of this commonwealth, in accordance with the preceding section, shall be proceeded with in said court as if the same had originated therein: provided, that the court shall be of opinion that the interests of the parties will not be prejudiced thereby: and provided further, that the court wherein any cause may be docketed under the preceding section, may at any time order its removal to the court in which it originated, when said court shall become capable of transacting its own business.

When cause removed

When cause returned

3. Any cause which may, under this act, be proceeded in to final judgment or decree, shall, by order of the court, as soon as can be done in safety, be returned to the court in which it originated, with duly certified copies of all orders, decrees and judgments which may have been pronounced and entered therein.

Commencement

4. This act shall be in force from its passage.

CHAP. 26.—An ACT to amend and re-enact section 4 of an act entitled an act to provide for Trial of Persons charged with Offences committed in Counties in the possession of the enemy, or threatened with immediate invasion, passed March 27th, 1862.

Passed October 8, 1863.

Act of 1862 amended

1. Be it enacted by the general assembly, that section four of an act entitled an act to provide for the trial of persons charged with offences committed in counties in the possession of the enemy, or threatened with immediate invasion, passed March twenty-seventh, eighteen hundred and sixty-two, be amended and re-enacted so as to read as follows:

Where to be confined

Proviso as to bail

"§ 4. When any such action shall be taken as is provided for in either of the foregoing sections, the person charged with the offence shall be hereafter confined in the jail of the county to which the case shall be removed: provided, however, that in addition to the right to bail, which such person may have under existing laws, he shall, before an examining court, whenever a continuance has been granted to the commonwealth for three successive terms, or whenever it shall appear that without default of the prisoner no examination has been had for the period within which three successive terms of said court, or the court of the county from which he was removed, are prescribed to be held, be entitled to bail, unless it shall appear that a felony has been committed, and strong suspicion of guilt falls on him: and whenever before such court a continuance has been granted to the commonwealth for four successive terms, or without default of the prisoner, no examination has been had for the period within which four successive terms of said court, or the court of the county from which he was removed, are prescribed by law to be held, he shall be entitled to bail as a matter of right; and any judge of a circuit court may in vacation admit such person to bail, upon the grounds for which an examining court is herein before authorized to admit him to bail: and provided further, that he shall, at a circuit court, if not indicted at or before the second term of the court at which he is held to answer, in addition to his right to bail under existing laws, be entitled to bail, unless it shall appear that a felony has been committed, and strong suspicion of guilt falls on him: and if not indicted at the third term of said court, he shall be admitted to bail as a matter of right." When bail granted as of right Power of circuit judge Proviso

2. This act shall be in force from its passage. Commencement

CHAP. 27.—An ACT to increase Jailors' Fees for keeping and supporting Prisoners.

Passed October 2, 1863.

1. Be it enacted by the general assembly, that the first section of an act passed seventeenth March eighteen hundred and sixty-three, entitled an act to amend and re-enact the first section of an act entitled an act to increase jailors' fees for keeping and supporting prisoners, passed September twenty-fourth, eighteen hundred and sixty-two, be amended and re-enacted so as to read as follows: Act of 1863 amended

"§ 1. Jailors shall hereafter be allowed one dollar per day for keeping and supporting persons confined in the jails of this commonwealth, and a fair proportion of said sum for any time less than twenty-four hours; and in all cases the allowance shall be made on an account stating the time for which the person or persons remained in jail: provided, that the county and corporation courts of the commonwealth may establish, in their discretion, a different rate, not less than thirty-five cents nor more than two dollars and fifty cents per diem." Fees of jailors

2. This act shall be in force from its passage. Commencement

CHAP. 28.—An ACT to amend the act passed February 13th, 1863, entitled an act amending and re-enacting the 1st and 2d sections of an act entitled an act to repeal the Fence Law of Virginia as to certain Counties, and to authorize the County Courts to dispense with enclosures in other Counties, passed October 3d, 1862, and to legalize the action of County Courts held under said law.

Passed October 9, 1863.

1. Be it enacted by the general assembly, that the second section of the act passed October the third, eighteen hundred and sixty-two, as amended by an act passed February the thirteenth, eighteen hundred and sixty-three, entitled an act amending and re-enacting the first and second sections of an act entitled an act to repeal the fence law of Virginia as to certain counties, and to authorize the county courts to dispense with enclosures in other counties, passed October the third, eighteen hundred and sixty-two, and to legalize the action of county courts held under said law, be amended and re-enacted so as to read as follows: Section 2 of Act of 1863 amended

"§ 2. Be it further enacted, that the county courts of the counties of Augusta, Frederick, Clarke, Warren, Culpeper, Rappahannock, Norfolk, Princess Anne, Mercer, Shenandoah, Page, Prince William, Spotsylvania, Hampshire, Berkeley, Caroline, Rockingham, Richmond, Westmoreland, Loudoun, Jefferson, Orange, Essex, King & Queen, Goochland, Giles, Bland, Fairfax, Greenbrier, New Kent, Charles City, James City, Prince George, Nansemond, Highland, Hardy and King William shall have power, all the justices having been summoned, and a majority thereof being present, to dispense with the existing laws in regard to enclosures, so far as their respective counties may be concerned, or such parts thereof, to be described by metes and bounds, as in their discretion they may deem it expedient to exempt from the operation of such law."

Power of courts

Commencement

2. This act shall be in force from its passage.

CHAP. 29.—An ACT to authorize the Arrest of Deserters by the Civil Authorities.

Passed October 27, 1863.

Deserters, how to be arrested

1. Be it enacted by the general assembly, that all conservators of the peace in this commonwealth are hereby authorized and required to arrest deserters from the army and navy of the Confederate States, whenever and wherever they may be found; and they shall promptly notify the nearest confederate officer, or the adjutant general, or the secretary of war, of such arrest, and shall commit the said deserter to the jail of the county, city or town in which he is arrested, until he can be delivered to the confederate authorities.

Arrest notified

Deserter committed to jail

Posse comitatus, when summoned

2. The said conservators of the peace, in making such arrest, may summon so many of the people of their county or corporation, or require the nearest commissioned officer of state forces to call out such portion of his command as may be sufficient to aid him, and may proceed in the manner prescribed in the twenty-fourth section of the forty-ninth chapter of the Code.

Penalties

3. Any conservator of the peace neglecting or refusing to perform the duties imposed by this act shall be fined, at the discretion of the jury, not less than thirty nor exceeding five hundred dollars for each offence.

Commencement

4. This act shall be in force from its passage.

CHAP. 30.—An ACT to provide for the Appointment of General Agents and Storekeepers for Counties and Corporations.

Passed October 27, 1863.

General agents and storekeepers, how appointed

1. Be it enacted by the general assembly, that it shall be lawful for the court of any county or corporation, all of the acting justices thereof having been duly summoned, and a majority of them being present and assenting to the provisions of this act, to appoint a general agent and storekeeper, and such sub-agents as may be deemed necessary, with the duties herein after assigned; which agents shall be chosen from persons who are exempt from military duty.

County court may borrow money

2. The court of any such county or corporation may, upon the credit thereof, at any regular term, all the justices thereof having been duly summoned, and a majority of them being present, borrow, for the purpose of carrying into effect the objects of this act, an amount of money, not exceeding at any one time ten thousand dollars for every one thousand of white population, and at a rate of interest not exceeding six per centum; and said court shall have authority to prescribe the articles to be purchased, and to fix the compensation of the agent, and to adopt rules and regulations for the

Court to prescribe articles to be purchased

sale and distribution of such articles to the citizens in such quantities and in such manner as shall best conduce to the relief of the distress and wants of the community: provided, that no article shall be sold to any person who may buy to sell again; and if such sale be made, the said agent and purchaser shall each be liable to a penalty of three times the value of the article sold; to be recovered by information or indictment, and the amount thereof paid into the county treasury. To whom articles not to be sold Penalty

3. The court of any such county or corporation, at any regular term thereof, may inspect the books and papers of such agent and storekeeper, and cause his accounts to be settled in such manner as the court may direct. Books of agent, how inspected

4. It shall be the duty of such general agent and storekeeper, under regulations prescribed by the court, to purchase and sell to the residents of such county or corporation, or otherwise dispose of articles of prime necessity; the sale to be at prices equal, as near as may be, to the aggregate amount of the prime cost, the cost of transportation, necessary expenses of sale of each article, the compensation for such agent, and the interest on the money borrowed, and the taxes that may be imposed. To whom articles to be sold Price therefor

5. Every such agent and storekeeper, before entering upon the discharge of his duties, shall take an oath before the clerk of such court for the faithful performance thereof, and enter into a bond in a penalty adequate, and with security sufficient, to be judged of by the court, with condition for the faithful performance of his duties as such agent and storekeeper; and such bond may be put in suit from time to time, at the relation and for the benefit of such county or corporation, or any person injured by a breach of the condition thereof. Oath and bond of agent

6. All of the rail roads throughout this state shall provide transportation for all goods purchased by such agents, in preference to all other articles, except army supplies. Transportation

7. That in counties where, in consequence of the presence of, or a threatened invasion by the public enemy, the provisions of sections one and two of this act cannot be carried into effect, it may be lawful for five or more of the acting justices thereof, a majority agreeing, to convene in said county at a place of safety from the enemy, who shall be clothed with all the powers to act in the premises, that are given to a majority of the justices of a county, under the first and second sections of this act. As to counties in power of enemy

8. This act shall be in force from its passage. Commencement

CHAP. 31.—An ACT for the Relief of the Indigent Soldiers and Sailors of the State of Virginia who have been or may be disabled in the Military Service, and the Widows and Minor Children of Soldiers and Sailors who have died or may hereafter die in said Service, and of the Indigent Families of those now in the Service.

Passed October 31, 1863.

1. Be it enacted by the general assembly, that it shall be the duty of the county and corporation courts of this commonwealth to order the sheriffs and sergeants of such counties and corporations to make a list of all indigent soldiers and sailors enlisted from their respective counties or corporations in the confederate service or state service, who have been or may be disabled or honorably discharged, and of their families, and of the families of those who may be now in the service, and of the widows and minor children of such as may have died or may hereafter die in the service; and said list shall be returned and deposited in the clerk's office of such counties and corporations, at the next regular term thereafter. And it shall be the duty of the magistrates in each magisterial district to report a list of said persons and families in their respective districts to the said term Lists of whom to be made List, how returned

of the county courts; and said courts shall then, and from time to time thereafter, at any regular term thereof, examine said list, and add to it or strike from it such names as it shall deem just and proper.

How examined and added to

Allowance, how made

How charged

2. It shall be the duty of said courts to make an allowance, in money or supplies, to the persons and families mentioned in the first section of this act, of such liberal amount and in such proportion as they may think just and sufficient for their maintenance; and said allowance shall be charged on the county, city or town; and provision shall be made for its payment, in the manner prescribed by law for sums legally chargeable on counties, cities and towns.

In case of refugees

3. Whenever any county court shall be satisfied that any such soldiers and sailors were, at the date of their enlistment, residents of any county of the commonwealth, and whose families may have been, or may hereafter be driven from their homes, by fear of the public enemy, and are residing in such county, it shall be the duty of such court to enroll such soldiers and sailors and their families, according to the provisions of the first section of this act, and to make the same provision for their support as for those soldiers and sailors and their families described in said section. The said county court shall state and certify their account for the support of such refugee soldiers and sailors and their families, and forward the same to the auditor of public accounts; and it shall be the duty of the auditor to pay said accounts by warrants upon the treasurer of the commonwealth.

Accounts, how certified

When paid out of the treasury

Agents and their duties

4. The said courts may, at any regular term thereof, appoint an agent or agents, whose duty it shall be to purchase, upon the order of said courts, a supply of such articles deemed necessary for the support of the persons and families mentioned in the first and third sections of this act, at rates to be agreed upon by the vendor and the agent, under instruction of said courts; or if the said courts shall deem it prudent and necessary, may authorize its agent or agents to impress, upon its order, a stated quantity of necessaries for the persons and families mentioned in the said first and third sections of this act, at prices not exceeding those prescribed by the commissioners appointed for the state of Virginia, under the act of the congress of the Confederate States regulating impressments, preferring in said impressment articles in the hands of persons who may have purchased the same for purposes of speculation: and said courts shall have the authority to prescribe the articles to be purchased, and to fix the compensation of the agent or agents, and to adopt rules and regulations for the proper care of such articles so purchased or impressed, and for the distribution of the same in such quantities and in such manner as shall best conduce to the relief of the distress and wants of the persons and families mentioned in the said first and third sections. Any person shall be held and deemed a speculator within the meaning of this act, who shall purchase any of the necessaries of life for profit by resale, or who shall purchase or hold the same when not needed for the consumption of his or her family during the then ensuing twelve months. Where the confederate government has an impressing agent in any county, it shall be the duty of the county court, in order to prevent collision, at once to cause an estimate to be made of the amount of supplies so needed by the persons mentioned in the first and third sections, and also of the amount needed for such other residents of such county as may not have supplies adequate to their necessities, who shall make affidavit as to such deficiency. It shall be the duty of the said county agent to report the aggregate amount of said estimates to the impressing officer of the Confederate States for said county, and endeavor so to arrange with the said agent as that a sufficiency for the said purpose, of the surplus products of said county, may be turned over by the confederate agent to the said agent of the county court, who shall proceed to sell so much thereof as may have been obtained for that purpose, at cost, to the persons not men-

When impressments may be made

Who shall be deemed a speculator

How collision prevented between county and impressing agents of confederate government

Estimates, how made

When agent may sell to others

tioned in the first and third sections of this act, adding the expenses of transportation and proper allowance for wastage: provided, that when the owner of property impressed is dissatisfied with the price, he may appeal to the county court, whose decision shall be final; but the agent may take possession of the property impressed immediately on the appeal being taken: provided, that so much of the act as defines who shall be held and deemed a speculator, shall not be so construed as to apply to a licensed merchant who only buys and sells such goods, wares and merchandise as he is authorized to do by virtue of his license; nor to a farmer who only holds such necessaries of life as are of his own production; but such articles deemed necessaries of life owned by any such merchant or farmer shall be liable to impressment in like manner as if owned by any person other than one held and deemed a speculator under this act: and provided further, that no impressment shall be made of any supplies laid in and necessary for the support of any family for a period not exceeding twelve months: and provided further, that no such order of impressment shall be made except at a term of said court to which all the justices of said county have been previously summoned: and provided further, whenever the said county agent or agents shall report to the clerk of said court his or their inability to procure by purchase at rates not exceeding those prescribed by the schedule of prices fixed by the commissioners for the state of Virginia, under the act of the confederate congress regulating impressments, the supplies necessary for the support of the persons and families aforesaid, the clerk of such court shall issue a summons to convene the justices of said county at the next regular term of such court.

Exception as to merchants

Exception as to impressment of family supplies

When justices to be convened

Oath and bond of agents

5. Every such agent, before entering upon the discharge of his duties, shall take an oath before the clerk of said court for the faithful performance thereof, and enter into a bond, in a penalty adequate and with security sufficient, to be judged of by the court, with conditions for the faithful performance of his duties as such agent; and such bond may be put in suit from time to time, at the relation and for the benefit of such county and corporation, or of any person injured by a breach of the conditions thereof.

Penalties for failure to carry out provisions of act

6. Be it further enacted, that if said county or corporation courts or said sheriffs or sergeants shall willfully neglect or refuse to perform the duties herein before imposed, the magistrates composing said court, and said sheriffs or sergeants who so neglect or refuse to perform their said duty, shall be fined severally the sum of one hundred dollars for each term of said courts at which they may be so in default; to be recovered by presentment, indictment or information in the circuit court of said counties or corporations: and such sums so recovered shall be set apart as a portion of the fund to be raised by such counties and corporations for the support of the persons and families mentioned in the first and third sections of this act.

How disposed of

How provisions of act executed

7. Be it further enacted, that for the purpose of carrying the provisions of this act into effect in counties partly held or threatened by the public enemy, and when the court thereof cannot be held at the courthouse of such county, it shall be lawful for any five or more of the acting justices thereof to assemble at some place in said county other than the courthouse thereof, who, so assembled, shall be regarded in all respects as the county court of said county for the purpose of carrying into effect the provisions of this act.

Act to be given in charge to juries

Commencement

8. This act shall be given in charge to the grand juries of the circuit courts of said counties and corporations, and shall be in force from its passage, and shall continue in force until six months after the ratification of a treaty of peace between the Confederate States and the United States.

CHAP. 32.—An ACT to repeal so much of the Ordinance of the Convention of April 24th, 1861, as provides for a Pay Department of Virginia Forces.

Passed October 31, 1863.

Ordinance repealed

1. Be it enacted by the general assembly, that so much of the ordinance of the convention of April twenty-fourth, eighteen hundred and sixty-one, as provides for a pay department to the forces of Virginia, be and the same is hereby repealed.

Unfinished business, how transacted

2. That from and after the first day of January eighteen hundred and sixty-four, the unfinished business of said department shall be turned over to the auditing board. together with all papers, documents and vouchers pertaining thereto: and thereafter all the duties of the pay department shall be performed by the said auditing board, in conformity with the practice and rules of the confederate service; and the commissions of all officers in the pay department, other than the paymaster general, are hereby canceled from the first day of January eighteen hundred and sixty-four.

Commencement

3. This act shall take effect and be in force from and after its passage.

CHAP. 33.—An ACT requiring certain Rail Road Companies to provide for the Transportation of Fuel in certain cases.

Passed October 31, 1863.

1. Be it enacted by the general assembly of Virginia, that every rail road company subject to the provisions of the sixty-first chapter of the Code (edition of eighteen hundred and sixty), shall conform to the following regulations:

Fuel, when to be transported

2. Whenever any person shall give notice in writing to the superintendent of any such rail road, that he has delivered at any depot or switch upon the said road not less than eight cords of wood or eight tons of coal, consigned to some city, town, village or chartered institution of learning upon the line of said road, and that he is prepared to load the same upon the cars within six hours after such cars shall be ready to receive it, it shall be the duty of said superintendent to provide forthwith sufficient transportation for the same.

Compensation for rail road companies

3. The said rail road companies shall be entitled to receive, for the transportation of such fuel, an addition of twenty-five per centum upon the rates of freight per ton per mile allowed them by law, and shall be entitled moreover to demand from any shipper referred to in the second section of this act, the delivery at the place of shipment, and at the value thereof at such place, of one-fourth part of all such fuel, to be applied to the use of such road. In case of any disagreement between such company and the shipper of such fuel as to the price thereof, such company shall be entitled to employ the provisions of the fifty-sixth chapter of the Code (edition of eighteen hundred and sixty) in fixing the valuation thereof.

How fixed

Fines

4. If any such company shall fail to perform the duties imposed thereon by this act, it shall be subject to a fine of five hundred dollars in every case; to be recovered in any court having jurisdiction, by presentment, information or indictment. One-half of such fine shall be paid to the informer or prosecutor, and the balance to the commonwealth, according to the provisions of the forty-third chapter of the Code (edition of eighteen hundred and sixty): provided, that the board of public works, in order to secure the transportation of salt, and of fuel for the salt furnaces, may, in their discretion, exempt, for such period of time as said board may order, the Virginia and Tennessee rail road from the provisions of this act.

Proviso as to Virginia and Tennessee rail road

Commencement

5. This act shall be in force from its passage.

CHAP. 34.—An ACT to authorize the Governor to hire Free Negro and other Convicts to work in Coal-pits.

Passed October 31, 1863.

1. Be it enacted by the general assembly, that it shall be lawful for the governor of this commonwealth to hire the free negro and slave convicts at any time in the penitentiary, to the owners of coal-pits, to work in said pits in any county of this state, and the money arising therefrom to pay into the public treasury to the credit of the penitentiary. When governor may hire free negro and slave convicts

2. Be it further enacted, that the governor shall also be authorized to hire, to work in said coal-pits, as many able-bodied white male convicts in said penitentiary as can be spared from the workshops therein, not exceeding one hundred and fifty: the proceeds of such hire to be paid into the public treasury to the credit of the penitentiary, monthly or quarterly, as to the governor may seem proper. When white convicts

3. Be it further enacted, that it shall be the duty of the governor, in making contracts with the owners of coal-pits, to provide for the safe-keeping and return to the penitentiary of convicts hired under the provisions of this act. Governor to stipulate for safe keeping and return of convicts

4. This act shall commence and be in force from its passage. Commencement

---

CHAP. 35.—An ACT to amend and re-enact the act passed March 11th, 1863, in relation to the unnecessary Consumption of Grain by Distillers and other Manufacturers of Spirituous and Malt Liquors.

Passed October 31, 1863.

Be it enacted by the general assembly, that the act passed March eleventh, eighteen hundred and sixty-three, entitled an act to amend and re-enact an act entitled an act to amend and re-enact an act entitled an act to prevent the unnecessary consumption of grain by distillers and other manufacturers of spirituous and malt liquors, passed October second, eighteen hundred and sixty-two, be and the same is hereby amended and re-enacted so as to read as follows: Act of 1863 amended

1. It shall not be lawful for any person hereafter to make or cause to be made any whiskey, or other spirituous or malt liquors, out of any corn, wheat, rye or other grain, or out of dried fruit, potatoes, sugar, molasses, sugar cane, molasses cane or sorghum; and any person so offending shall be deemed guilty of a misdemeanor, and upon conviction thereof, shall be fined for every offence not less than one hundred dollars nor more than five thousand dollars, and be subject to imprisonment in the county jail not exceeding twelve months, at the discretion of the court. Distillation prohibited Penalties

2. No person, firm or company shall hereafter execute, in whole or in part, any contract, heretofore or hereafter made with the confederate government, or with any agent of said government, for making or causing to be made any whiskey or other ardent spirits within this state; and all such contractors who shall violate this section, shall be deemed subject to all the penalties imposed by this and other acts against unlawful distillation. No contracts to be executed

3. The keeper of the rolls shall cause this act to be published in at least two newspapers in the city of Richmond for two weeks. Act to be published

4. This act shall be in force from its passage. Commencement

CHAP. 36.—An ACT to provide for the Payment of certain Claims against the Eastern Lunatic Asylum.

Passed October 23, 1863.

1. Be it enacted by the general assembly of Virginia, that any person having any pecuniary demand against the Eastern lunatic asylum of this state, contracted prior to the first day of January When demands may be paid

eighteen hundred and sixty-three, may present the same to the auditor of public accounts for payment thereof; and thereupon the said auditor, upon the certificate of the steward of said asylum, and upon other satisfactory evidence that any such demand is correct and ought to be paid, is hereby authorized and required to draw his warrant upon the treasury, payable out of any funds therein not otherwise appropriated, in favor of the person to whom such claim may appear to be justly due, and for the amount thereof.

When auditor to issue warrant

2. This act shall be in force from its passage.

Commencement

CHAP. 37.—An ACT to supply Deficiencies in the Appropriation for the Support of the Central Lunatic Asylum.

Passed October 19, 1863.

Amount appropriated

1. Be it enacted by the general assembly, that the auditor of public accounts be and he is hereby authorized to issue his warrant on the treasury for the sum of twenty-two thousand seven hundred and nineteen dollars and thirty cents, payable on the order of the directors of the Central lunatic asylum, in the manner provided by existing laws, to be applied for the support of the said institution, in addition to the annual appropriation for that purpose, for the fiscal year ending September thirtieth, eighteen hundred and sixty-three; and the said auditor is further authorized to issue his warrant in like manner for the sum of twenty-five thousand dollars, to be credited as a part of the entire sum which may be hereafter appropriated for the support of said asylum during the fiscal year ending September thirtieth, eighteen hundred and sixty-four.

Auditor to issue warrant

2. This act shall be in force from its passage.

Commencement

CHAP. 38.—An ACT to provide Fuel and Lights for the Governor's House.

Passed October 27, 1863.

Governor reimbursed for lights, &c

1. Be it enacted by the general assembly, that the governor be authorized to issue his order on the auditor of public accounts, directing him to issue his warrant on the treasury, payable out of the civil contingent fund, for such sum as may reimburse him the amount actually expended for fuel and lights for the governor's house from the first day of October eighteen hundred and sixty-two to the passage of this act.

Lights, &c to be furnished governor's house

2. Be it further enacted, that the governor be authorized to issue, from time to time, his orders on the auditor of public accounts, directing him to issue his warrants on the treasury, payable out of the civil contingent fund, in favor of the persons entitled thereto, for such sums as may be hereafter necessary to procure fuel and lights for the governor's house.

Commencement

3. This act shall be in force from its passage until six months after the ratification of a treaty of peace between the United States and the Confederate States.

CHAP. 39.—An ACT for the Relief of William F. Ritchie, Public Printer.

Passed October 23, 1863.

Amount appropriated

1. Be it enacted by the general assembly, that the auditor of public accounts be and he is hereby authorized to issue his warrant on the treasury, payable out of any money therein not otherwise appropriated, in favor of William F. Ritchie, public printer, or his legal representative, for the sum of ten thousand eight hundred and seventy-nine dollars and sixty cents: four thousand three hundred and fifty-two dollars and eighty-three cents of said sum being the

Items

amount of actual loss on the public printing for the house of delegates since January eighteen hundred and sixty-two; two thousand two hundred and nineteen dollars and fifty cents of said sum being the actual loss for printing five hundred volumes of fifth Leigh's Reports; and four thousand three hundred and seven dollars and twenty-seven cents of said sum being twenty per centum profit on the actual cost of said printing.

2. This act shall be in force from its passage. Commencement

CHAP. 40.—An act to authorize the Auditor to pay the Funeral Expenses of Israel Robinson, late Delegate from Berkeley County.

Passed October 30, 1863.

1. Be it enacted by the general assembly, that the auditor of public accounts is hereby directed to draw his warrant upon the treasury, payable out of any money therein not otherwise appropriated, in favor of John A. Belvin, for four hundred and eighty-one dollars, being the amount of the funeral expenses of Israel Robinson, late delegate from the county of Berkeley. Amount appropriated

2. This act shall be in force from its passage. Commencement

PRIVATE OR LOCAL ACTS.

CHAP. 41.—An ACT to incorporate the Confederate Savings and Insurance Company of Petersburg.

Passed October 7, 1863.

1. Be it enacted by the general assembly of Virginia, that the persons who shall, as hereafter mentioned, become subscribers to the capital stock hereby created, are hereby created and declared to be a body politic and corporate, by the name and style of The Confederate Savings and Insurance Company of Petersburg; and by that name shall have perpetual succession, and be able to sue and be sued, plead and be impleaded in all courts in this state and elsewhere; and have a common seal, and the same to alter and renew at their pleasure; to make and ordain such ordinances and regulations, and generally to do every act and thing necessary to carry into effect this act, or to promote the object and designs of this corporation. Company incorporated

2. The capital stock of said company shall not be less than two hundred and fifty thousand dollars, to be divided into twenty-five hundred shares of one hundred dollars each, with power to increase the same to five hundred thousand dollars whenever a majority of stockholders in interest shall, in general meeting assembled, determine so to do. Capital

3. The capital stock shall be paid as follows: twenty dollars on each share at the time of subscribing shall be paid to the commissioners herein after named, and the residue thereafter, as may be required by the president and directors. How paid

4. Robert P. Stainback, John McIlwaine, Z. W. Pickrell, William R. Johnson, John P. Branch, Robert D. McIlwaine, J. M. Venable, T. T. Broocks and R. A. Young shall be commissioners, any three or more of whom, after giving notice thereof for ten days, shall open books in the city of Petersburg, to receive subscriptions to the capital stock of said company; which books shall not be closed in less than fifteen days, unless the capital stock be sooner subscribed. When it shall appear to the commissioners that fifty thousand dollars of the capital has been subscribed and paid, or secured to be paid, they shall call a general meeting of the stockholders at a certain time and place in said city, to organize said company. From the time of such meeting the subscribers or stockholders shall stand incorporated, unless in the said meeting it be otherwise determined. In this meeting the stockholders present (in person or by proxy), representing a majority of stock subscribed, shall proceed, under the inspection of the commissioners, to choose seven directors. The commissioners shall forthwith, upon the said election, pay over, as the directors may order, all moneys by them received from the subscribers to the capital stock of said company, and deliver up all books and papers in their hands concerning the same: provided, that no person shall vote in such meeting, unless he shall have paid to the commissioners, or some one of them, twenty dollars on every share by him subscribed. Commissioners

5. The affairs of the said company shall be managed by a president and seven directors, being stockholders (a majority of whom shall constitute a quorum), who shall continue in office one year from the time of their election, and until others are elected in their stead; to be chosen by ballot, by a majority of the stockholders present, in person or by proxy. Each stockholder shall be entitled to as many Affairs, how managed

votes at any meeting of the stockholders as he may hold shares in said company. The directors to be elected under this act at the first meeting of the company, shall continue in office until the first Thursday in October eighteen hundred and sixty-four, or until others are chosen in their place; on which first Thursday in October eighteen hundred and sixty four, and annually thereafter, there shall be a general meeting of the stockholders for the election of officers, and for such other business as may come before them. At the first meeting after every election the directors shall choose from amongst themselves, or the stockholders at large, a president, and allow him a reasonable compensation for his services; and in case of death, resignation or disqualification of the president, or any of the directors, the remaining directors may elect others to supply their places for the remainder of the term for which they were chosen.

Officers

6. The president and directors may appoint, and dismiss at their pleasure, a secretary, and such other officers as may be necessary for the transaction of the business of the company, and allow such compensation for their services as they may think reasonable, and may require such secretary or other officers to enter into bond for the faithful discharge of their duties.

Assignment

7. Every stockholder not in debt to the company may at pleasure, in person or by attorney, assign his stock on the books of the company, or part thereof, not being less than a whole share; but no stockholder indebted to the company shall assign or make a transfer of his stock or receive a dividend until such debt is paid, or secured to the satisfaction of the board of directors.

Insurance on vessels, &c.

8. The president and directors are authorized to make insurance upon vessels, freights, merchandise, specie, bullion, jewels, profits, commission, bank notes, bills of exchange, and other evidences of debt, bottomry and respondentia interest, and to make all and every insurance connected with marine risks, and risks of transportation and navigation.

On dwellings, &c

9. To make insurance on dwellings, houses, stores and other property and merchandise, against loss or damage by fire.

On lives, &c

10. To make insurance on lives; to grant annuities; to guarantee the payment of notes, bonds and bills of exchange; and to make all kinds of contracts for the insurance of every description of property; to receive money on deposit, and to pay interest thereon, as may be advantageous to the stockholders; to provide for investments of the capital stock and other funds, in bank, state or other stocks; in the purchase of bonds issued by this or any other state, or of the Confederate States, and of bonds of any incorporated company; to lend money upon personal or real security; and to purchase or otherwise acquire, to have and to hold, to convey and to sell, any real or personal estate for the purpose of securing any debt or debts that may be due to them, and for their own use and convenience: provided always, that nothing in this act shall be construed to authorize said company to issue and put into circulation any note of the nature of a bank note, or to own more land than is necessary for an office building.

Policies

11. All policies of insurance and other contracts made by the said company, signed by the president and countersigned by the secretary, shall be obligatory on said company, and have the same effect as if said policies and contracts had been attested by a corporate seal.

Dividends

12. The president and directors may declare semi-annual or other dividends of the profits of the company, as they may deem proper; but no dividend shall be declared when, in the opinion of a majority of the board, the capital stock would be impaired thereby.

General meeting

13. The president and directors may at any time, when deemed necessary by them, call a general meeting of the stockholders; and any number of stockholders owning not less than one-fourth of the whole number of shares, may require the president and directors to call

such meeting; and on their refusal to do so, may themselves call such meeting, giving fifteen days' notice thereof in one or more of the newspapers published in the city of Petersburg.

14. The president and directors may appoint an agent in any of the cities, towns or counties of this state or elsewhere, to receive offerings for insurance, and for the transaction of such business of the company as may be confided to him. Agents

15. The corporation hereby created shall be subject to the provisions of the Code of Virginia, so far as the same are applicable to and not inconsistent with the provisions of this act; and this act shall be subject to alteration, amendment or repeal, at the pleasure of the general assembly. Subject to Code

16. This act shall be in force from its passage. Commencement

---

CHAP. 42.—An ACT incorporating the Home Insurance Company of the City of Petersburg.

Passed October 22, 1863.

1. Be it enacted by the general assembly of Virginia, that John Rowlett, Joseph H. Cooper, John Enniss, J. Andrew White, Robert A. McKenney, David B. Dugger, John Stevenson, Carter R. Bishop, Augustine C. Butts, Alexander Donnan and James Kerr, and their associates and successors, who may hereafter become subscribers or stockholders, be and they are hereby constituted and made a body politic and corporate, under the name and style of The Home Insurance Company of Petersburg; and by that name shall have perpetual succession, and be able to sue and be sued, plead and be impleaded in all courts in this state and elsewhere; and to have a common seal, and the same to alter and renew at their pleasure; and to make and ordain such ordinances and regulations, and generally to do all such acts and things as may be necessary to carry into effect this act, and promote the object and design of this corporation. Company incorporated

2. The capital stock of said corporation shall not be less than one hundred thousand dollars, to be divided into shares of one hundred dollars each, with power to increase the same to a sum not exceeding five hundred thousand dollars, whenever a majority of the stockholders in interest shall in general meeting from time to time determine so to do. Capital

3. The capital stock shall be paid as follows: ten dollars per share before or at the general meeting for the organization of the company, to the five associates herein first named, who are hereby appointed commissioners (any three of whom may act), and the residue thereafter, as may be required by the president and directors. How paid

4. Whenever it shall appear to the commissioners aforesaid that one hundred thousand dollars of the capital stock has been subscribed, and fifty thousand dollars thereof has been paid or secured to be paid, the said commissioners shall, by service of personal notice or otherwise, call a general meeting of the subscribers or stockholders at a certain time and place in said city, to organize said corporation. In such meeting the subscribers or stockholders shall proceed, under the inspection of the commissioners, to elect a president and five or more directors. The commissioners shall forthwith, after said election, pay over, as the president and directors may order, all moneys received by them from the subscribers to the capital stock of the company, and deliver up all books and papers in their hands concerning the same. General meeting

5. The affairs of the corporation shall be managed by the president and five or more directors, being stockholders (a majority of whom shall constitute a quorum), who shall be chosen by the stockholders in general meeting, and continue in office for one year, or until others are elected in their stead; and in case of the death, re- Affairs, how managed

signation or disqualification of the president or any of the directors, the remaining members of the directory shall elect others to fill the vacancies for the residue of the time for which they were chosen.

Quorum

6. In all general meetings of the stockholders a majority of all the stockholders in interest, being present in person or by proxy, shall constitute a quorum for the transaction of business. Each stockholder shall be entitled to as many votes as he may hold shares in said company. The stockholders in general meeting shall have power to fix the time and place of the annual meetings, and to prescribe the mode in which general meetings of the stockholders may be called by the directory, and the manner in which the stockholders shall be notified of all meetings of their body. The stockholders shall determine and fix the compensation of the president.

Officers

7. The president and directors may appoint, and dismiss at their pleasure, a secretary, and such other officers as may be necessary for the transaction of the business of the company, and allow such compensation for their services as they may deem reasonable, and may require such secretary and other officers to enter into bonds with security for the faithful discharge of their duties.

Assignment

8. Every stockholder not in debt to the company may, subject to such regulations and upon such terms as the stockholders may prescribe, in person or by attorney, assign his stock or any number of his shares on the books of the company; but no stockholder indebted to the company shall assign or make a transfer of his stock, or receive a dividend until such debt is paid or secured to the satisfaction of the board of directors.

Insurance on vessels, &c

9. The president and directors are authorized to make insurance upon vessels, freights, merchandise, specie, bullion, jewels, profits, commissions, bank notes, bills of exchange, and other evidences of debt, bottomry and respondentia interests, and to make all and every insurance connected with marine risks and risks of transportation and navigation.

On dwellings, &c

10. To make insurance on dwellings, houses, stores and other kinds of buildings, and upon household furniture and other property and merchandise, against loss or damage by fire.

On lives, &c

11. To make insurance on lives; to grant annuities; to guarantee the payment of notes, bonds and bills of exchange, and to make all kinds of contracts for the insurance of every description of property.

Investments

12. The president and directors shall have power to invest the capital stock and other funds of the company, in bank, state or other stocks, in the purchase of bonds issued by this or any other state, or of the Confederate States, or by any incorporated company; to lend money upon personal or real security; and to purchase or otherwise acquire, to have and to hold, and convey and sell any real or personal estate, for the purpose of securing any debt or debts that may be due them, and for their own use and convenience.

Policies of insurance

13. All policies of insurance and other contracts made by the said company, signed by the president and countersigned by the secretary, shall be obligatory upon the said company, and have the same effect as if the said policies and contracts had been attested by a corporate seal.

Dividends

14. The president and directors may declare semi-annual or other dividends of the profits of the company, as they may deem proper; but no dividend shall be declared when, in the opinion of the majority of the board, the capital stock would be impaired thereby.

General meeting

15. The president and directors may, at any time when deemed necessary by them, call a general meeting of the stockholders; and any number of the stockholders, owning not less than one-fourth of the whole number of shares, may require the president and directors to call such meeting; and on their refusal to do so, may themselves call such meeting, by giving fifteen days' notice thereof in one or more of the newspapers published in the city of Petersburg.

16. The president and directors may appoint an agent in any of the cities, towns or counties of this state or elsewhere to receive offerings for insurance, and for the transaction of such business of the company as may be confided to him. Agent

17. The corporation hereby created shall be subject to the provisions of the Code of Virginia, as far as the same are applicable to and not inconsistent with the provisions of this act; and this act shall be subject to alteration, amendment or repeal, at the pleasure of the general assembly. Subject to Code

18. This act shall be in force from its passage. Commencement

---

CHAP. 43.—An ACT incorporating the Southern Insurance and Savings Society of Petersburg.

Passed October 22, 1863.

1. Be it enacted by the general assembly of Virginia, that William R. Johnson, T. T. Broocks, Z. W. Pickrell, S. A. Plummer, J. B. Wilson, Joseph E. Venable, R. D. McIlwaine, John McNecce, John McIlwaine and E. A. Broadnax, and their associates and successors, who may hereafter become subscribers or stockholders, be and they are hereby constituted and made a body politic and corporate, under the name and style of The Southern Insurance and Savings Society of Petersburg; and by that name shall have perpetual succession and be able to sue and be sued, plead and be impleaded in all courts in this state and elsewhere; and to have a common seal, and the same to alter and renew at their pleasure; and to make and ordain such ordinances and regulations, and generally to do all such acts and things as may be necessary to carry into effect this act, and promote the object and design of the corporation. Company incorporated

2. The capital stock of said company shall not be less than two hundred thousand dollars, to be divided into shares of one hundred dollars each, with power to increase the same to a sum not exceeding one million of dollars, whenever a majority of the stockholders in interest shall in general meeting from time to time determine so to do. Capital stock

3. The capital stock shall be paid as follows: twenty dollars per share before or at the general meeting for the organization of the company, to the five associates herein first named, who are hereby appointed commissioners (any three of whom may act), and the residue thereafter as may be required by the president and directors.

4. Whenever it shall appear to the commissioners aforesaid that two hundred thousand dollars of the capital stock has been subscribed, and forty thousand dollars thereof has been paid to them in cash, the said commissioners shall, by service of personal notice or otherwise, call a general meeting of the subscribers or stockholders at a certain time and place in said city, to organize said corporation. In such meeting the subscribers or stockholders shall proceed, under the inspection of the commissioners, to elect a president and four directors. The commissioners shall forthwith, after said election, pay over, as the president and directors may order, all moneys received by them from the subscribers to the capital stock of the company, and deliver up all books and papers in their hands concerning the same. General meeting

5. The affairs of the corporation shall be managed by the president and four directors, being stockholders (a majority of whom shall constitute a quorum), who shall be chosen by the stockholders in general meeting, and continue in office for one year, and until others are elected in their stead; and in case of the death, resignation or disqualification of the president or any of the directors, the remaining members of the directory shall elect others to fill the vacancies for the residue of the term for which they were chosen. Affairs, how managed

6. In all general meetings of the stockholders a majority of all the Quorum

stockholders in interest, being present in person or by proxy, shall constitute a quorum for the transaction of business. Each stockholder shall be entitled to as many votes as he may hold shares in said company. The stockholders in general meeting shall have power to fix the time and place of the annual meetings, and to prescribe the mode in which general meetings of the stockholders may be called by the directory, and the manner in which the stockholders shall be notified of all meetings of their body. The stockholders shall determine and fix the compensation of the president.

Officers

7. The president and directors may appoint and dismiss at their pleasure, a secretary, and such other officers as may be necessary for the transaction of the business of the company, and allow such compensation for their services as they may deem reasonable, and may require such secretary and other officers to enter into bonds with security for the faithful discharge of their duties.

Assignment

8. Every stockholder not in debt to the company may, subject to such regulations and upon such terms as the stockholders may prescribe, in person or by attorney, assign his stock, or any number of his shares, on the books of the company; but no stockholder indebted to the company shall assign or make a transfer of his stock or receive a dividend, until such debt is paid or secured to the satisfaction of the board of directors.

Insurance on vessels, &c

9. The president and directors are authorized to make insurance upon vessels, freights, merchandise, specie, bullion, jewels, profits, commissions, bank notes, bills of exchange, and other evidences of debt, bottomry and respondentia interests, and make all and every insurance connected with marine risks and risks of transportation and navigation.

On dwellings, &c

10. To make insurance on dwellings, houses, stores and other kinds of buildings, and upon household furniture and other property and merchandise, against loss or damage by fire.

On lives, &c

11. To make insurance on lives; to grant annuities; to guarantee the payment of notes, bonds and bills of exchange; and to make all kinds of contracts for the insurance of every description of property; to receive money on deposit, and to pay interest thereon, as may be advantageous to the stockholders; to provide for the investment of funds of the company, in bank or other stocks; in the purchase of bonds issued by this or any other state or of the Confederate States, and of bonds of any incorporated company; to lend money upon personal or real security; and to purchase or otherwise acquire, to have and to hold, to convey and sell any real or personal estate for the purpose of securing any debt that may be due them, and for their own use and convenience: provided, that said company shall not issue or circulate any note of the nature of a bank note.

Money on deposit

Policies

12. All policies of insurance and other contracts made by the said company, signed by the president and countersigned by the secretary, shall be obligatory on said company, and have the same effect as if the said policies and contracts had been attested by a corporate seal.

Dividends

13. The president and directors may declare semi-annual or other dividends of the profits of the company, as they may deem proper; but no dividend shall be declared when, in the opinion of a majority of the board, the capital stock would be impaired thereby.

General meeting

14. The president and directors may at any time, when deemed necessary by them, call a general meeting of the stockholders; and any number of stockholders owning not less than one-fourth of the whole number of shares, may require the president and directors to call such meeting; and on their refusal to do so, may themselves call such meeting, giving fifteen days' notice thereof in one or more of the newspapers published in the city of Petersburg.

Agent

15. The president and directors may appoint an agent in any of the cities, towns or counties of this state or elsewhere, to receive

offerings for insurance, and for the transaction of such business of the company as may be confided to him.

16. The corporation hereby created shall be subject to the provisions of the Code of Virginia, so far as the same are applicable to it, and not inconsistent with the provisions of this act; and this act shall be subject to alteration, amendment or repeal, at the pleasure of the general assembly. Subject to Code

17. This act shall be in force from its passage. Commencement

---

CHAP. 44.—An ACT to amend the Charter of the Merchants Insurance Company of Richmond.

Passed October 28, 1863.

1. Be it enacted by the general assembly, that the second section of the act passed December the eighteenth, eighteen hundred and fifty-five, entitled an act to incorporate the Merchants insurance company in the city of Richmond, be and the same is hereby amended and re-enacted so as to read as follows: Act amended

"§ 2. The capital of the said corporation shall not be less than fifty thousand dollars nor more than three millions of dollars. The par value of the shares shall be twenty-five dollars each; and holders of certificates of stock shall be entitled to new certificates, embracing double the number of shares their face calls for. From time to time the board of directors of the said corporation may order books of subscription to be opened to the capital stock thereof; and such books of subscription shall be opened on the day so ordered; and the said books of subscription may at any time be closed, after giving twenty days' previous notice of such closing, in at least two of the newspapers published in the city of Richmond. The stock of the said corporation shall be assignable and transferable, according to such rules and subject to such restrictions and regulations as the board of directors shall make and establish; but in case the said corporation shall have any demand or claim against any stockholder thereof, whether such claim is due or to become due at any future period, such stockholder shall not be entitled to make such transfer, sale or conveyance of his or her stock in said corporation, or to receive any dividend thereon, until such claim or demand shall be paid or secured to be paid to the satisfaction of the board of directors: and unless such demand shall be paid or secured to be paid satisfactorily as aforesaid, within ninety days after the same shall have become due, then such stock of any such debtor, or so much thereof as shall be sufficient for that purpose, may be sold by the said corporation, under the direction of, and in such manner as the directors for the time being may think most advisable; and the proceeds thereof shall be applied towards the satisfaction of such claim or demand." Capital; Stock, how assignable

2. This act shall be in force from its passage. Commencement

CHAP. 45.—An ACT to incorporate the Catharine Furnace Company in the County of Spotsylvania.

Passed January 25, 1863.

1. Be it enacted by the general assembly of Virginia, that George B. Scott, J. Warren Slaughter, Charles C. Wellford, A. Alexander Little and C. B. Wellford, and such other persons as may be hereafter associated with them (any four of whom may own the whole capital stock), shall be and are hereby incorporated and made a body politic and corporate, by the name and style of The Catharine Furnace Company, for the purpose of mining iron ore, and of working and smelting the same into pig iron or otherwise, and also for the purpose of manufacturing iron in all its branches and uses, in said Company incorporated

county of Spotsylvania, and of transporting to market and selling iron ores or other products of their mine and manufactory; and of transacting the usual business of companies engaged in mining and manufacturing, and transporting to market and selling the products of their mines and manufactory.

Delegated powers — 2. The said company and their successors are hereby invested with all the rights, privileges and powers, and make subject to all the restrictions and regulations now provided by law for the general regulation of bodies politic and corporate, and of the mining and manufacturing companies of the commonwealth, so far as the same may apply to and are not inconsistent with the provisions of this act.

Capital — 3. Be it further enacted, that the capital stock of said company shall not be less than forty thousand dollars nor more than two hundred thousand dollars, to be divided into shares of one thousand dollars each; and the said company shall have the right to purchase and to hold land not exceeding ten thousand acres.

Commencement — 4. This act shall be in force from the passage thereof, and shall be subject to any amendment, alteration or modification, at the pleasure of the general assembly.

CHAP. 46.—An ACT to incorporate the Petersburg Iron Works.

Passed February 4, 1862.

Company incorporated — 1. Be it enacted by the general assembly of Virginia, that William T. Joynes, Charles O. Sanford, William E. Hinton, A. G. McIlwaine, Robert D. McIlwaine, Joseph B. Dunn, John G. Dunn, Joseph H. Cooper, James H. Cox, Thomas H. Wynne, Lemuel Peebles, John Alfriend, N. F. Rives, and their associates, be and they are hereby constituted a body corporate, for the purpose of manufacturing engines, cars, agricultural and other implements, and machinery generally, under the name and style of The Petersburg Iron Works; under which name they shall be entitled to all the rights and privileges of a corporation, and be subject to the provisions of the Code of Virginia, and the acts amendatory thereof, as far as the same may be applicable, and not inconsistent with this act: provided, that the said corporation shall not hold at one time more than fifteen acres of land, of which five acres may be in the city of Petersburg, and ten acres in the county of Chesterfield.

Capital — 2. The capital stock of said corporation shall be divided into shares of five hundred dollars each, and shall be in the aggregate not less than seventy-five thousand dollars nor more than three hundred thousand dollars.

How organized — 3. It shall not be necessary to open books of subscription for the stock of said company; but it shall be lawful for the parties hereby incorporated to proceed at once to organize the same; and the organization shall be as valid in all respects as if the same proceedings were had as are required by the Code.

General meeting — 4. Any general meeting of the stockholders after the first may be called upon such notice as may be prescribed by the by-laws of said corporation: provided the same shall be a notice of not less than ten days.

Commencement — 5. This act shall be in force from its passage.

CHAP. 47.—An ACT to incorporate the Union Manufacturing Company in the County of Fluvanna.

Passed October 30, 1862.

Company incorporated — 1. Be it enacted by the general assembly of Virginia, that James Magruder, Dudley Boston, H. J. Magruder, ——— King and B. H. Magruder, and such other persons as may hereafter be associated with them, or any of them, be and they are hereby incorporated and made a body politic and corporate, under the name and style of The Union Manufacturing Company, for the purpose of manufacturing wool, cotton, flour, tobacco, leather, iron and other articles, at Union mills, in the county of Fluvanna; and are invested with all the rights, privileges and powers conferred upon such bodies politic, and subject to all the restrictions and limitations contained in the Code of Virginia, so far as the same are applicable to and not inconsistent with the rights and powers hereby conferred, or modified by the provisions of this act.

2. The capital stock shall be not less than fifty thousand dollars nor more than one hundred thousand dollars, to be divided into shares of one hundred dollars, four-fifths of which shall never be owned by less than four shareholders; and it shall be lawful for the commissioners herein after named to open books of subscription for raising the said capital stock, at such times and places as they may designate. Capital

3. The said company shall have power to purchase, hold and possess land, not exceeding three hundred acres at any one time. Powers

4. The parties named in the first section of this act, or any three of them, are hereby appointed commissioners to carry out the provisions of this act. Commissioners

5. This act shall be in force from its passage, and shall be subject to amendment, modification or repeal, at the pleasure of the general assembly. Commencement

---

CHAP. 48.—An ACT to incorporate the Old Dominion Trading Company of the City of Richmond.

Passed March 25, 1863.

1. Be it enacted by the general assembly of Virginia, that A. Morris, P. C. Williams, William G. Payne, D. O. Huffard and E. D. Keeling, together with such other persons as are now connected with them, under the name and style of The Old Dominion Trading Company of the City of Richmond, be and the same are, together with their successors and assigns, hereby made and constituted a body corporate, under the said name and style of the Old Dominion trading company of the city of Richmond, for the purpose of owning, navigating and freighting ships and other vessels engaged in foreign and domestic commerce, trading from the ports of the Confederate States of America, and with powers to purchase and sell and otherwise deal in the products and commodities so freighted. Company incorporated

2. The capital stock of the said company shall not be less than one hundred thousand dollars nor more than one million of dollars, and shall be held in shares of five thousand dollars each. The affairs of the company shall be managed by a president and board of directors, whose term of office and their number shall be determined and elected by the stockholders; and the said board of directors shall possess all the corporate powers of the company: provided, that the said company shall be subject to such general laws as may affect corporations of this character. Capital

3. This act shall be in force from its passage, and shall be subject to repeal, modification or amendment, at the pleasure of the general assembly. Commencement

---

CHAP. 49.—An ACT to amend and re-enact an act entitled an act to incorporate the Old Dominion Trading Company, passed March 25th, 1863.

Passed October 3, 1863.

1. Be it enacted by the general assembly of Virginia, that an act passed twenty-fourth March eighteen hundred and sixty-three, enti- Act amended

tled an act to incorporate the Old Dominion trading company, be amended and re-enacted so as to read as follows:

"A. Morris, P. C. Williams, William G. Payne, D. O. Huffard and E. D. Keeling, together with such other persons as are now connected with them, under the name and style of The Old Dominion Trading Company of the City of Richmond, be and the same are, together with their successors and assigns, hereby made and constituted a body corporate, under the said name and style of the Old Dominion trading company of the city of Richmond, for the purpose of owning, navigating and freighting ships and other vessels engaged in foreign and domestic commerce, trading from the ports of the Confederate States of America, and with powers to purchase and sell and otherwise deal in the products and commodities so freighted.

Powers of company

Capital

The capital stock of said company shall not be less than one hundred thousand dollars nor more than two millions of dollars, and shall be held in shares of five hundred dollars each. The affairs of the company shall be managed by a president and board of directors, whose term of office and their number shall be determined and elected by the stockholders; and the said board of directors shall possess all the corporate powers of the company: provided, that the said company shall be subject to such general laws as may affect corporations of this character."

Commencement

2. This act shall be in force from its passage, and shall be subject to repeal, modification or amendment, at the pleasure of the general assembly.

CHAP. 50.—An ACT to amend and re-enact the 3d section of an act to incorporate the James River Canal Packet Company, passed March 16th, 1868

Passed September 28, 1863.

Act amended

1. Be it enacted by the general assembly of Virginia, that the third section of an act entitled an act to incorporate the James river canal packet company, passed the sixteenth of March eighteen hundred and sixty, be amended and re-enacted so as to read as follows:

Capital increased

"§ 3. The capital stock of said company shall not be less than fifty thousand dollars nor more than three hundred thousand dollars, to be divided into shares of one hundred dollars each."

Commencement

2. This act shall be in force from its passage.

CHAP. 51.—An ACT incorporating the Virginia Volunteer Navy Company

Passed October 13, 1863.

Company incorporated

1. Be it enacted by the general assembly, that Samuel J. Harrison, Bacon and Baskervill, Dunlop, Moncure and Company, Joseph R. Anderson and Company, J. L. Apperson, R. H. Maury and Company, W. F. Watson, J. P. George, John Robin McDaniel, R. M. Crenshaw, Thomas Branch, D. B. Dugger, Thomas R. Price and Company, Matthew Bridges, William B. Jones and Company, William B. Isaacs, Bolling W. Haxall, and such other persons as are now or may be hereafter associated with them, shall be and are hereby incorporated and made a body politic and corporate, by the name and style of The Virginia Volunteer Navy Company, for the purpose of owning, procuring, arming, equipping, manning and running a vessel or vessels for the volunteer navy of the Confederate States, to cruise against the commercial or naval vessels of all enemies of the Confederate States wherever found, according to the provisions of the act of congress of the Confederate States, entitled an act to establish a volunteer navy, approved April eighteenth, eighteen hundred and sixty-three; and after the present war shall have closed, all vessels so owned may be employed in commercial enterprises, or otherwise disposed of, as the said company may determine.

Powers

2. The said company and their successors are hereby invested with all the rights, privileges and powers, and made subject to the restrictions and regulations now provided by law for the general regulation of bodies politic and corporate, save so far as modified by the provisions of this act. Delegated powers

3. The capital stock of the said company shall consist of not less than one million nor more than ten millions of dollars, to be divided into shares of five hundred dollars each; and the said company having already had subscribed one million of dollars, and by regular election by the stockholders, the following persons have been elected president and directors of the said company until the first Monday in May eighteen hundred and sixty-four, to wit: Samuel J. Harrison as president, Robert Archer, J. L. Apperson, Thomas W. McCance and J. R. McDaniel as the directors, it is hereby enacted that the said persons shall be such president and directors of the said company until the date last mentioned, and until successors shall be elected by the stockholders of said company, on said first Monday in May eighteen hundred and sixty-four, or thereafter. Capital

4. The president of the said company shall be one of the directors, and the directors may consist of five or more, according to the wishes of the said company. In a meeting of stockholders each stockholder may in person or by proxy give the following vote on whatever stock he may hold in the same right, to wit, one vote for each share of such stock, whatever the number may be. President and directors

5. Books for subscription to increase the capital stock until it reaches the maximum of ten millions may be opened from time to time by the directors, who are hereby appointed commissioners for the purpose, and shall be kept open for thirty days on each occasion; and before closing the books, ten days' previous public notice shall be given in two or more newspapers published in the city of Richmond. Increase of capital authorized

6. This act shall be in force from the passage thereof, but the general assembly may at any time amend or repeal the same. Commencement

---

CHAP. 52.—An ACT to reorganize the Board of Trustees for Bethany College.

Passed October 23, 1863.

Whereas, the members of the board of trustees of Bethany college, an institution possessing valuable real estate and a large endowment fund, are many of them citizens of the United States, and others of them disloyal citizens of this state, of whom some are in the service of the enemy, and by reason of the occupation of Brooke county by the enemy, some loyal members of the board cannot attend sittings in that county, and there is reason to apprehend that that portion of said trustees accessible to the institution may take such action as may jeopard the rights and property of the institution and impair its usefulness: Therefore, Preamble

1. Be it enacted by the general assembly, that James W. Goss, R. L. Coleman, Charles W. Russell and Joseph H. Pendleton, members of the board of trustees of Bethany college, and such other loyal members of the board as are within the confederate military lines, shall be and are hereby constituted the board of trustees of Bethany college, on whom are conferred all the rights, duties, privileges and powers conferred by the charter of said college upon the board of trustees therein organized. Directors

2. Be it further enacted, that the first meeting of the board constituted herein shall be held at the capitol in the city of Richmond, on Friday the thirtieth day of October eighteen hundred and sixty-three; and at such meeting any three or more of said trustees may constitute a quorum; and they may proceed at that or any subsequent meeting to fill all vacancies that may occur in the board, and When and where meeting to be held Powers

may declare vacant the place of any member not within said lines: provided, that no person shall be elected a member of said board who is not a citizen of the Confederate States. They shall elect from their number a president pro tempore. Should the first meeting provided for by this act fail from any cause to take place, then it shall be lawful for any two of the trustees herein named to designate such other time and place as they may deem proper, giving notice thereof for one week in some newspaper published in the city of Richmond; and further meetings of the board shall be held at such times and places as the majority may determine; or the president pro tempore, upon the request in writing of three members of the board, may fix such time and place of meeting. Notice of meetings may be given in such manner as the board may prescribe.

Commencement 3. This act shall be in force from its passage.

CHAP. 53.—An ACT to incorporate the Virginia Female Institute of the City of Richmond.

Passed November 2, 1863.

Company incorporated 1. Be it enacted by the general assembly, that Olof A. Erricson, James Gordon, Charles H. Read, Robert A. Lancaster, Patteson Fletcher, S. P. Christian and Alexander Garrett, and their successors, be and they are hereby constituted a body politic and corporate, under the name and style of The Virginia Female Institute: and by that name shall have perpetual succession and a common seal, and may sue and be sued, implead and be impleaded in any court of law or equity within this state. The said Virginia female institute shall be capable in law to receive, hold and dispose of real and personal property, in order to carry out the purposes of its incorporation.

How managed 2. The said Virginia female institute shall be under the control and management of the said trustees and their successors, who shall appoint a treasurer and all necessary officers and professors, and make such rules and regulations for the government of the institution as to them shall seem meet, not inconsistent with the laws of this state, or of the Confederate States. A majority of the trustees shall constitute a quorum for the transaction of business; and any vacancy or vacancies in the said board of trustees, occasioned by death, resignation or otherwise, shall be supplied by appointment by the remaining trustees: and they may remove any member of their body, two-thirds of the whole number being present and concurring.

Duties of treasurer 3. The treasurer shall receive all moneys accruing to the institute and property delivered to his care, and shall pay or deliver the same to the order of the board of trustees. Before entering upon the discharge of his duties, he shall give bond with such security and in such penalty as the board may direct, made payable to the trustees for the time being, and their successors, and conditioned for the faithful performance of the duties of his office, under such rules and regulations as the board may adopt.

4. The board of trustees, in connection with the president and professors of the institute, shall have power to confer such diplomas and literary titles as they may think best calculated to promote the cause of female education.

Commencement 5. This act shall be in force from its passage.

CHAP. 54.—An ACT to amend the Charter of the Bank of Rockbridge.

Passed October 31, 1863.

Act amended 1. Be it enacted by the general assembly, that the sixth, seventh, eighth, ninth, tenth and eleventh sections of the act passed on the twenty-first day of March eighteen hundred and fifty-two, entitled an act incorporating the Bank of Rockbridge, be and the same are hereby repealed.

Expiration of charter.

2. That the charter of said bank shall continue and be in force until the twenty-first day of March eighteen hundred and seventy-two.

Duty of treasurer

3. The treasurer of the state may retransfer to the said bank the certificate of debt of the state now held by him in trust for the purposes of said bank, or any part thereof, upon receiving and canceling an equal amount of the notes of said bank, countersigned by him; and if the notes of said bank, so countersigned by him, have been so far returned and canceled as that the amount outstanding shall not exceed the sum of five thousand dollars, the said treasurer may retransfer the residue of said certificates or guaranteed bonds to said bank, upon receiving from at least five of the stockholders thereof, with at least five good and sufficient securities, to be approved by him, a joint and several bond, payable to the commonwealth of Virginia, in a penalty equal to at least three times the amount of such outstanding notes; and conditioned to pay the same, on demand, at the place of business of said bank, or of either of the obligors therein: which bond shall be recorded in the manner prescribed in the fourth section of chapter one hundred and eighty-six of the Code of Virginia, and shall have the force of a judgment; and for every breach of the conditions thereof, execution may be issued, upon ten days' notice of the application therefor, in the name of the commonwealth, for the benefit of the holders of any such outstanding unredeemed notes, for the amount thereof and costs.

Notes

4. The bank shall not issue and pay out any notes for circulation, except of the denomination of five dollars, ten dollars, or some multiple of ten.

Quarterly statements

5. Every quarterly statement of this bank shall, in addition to the information which the Code of Virginia requires to be made, also exhibit the aggregate debt due by the bank, the oustanding debts due the bank, its discount of inland and foreign bills of exchange, its loans to directors, its specie circulation and deposits, on the first day of each month of the quarter it embraces.

Board of directors

6. The board of directors shall consist of not more than nine nor less than seven, as the stockholders may direct.

7. Provided, that nothing in this act contained shall debar the Bank of Rockbridge of the privileges contained in an act passed March twenty-ninth, eighteen hundred and sixty-two, entitled an act to provide a currency of notes of less denomination than five dollars.

Commencement

8. This act shall commence and be in force from and after the time when the provisions have been approved by the stockholders in said bank, convened in general meeting, at any time before the tenth day of January eighteen hundred and sixty-four, and such approval shall have been made and certified by the president and cashier of said bank to the governor of the commonwealth.

CHAP. 55.—An ACT to repeal so much of the act passed February 15th, 1853, as exempts the White Male Citizens of the County of King George, of forty-five years and upwards, from working on the Public Roads in that County.

Passed October 13, 1863.

Act amended

1. Be it enacted by the general assembly, that so much of the act passed February fifteenth, eighteen hundred and fifty-three, as exempts the white male citizens of the county of King George, of the age of forty-five years and upwards, from working on the public roads in said county, be and the same is hereby repealed.

Commencement

2. This act shall be in force from its passage.

CHAP. 56.—An ACT authorizing the County Court of Washington to dispense with the Law of Enclosures in said County.

Passed October 31, 1863.

Powers of court

1. Be it enacted by the general assembly of Virginia, that the county court of the county of Washington shall have power, all the justices having been summoned, and a majority thereof being present, to dispense with the existing laws in regard to enclosures, so far as their county may be concerned, or such parts thereof, to be described by metes and bounds, as in their discretion they may deem it expedient to exempt from the operation of such law.

Trespass

2. If any horses, mules, cattle, hogs, sheep or goats, or any animal of either of the preceding classes, shall enter into any grounds in the county of Washington, in which the existing law of enclosures has been repealed as aforesaid, the owner or manager of any such animal shall be liable to the owner or occupier of such grounds for any damages arising from such entry. For every succeeding trespass by such animal, the owner thereof shall be liable for double damages; and after having given at least five days' notice to the owner or manager of such animal of two previous trespasses, the animal shall be forfeited to the overseers of the poor, for the benefit of the poor, if it be found again trespassing on said grounds.

Repealing clause

3. All acts and parts of acts in conflict with the provisions of this act are hereby repealed.

Commencement

4. This act shall be in force from its passage.

CHAP. 57.—An ACT for the relief of William E. Gaskins and James H. Gaskins.

Passed September 29, 1863.

Preamble

Whereas, by virtue of a written instrument in the nature of a rent charge and mortgage executed on the twentieth day of November seventeen hundred and ninety, by one Cuthbert Bullett to the overseers of the poor of Prince William county, and of record in the county court of Fauquier, a lien was created on certain real estate situate in said county of Fauquier, now the property of William E. Gaskins and James H. Gaskins of said last mentioned county, by purchase from the heirs of said Bullett, said lien being intended to secure a debt of eight hundred and eighty-five pounds, with interest at the rate of five per centum per annum, payable annually, from the date aforesaid, to said overseers of the poor, and their successors, for the purposes in said deed specified; which interest has been paid in full up to the twentieth day of November eighteen hundred and sixty: And whereas the said William E. Gaskins and James H. Gaskins are desirous to remove said lien, by payment of the amount thereof, principal and interest, as by the terms of said instrument they are specially authorized to do, but which they are unable to do by reason of the continued occupancy of said county of Prince William by the public enemy:

Amount appropriated

1. Be it enacted by the general assembly, that it shall be lawful for the second auditor to receive of the said William E. Gaskins and James H. Gaskins, or either of them, the sum of twenty-nine hundred and fifty dollars, with interest thereon at the rate of five per centum from the twentieth day of November eighteen hundred and sixty, to be applied to the credit of the literary fund; and that upon the payment thereof, the attorney general shall execute and deliver to the said William E. Gaskins and James H. Gaskins, their heirs and assigns, a deed of release and reconveyance of the real estate in said instrument of writing described; which deed, when so executed and delivered, shall be effectual to extinguish said lien.

Funds, how held

2. The fund thus received shall be held by the second auditor as part of the literary fund, and shall be by him invested, and its income

applied to the use and benefit of the school commissioners of Prince William county, who shall receive, apply and account for the same, as directed by an act of the general assembly passed on the third day of February eighteen hundred and nineteen, entitled an act concerning the school commissioners of Prince William.

3. This act shall be in force from its passage. Commencement.

CHAP. 58.—An ACT to enlarge the powers of the Common Council of the City of Petersburg.

Passed October 16, 1863.

1. Be it enacted by the general assembly, that the council of the city of Petersburg be and the same is hereby authorized to suppress riots and unlawful assemblies in the said city; to suppress gaming and gambling houses, tippling and tippling houses, and to prevent or regulate the sale of spirituous and fermented liquors within the said city, and around the same to the boundaries to which the jurisdiction of its corporation court or officers of police extends in criminal cases. And for the purposes of extending the powers and authority hereby vested in said council, the said council may enact ordinances and impose penalties for the violation thereof, not exceeding five hundred dollars, and imprisonment not exceeding three months; may authorize and empower the proper officers and police of the city to seize such liquors sold or kept for sale, for the use of the city, and to shut up the houses in which such liquors are so sold or kept for sale, and arrest the persons who shall sell or keep for sale or purchase the said liquors in violation of the said ordinances, and hold them in custody until they shall give security for their good behavior, in such penalty, not exceeding one thousand dollars, as the justice before whom they are taken shall prescribe. And the said officers and police shall have the same powers and authority in discharging their duties under said ordinances, as state officers have in cases of breaches of the peace. Powers of council

2. The said council may organize and establish an armed police, and appoint such officers thereof as to the council may seem expedient; and the said officers shall be accountable to and under the supervision and control of the council, or such other body or officer as the council may prescribe. Armed police, &c.

3. This act shall be in force from its passage. Commencement

CHAP. 59.—An ACT authorizing the Board of Public Works, acting as a Board of Supervisors for the production and distribution of Salt, to modify the Contract of Lease between Stuart, Buchanan & Co. and Thomas R. Friend.

Passed October 16, 1863.

Whereas, by a resolution adopted on the twenty-first day of September eighteen hundred and sixty-three, the board of public works, acting as a board of supervisors for the production and distribution of salt, have recommended to the general assembly to make some equitable modification of the terms of the contract of lease between Stuart, Buchanan and Company and Thomas R. Friend, assigned by the former to the state of Virginia: Preamble

1. Be it therefore enacted, that the board of public works, acting as a board of supervisors for the production and distribution of salt, be and they are hereby authorized to make such modifications and alterations as may be just and equitable to both parties in the contract between Stuart, Buchanan and Company and Thomas R. Friend, bearing date the twenty-third day of August eighteen hundred and sixty-two, for the lease of the Findley furnace at the Smyth and Powers of board of public works

Washington county salt works, which said lease was assigned to the state of Virginia by the said Stuart. Buchanan and Company, in March eighteen hundred and sixty-three: provided, however, that such modifications and alterations be assented to by the said Thomas R. Friend.

Commencement 2. This act shall be in force from its passage.

CHAP. 60.—An ACT to repeal the act passed March 5th, 1862, entitled an act to authorize the issue of Registered Certificates of State Stock to Dr. Peter F. Brown, in lieu of two lost bonds.

Passed October 19, 1863.

Preamble Whereas it appears to the general assembly that the two coupon bonds, the property of Doctor Peter F. Brown of Accomack county, referred to in the act passed on the fifth day of March eighteen hundred and sixty-two, entitled an act to authorize the issue of registered certificates of state stock to Doctor Peter F. Brown, in lieu of two lost bonds, have been recovered from the enemy: Therefore,

Act repealed 1. Be it enacted by the general assembly, that the act passed on the fifth day of March in the year one thousand eight hundred and sixty-two, entitled an act to authorize the issue of registered certificates of state stock to Doctor Peter F. Brown, in lieu of two lost bonds, be and the same is hereby repealed.

Commencement 2. This act shall be in force from its passage.

CHAP. 61.—An ACT allowing the Petersburg Iron Manufacturing Company to hold not more than twenty thousand acres of land at any one time.

Passed October 22, 1863.

Powers of company 1. Be it enacted by the general assembly, that it shall be lawful for the Petersburg iron works to establish and work one or more iron furnaces in any part of this state; and for this purpose, to acquire and hold not exceeding fifteen thousand acres of land in the counties of Botetourt and Alleghany, and not to hold more than twenty thousand acres in all at any one time.

Commencement 2. This act shall be in force from its passage, and be subject to alteration or amendment, at the pleasure of the general assembly.

CHAP. 62.—An ACT to authorize the Sale of Capon Springs.

Passed October 22, 1863.

Sale authorized 1. Be it enacted by the general assembly, that the trustees of Watsontown, generally known as the Capon springs (a majority of them consenting thereto), be and they are hereby authorized to sell at public or private sale, as they may think best, for the best price they can obtain, the land and lots vested in them by the acts of December twelfth, seventeen hundred and eighty-seven, March twentieth, eighteen hundred and forty-seven, March eighth, eighteen hundred and forty-nine, December fourteenth, eighteen hundred and forty-nine, and January eleventh, eighteen hundred and fifty: provided, however, in the sale and conveyance, that the purchaser shall permit the visitors frequenting the said springs to have free access to and the use of the mineral springs on the said lands, and of the pavilion, baths and other improvements erected by the said trustees, not charging for the use of the water or baths more than was at any time charged by the trustees: and if the trustees shall have sold any life tickets for the use of the water or baths, reserving to such persons the free use of the water and baths. And the trustees shall apply the proceeds of sale, first to pay the debt now due by them, contracted in the construction of the improvements thereon, and the balance, if any, to the further improvement of the property, to be expended under the direction of Henry M. Brent, Philip Williams and Julius C. Waddle.

2. This act shall be in force from its passage. Commencement

CHAP. 63.—An ACT to authorize the Sale and Transportation of Salt belonging to John N. Clarkson.

Passed October 30, 1863.

1. Be it enacted by the general assembly, that it shall be lawful for John N. Clarkson, superintendent of salt works, to sell any salt to which he has or may during the present year become entitled for the hire of slaves employed at Saltville, under contract made with Stuart, Buchanan and Company, or with the state of Virginia; and the board of public works is authorized to allow said Clarkson to transport said salt in such manner as may not conflict with the prior right of transportation now held by the state, or with the equal rights of other citizens. Salt, how transported

2. This act shall be in force from its passage. Commencement

CHAP. 64.—An ACT for the relief of Washington G. Singleton, Clerk of the District Court of the Sixth Judicial District.

Passed October 22, 1863.

1. Be it enacted by the general assembly, that the auditor of public accounts be and he is hereby authorized and required to issue his warrant on the treasury, payable out of any money therein not otherwise appropriated, in favor of Washington G. Singleton, or his legal representatives, for the sum of one hundred and fifty dollars, in full of office rent and fees due said Singleton as clerk of the district court for the sixth judicial district for the year ending December eighteen hundred and sixty-two. Amount appropriated

2. This act shall be in force from its passage. Commencement

CHAP. 65.—An ACT refunding to John Nunan part of a License Tax paid by him.

Passed October 30, 1863.

1. Be it enacted by the general assembly, that the auditor of public accounts be and he is hereby authorized and directed to issue his warrant on the treasury, payable out of any money therein not otherwise appropriated, in favor of John Nunan, or his legal representatives, for the sum of forty dollars, being part of a license tax imposed for the distillation of ardent spirits, and which license privilege had been prohibited by law for the residue of the term for which he was so licensed. Auditor to issue warrant

2. This act shall be in force from its passage. Commencement

RESOLUTIONS.

No. 1.—Preamble and Resolutions asserting the Jurisdiction and Sovereignty of the State of Virginia over her Ancient Boundaries.

Adopted October 8, 1863.

Whereas the general assembly of Virginia did, on the seventeenth day of January eighteen hundred and sixty-two, adopt the following preamble and resolution:

"Whereas, the public enemy, invited by domestic foes, being in power in some of the counties of Virginia, where they are confiscating the property of loyal citizens, and otherwise oppressing them in a cruel manner: and whereas the traitors there, contemplating a division of this time-honored commonwealth, with the aid of the public enemy, have set up a pretended government over the same, which, under the force of circumstances, could not be prevented by the timely sending of an adequate military force: and whereas the legislature desires to reassure all loyal citizens throughout the commonwealth of their desire and intention to protect them: Therefore, Preamble

Resolved by the senate and house of delegates, that in no event will the state of Virginia submit to or consent to the loss of a foot of her soil; that it is the firm determination of the state, and known to be that of the confederate government, to assert and maintain the jurisdiction and sovereignty of the state of Virginia to the uttermost limits of her ancient boundaries, at any and at every cost."

And whereas, since the passage of said resolution by the general assembly, the government of the United States, in pursuance of its settled purpose to override and destroy the separate existence of the states, has attempted to form a new state out of the state of Virginia, in contravention alike of the constitution of the United States and the constitution of the state of Virginia: and is upholding, by the power of her armies, certain evil-disposed and traitorous citizens of this state, who are leagued with the said United States in their nefarious and wicked purposes against the peace, welfare, institutions and integrity of Virginia: and whereas it is the fixed and unalterable intention of Virginia to maintain and assert her prerogative as set forth in said resolution of the last general assembly, and approved by the confederate congress, and to protect alike her citizens and her soil from the machinations of traitors within and enemies without: Therefore,

1. Resolved by the senate and house of delegates, that Virginia maintains, fixed and unalterable, the purpose and determination so clearly set forth in the resolution of the last general assembly, and that this general assembly cordially readopts and sanctions the same, and redeclares alike to her citizens and the world, that it is the firm determination of the state, and known to be that of the confederate government, to assert and maintain the jurisdiction and sovereignty of the state of Virginia to the uttermost limits of her ancient boundaries, at any and every cost. Purpose and determination of state

2. Resolved, that the governor be requested to send a copy of these resolutions, properly certified, to the congress of the Confederate States, to convene on the twenty-second of February eighteen hundred and sixty-four, for their approval. Governor to transmit to congress

No. 2.—Joint Resolution in relation to the Increase of Pay to Soldiers, and Commutation for Rations not furnished in kind.

Adopted October 21, 1863.

Increase of pay recommended

Resolved by the general assembly, that we instruct our senators and request our representatives in the confederate congress to use their best efforts to procure, at as early a day as practicable, the passage of a law giving increased compensation to the soldiers in the confederate army, and commutation for rations allowed by the Army Regulations, and not furnished in kind.

No. 3.—Joint Resolution defining what Commutation for Clothing is to be allowed to the Non-commissioned Officers and Privates of the Virginia State Line.

Adopted October 30, 1863.

Commutation for clothing

Resolved by the general assembly, that the non-commissioned officers and privates of the Virginia state line are entitled to the same commutation for clothing that is allowed by the Confederate States for the time being; that is to say, at the rate of fifty dollars per annum for such period of their service as is prior to October eighth. eighteen hundred and sixty-two, and at the rate of one hundred and thirty-four dollars and twelve cents per annum for such period of service as is subsequent to the eighth day of October eighteen hundred and sixty-two; and at said rates for any shorter period of service: the same to be allowed on the pay rolls, deducting therefrom the pay; also, if necessary, the price of all clothing actually issued in kind to each non-commissioned officer and private. The amount thereof to be certified by the company commandant or the quartermasters of the regiment or battalion to which the company belonged.

No. 4.—Joint Resolution directing the Paymaster of the Virginia Forces to suspend Payment of Commutation, &c.

Adopted October 8, 1863.

Suspension of commutation

Resolved by the senate and house of delegates, that the paymaster of the Virginia forces suspend all payments of commutation for clothing until the further order of the general assembly.

No. 5.—Joint Resolution concerning Commissioners of the Revenue.

Adopted October 23, 1863.

Districts to be numbered

1. Resolved by the general assembly, that it shall be the duty of every county and corporation court in this commonwealth, in whose county or corporation more than one commissioner of the revenue is now authorized by law, at the first court after the receipt or notification of this resolution, to designate by order of court each commissioner's district by number, commencing with number one, and continuing a successive enumeration until the whole number in the county authorized by law is completed. That such court also, through its clerk, report immediately to the auditor of public accounts the designation of the districts aforesaid, and the name of the present commissioner of the district so designated.

Report to auditor

Designation of districts not to be changed

2. After such order of court shall be made, no change in the designation of the districts shall be made, unless the number of the districts shall be increased or diminished in the county or corporation.

No. 6.—Joint Resolution ratifying the Contract entered into between the Chairmen of the Joint Committee on Salt, and Stuart, Buchanan & Co and Charles Scott & Co.

Adopted October 29, 1863.

Be it resolved by the general assembly, that the contract made and entered into by Robert A. Coghill, chairman of senate committee, and James V. Brooke, chairman of house committee, with Stuart, Buchanan & Co. and Charles Scott & Co., bearing date the twenty-seventh day of October eighteen hundred and sixty-three, and providing for the sale and delivery by the last named parties of forty thousand bushels of salt to the state, in the words and figures following, to wit: Ratification of contract

Memorandum of a contract made and entered into by Robert A. Coghill, chairman of the senate committee, and James V. Brooke, chairman of the house committee—the two committees acting as a joint committee of the general assembly of Virginia on supply and distribution of salt—parties of the first part, and Stuart, Buchanan & Co. and Charles Scott & Co., parties of the second part: Contract for salt

Witnesseth, that said parties of the second part agree and covenant to sell to the commonwealth of Virginia forty thousand bushels of salt, to be delivered at their works at Saltville in the months of November and December eighteen hundred and sixty-three, and in daily installments, as near as reasonably may be, or as much faster as the said parties of the second part may desire: the salt to be subject to inspection, and actually inspected and made merchantable salt.

And the parties of the first part, acting on behalf of the state, do agree and covenant to pay to the said parties of the second part two dollars per bushel for said salt so delivered, on delivery, and to furnish the sacks for the same.

They also stipulate, on behalf of the state and of the board of public works, that the parties of the second part shall, during said two months, have the free and unrestricted use of all trains owned or hired by them, now on the rail road, and of any other trains not belonging to the Virginia and Tennessee rail road company, which they may introduce on the road, subject only to terms now made or to be made with the Virginia and Tennessee rail road company for the use of their roadways; and that the state and the board of public works shall not prevent the Virginia and Tennessee rail road company from hauling wood for said parties of the second part, next after the furnaces of the state of Virginia, when the said parties of the second part are without a sufficient wood train, if that should happen to be the case at any time before the first day of January next. Use of trains for transportation

And they further stipulate on behalf of the state, that the said parties of the second part shall be allowed a fair and reasonable abatement from their contract for delivery of salt, in the event of interruption of their work by incursion of the public enemy, and in proportion to the time or duration of such interruption. Abatement

Witness the hands of the parties this twenty-seventh day of October eighteen hundred and sixty-three.

R. A. Coghill,
Ch'n Senate Committee.
Jas. V. Brooke,
Ch'n House Committee.
Stuart, Buchanan & Co.
Charles Scott & Co.

—be and the same is hereby ratified and confirmed.

No. 7.—Report of the Joint Committee on Salt, on a Communication from the Governor enclosing a Communication from the Governor of Georgia, in respect to Interruption in the transportation of Salt belonging to that State.

Adopted October 31, 1863.

Report in respect to interruption in transportation of salt belonging to the state of Georgia

To the General Assembly of Virginia—The joint committee, to whom has been referred the message of the governor of this commonwealth, inviting the attention of the general assembly to an accompanying "communication from the governor of Georgia, relative to supply of salt," beg leave to report:

That they have had the subject therein referred to under careful consideration, and can find nothing in the character of the rules adopted by the board of public works, touching the transportation of salt, which would justify the conclusion that "our sister state of Georgia has been shamefully treated," or require the interposition of the general assembly to "rebuke it."

Your committee appreciate very fully the importance as well as the propriety of cultivating relations of comity and kindness between the states of this Confederacy. Engaged as they are in a common struggle, and dependent, in great measure, upon the prevalence of a spirit of harmony and brotherhood for the ultimate triumph which they hope to achieve, it is the obvious policy of the several states to avoid, in their commercial intercourse, any measure which may lead to discord and discontent.

Nevertheless, your committee cannot consider it reasonable that this principle should be carried to such an extent as to absorb all other considerations.

It must be held in subserviency to the higher obligation, under which every government is laid, to provide specially for the safety and welfare of its own people: and tested by this standard, the conduct of the board of public works has been, in the opinion of your committee, entirely unexceptionable. For, while it would be gross illiberality in the authorities of the state of Virginia to deny to any of her sister states all proper facilities for sharing in the benefits to be derived from the production and distribution of an adequate supply of salt, it would be manifest injustice to her own people to permit the enjoyment of such privileges in such manner as to deprive them of advantages to which they are properly entitled.

As your committee understand the resolution adopted by the board of public works in relation to this subject, it provides, in substance, as follows: That foreign trains shall be permitted to run upon the rail roads of this commonwealth, upon condition that such trains shall transport the salt manufactured by states, when awaiting transportation, in preference to salt manufactured on private account, or for purposes of speculation.

The effect of this rule would seem to be, to insure to the people of the states interested in the production of salt, an adequate supply upon the most reasonable terms, and to protect them against the evils of speculation and extortion. It certainly cannot be regarded as improper that this state should require that trains of other states, after transporting the salt of such states, should transport for the state of Virginia before transporting the salt of private manufacturers, whose interest it is to sell at extortionate prices.

This rule, properly construed, does not give the state of Virginia any priority in the use of foreign trains over the state to which such trains belong. If such has been the result in any case, it must have been due to the uncertainty which attached to the true character of some of the enterprises purporting to be conducted on state account.

A repetition of such mistakes may be effectually prevented, by adopting such rules as will certainly fix the true relation which enterprises bear to the several states.

To accomplish this object, your committee submit the following resolution, and recommend its passage by the general assembly:

Resolved by the general assembly, that the power conferred by the act of March thirtieth, eighteen hundred and sixty-three, upon the superintendent of salt works, to control (under the control of the board of supervisors) transportation on the several rail roads of this commonwealth, for the conveyance of supplies to the salt works, &c., shall, so far as trains belonging to other states are concerned, be exercised so as to allow transportation by said trains in the following order of priority: Order of priority for transportation

1st. To the transportation necessary for the Confederate States government.

2d. To the transportation necessary for the state owning or employing such trains, in the production and distribution of salt made by such state, for the supply of its own citizens, and not the subject of speculation. In ascertaining the true character of any of the works employed in the manufacture of salt, the certificate of the governor of any state, under the seal thereof, shall be regarded as unquestionable evidence of the facts stated therein.

3d. To the transportation necessary for the state of Virginia in the production and distribution of state salt.

4th. To the transportation necessary for private citizens or corporations of the state owning or employing said trains.

Your committee submit herewith a communication from the board of supervisors, and also a communication from Honorable B. H. Bigham, agent for Georgia.

Resolved, that the governor be requested to transmit to the governor of Georgia a copy of this report, and a copy of his communication addressed to the general assembly of Virginia, calling their attention to the subject of the communication of the governor of the state of Georgia. To be transmitted to governor of Georgia

INDEX.

ACTS

OF THE

GENERAL ASSEMBLY

OF THE

STATE OF VIRGINIA,

PASSED AT SESSION OF 1863-4,

IN THE

EIGHTY-EIGHTH YEAR OF THE COMMONWEALTH.

RICHMOND:
WILLIAM F. RITCHIE, PUBLIC PRINTER.
1864.

PUBLIC OR GENERAL ACTS.

CHAP. 1.—An ACT to suspend the act passed March 28th, 1863, entitled an act imposing Taxes for the Support of Government, and to continue the Rights and Remedies of the Commonwealth, and prescribing further Regulations for Licenses.

Passed March 3, 1864.

Whereas it appears, from the report and estimates of the auditor of public accounts, that the available balance which will be in the treasury on the fifteenth of March eighteen hundred and sixty-four, with additional receipts accruing during the current fiscal year, will amount to the sum of nine million three hundred and twenty-five thousand four hundred and forty-five dollars, which sum will, in the opinion of this general assembly, be ample for the support of the state government, as well as for compliance with any demands which may probably be made upon the treasury during the current year: Therefore, Preamble

1. Be it enacted by the general assembly, that the act passed March twenty-eighth, eighteen hundred and sixty-three, entitled an act imposing taxes for the support of government, be and the same is hereby suspended until the thirty-first day of January eighteen hundred and sixty-five. Act of 1863 suspended

2. All the rights, remedies and penalties imposed by said act, which may have accrued under the same, are reserved to the commonwealth. Rights, remedies and penalties reserved

3. In every case, under the operation of the act aforesaid, or any other law now in force, in which a license was required, a license shall be obtained, and a fee of one dollar shall be paid to the commissioner issuing such license. License required

4. There shall be no assessment of property or licenses, during the suspension of the act aforesaid, by the commissioners of the revenue, but licenses shall be issued and obtained without assessment. No assessment to be made

5. This act shall be in force from its passage. Commencement

CHAP. 2.—An ACT appropriating the Public Revenue for the Fiscal Years 1863–4 and 1864–5.

Passed March 8, 1864.

1. Be it enacted by the general assembly, that the public taxes and arrearages of taxes due prior to the first day of October eighteen hundred and sixty-three, and not otherwise appropriated, and all other revenue and public money not otherwise appropriated by law, which shall come into the treasury prior to the first day of October eighteen hundred and sixty-five, and the surplus of all appropriations made prior to the said first day of October eighteen hundred and sixty-five, shall constitute a general fund, and be appropriated for the fiscal years to close respectively on the thirtieth day of September eighteen hundred and sixty-four and the thirtieth day of September eighteen hundred and sixty-five, and to be paid out upon the warrant of the auditor of public accounts, to wit: General fund

First—The appropriations for the year ending the thirtieth day of September eighteen hundred and sixty-four shall be as follows, to wit:

Civil Department.

General assembly — To pay the per diem allowance and mileage, and other expenses of the members and officers of the general assembly for the extra session continued in October, and the regular session which commenced on the first Monday in December eighteen hundred and sixty-three; to pay the pages of the senate and house of delegates, the porter of the senate, and servants for making fires and superintending furnaces in the capitol, upon the certificates heretofore issued in such cases, seven hundred thousand dollars.

Judiciary — To pay the salaries and mileage of judges, and the salaries of all other officers of the civil government, two hundred and fifty thousand dollars.

Expense of courts — To pay allowances to commonwealth's attorneys, clerks, sheriffs, tipstaffs and messengers of courts, including fuel, stationery and office rent for the supreme, district and circuit courts, seventy-five thousand dollars.

Clerks in auditor's office — To pay temporary clerks in the office of the auditor of public accounts, for services accruing prior to the twenty-second day of January eighteen hundred and sixty-four, one thousand four hundred and eighty-nine dollars and eighty-five cents.

Messenger — To pay for the services of a messenger in the office of the auditor of public accounts, eight hundred dollars.

Civil contingent fund — To pay expenses chargeable to the civil contingent fund, one hundred thousand dollars.

Civil prosecutions — To pay expenses of civil prosecutions, eight thousand dollars.

Vaccine agents — To pay salary of vaccine agent at Lewisburg, and allowance to vaccine agent at Richmond (five hundred dollars each), one thousand dollars.

Commissioners of revenue — To pay the commissions of the commissioners of the revenue allowed by law, eighty thousand dollars.

Printing — To pay expenses of printing for the general assembly and public officers, and for paper and books for public offices, sixty thousand dollars.

Births, deaths and marriages — To pay commissioners of the revenue and clerks of courts, for their services in ascertaining and recording the marriages, births and deaths, and other duties required by law in relation thereto, two thousand dollars.

Public warehouses — To pay allowances to commissioners of public warehouses, one hundred and fifty dollars.

Governor's house — To pay for repairs to and furnishing of the governor's house, to be paid upon the certificate of the superintendent of public buildings, five thousand five hundred dollars.

Capitol — To pay for repairs to the capitol, two thousand dollars.

Records of court of appeals — To pay for printing records of the court of appeals and district courts, four thousand dollars.

Secretary of sinking fund — To pay the usual allowance to the secretary of the sinking fund, three hundred dollars.

Comparing polls — To pay expenses of comparing polls in sundry elections, fifteen hundred dollars.

David Patteson — To pay David Patteson, for making fires and other attentions to the public offices, for arrearages of pay from October first, eighteen hundred and sixty-three, to January first, eighteen hundred and sixty-four, one hundred dollars.

Military Department.

Adjutant general's office — To pay the salaries of the adjutant general and his clerk, seven thousand one hundred and twenty-five dollars.

Public guard — To pay officers and privates of the public guard, their allowances for pay, rations and clothing, including temporary quarters, one hundred and ninety-five thousand dollars.

Ordnance department — To pay the salaries of the ordnance officers allowed by law, and the laborers employed therein, including the pay of the ordnance sergeant at the Virginia military institute, and charges for rent and fuel, and for purchase and transportation of supplies, and for the transportation of arms collected and distributed, one hundred thousand dollars.

To pay brigade inspectors, adjutants, clerks of regimental courts, musicians, and other lawful charges of the militia establishment, five thousand dollars. Militia

To pay expenses chargeable to the military contingent fund, fifty thousand dollars.

To pay the salaries and allowances of naval officers on the retired list, seven thousand five hundred dollars. Naval officers

To pay military expenses heretofore incurred, to be allowed and certified by the auditing board, sixty thousand dollars. Military expenses

To pay military expenses hereafter to be incurred, to be paid by the auditor of public accounts, upon such pay rolls and certificates as are prescribed by Army Regulations of the Confederate States, fifty thousand dollars.

To pay the governor's aid a salary, in lieu of all other compensation, three thousand five hundred dollars. Governor's aid

To pay pensions allowed by law for military services, four hundred and thirty-two dollars. Pensions

Annuities and similar Claims.

To the Central lunatic asylum, to pay salaries of officers, nurses, transportation of patients, and all other incidental expenses for support of patients confined therein, one hundred and fifty-two thousand dollars; and in addition thereto, whatever sum may have been paid into the treasury, arising from the pay patient fund. Central lunatic asylum

To the Eastern lunatic asylum, to pay salaries of officers, nurses, transportation of patients, and all other incidental expenses for support of patients confined therein, sixty thousand dollars. Eastern lunatic asylum

To pay expenses of lunatics confined in jail, or supported out of jail, by contract, in pursuance of law, and with which the state is chargeable, thirty thousand dollars. Lunatics in jail

To pay the annuity of the Virginia military institute, thirteen thousand five hundred dollars; and in accordance with the provisions of the act passed the twenty-second day of January eighteen hundred and sixty-four, entitled an act providing an additional appropriation to the Virginia military institute, the sum of twenty thousand dollars. Virginia military institute

To pay the annuity allowed by law to the institution for the deaf, dumb and blind, fifty thousand dollars. Deaf, dumb and blind

Criminal Charges.

To pay for the arrest and support of prisoners, pay of jurors, witnesses, and other charges allowed by law, five hundred and fifty thousand dollars. Criminal charges

To pay the salaries of the superintendent, surgeon and other officers of the penitentiary, and allowances to the interior guard thereof; to purchase supplies, clothing, subsistence and support of convicts; to pay sheriffs and other officers for the transportation of the convicts to the penitentiary, and all other incidental expenses attending the management of said institution, allowed by law, one hundred thousand dollars; and to pay, in addition thereto, all sums necessary to carry on the said penitentiary, which may have been paid into the treasury by the superintendent. Penitentiary

To pay for slaves condemned and executed, or sentenced to or reprieved for sale and transportation, eighty thousand dollars. Slaves condemned, &c

To pay expenses of bringing condemned slaves to the penitentiary, two thousand dollars. Transportation

Second—The appropriations for the year ending the thirtieth day of September eighteen hundred and sixty-five, shall be as follows, to wit:

Civil Department.

General assembly — To pay the per diem allowance and mileage, and other expenses of the members and officers of the general assembly, for an extra session to be held during the fiscal year commencing October eighteen hundred and sixty-four; to pay the pages of the senate and house of delegates, the porter of the senate, and servants for making fires and superintending furnaces in the capitol, upon the certificates heretofore usual in such cases, five hundred and sixty-five thousand dollars.

Judiciary — To pay the salaries and mileage of judges, and the salaries of all other officers of the civil government, two hundred and fifty thousand dollars.

Expenses of courts — To pay the allowances to commonwealth's attorneys, clerks of courts, sheriffs, tipstaffs and messengers of courts, including fuel, stationery and office rent for the supreme, district and circuit courts, seventy-five thousand dollars.

Messenger — To pay for the services of a messenger in the office of the auditor of public accounts, eight hundred dollars.

Vaccine agents — To pay salary of vaccine agent at Lewisburg, and allowance to vaccine agent at Richmond (five hundred dollars each), one thousand dollars.

Postage — To pay postage on commissioners' books, and on circulars to and from commissioners of the revenue, fifteen thousand dollars.

Printing — To pay expenses of printing for the general assembly and public officers, and for paper and books for public offices, sixty thousand dollars.

Births, deaths and marriages — To pay commissioners of the revenue and clerks of courts, for their services in ascertaining and recording the marriages, births and deaths, and other duties required by law in relation thereto, two thousand dollars.

Public warehouses — To pay allowances to commissioners of public warehouses, one hundred and fifty dollars.

Governor's house — To pay for repairs to the governor's house, to be paid upon the certificate of the superintendent of public buildings, five hundred dollars.

Capitol — To pay for repairs to the capitol, two thousand dollars.

Printing records — To pay for printing records of the court of appeals and district courts, four thousand dollars.

Comparing polls — To pay expenses of comparing polls at sundry elections, five hundred dollars.

Secretary of sinking fund — To pay the usual allowance to the secretary of the sinking fund, three hundred dollars.

Military Department.

Adjutant general's office — To pay the salaries of the adjutant general and his clerk, seven thousand one hundred and twenty-five dollars.

Public guard — To pay officers and privates of the public guard, their allowances for pay, clothing, rations, including temporary quarters, one hundred and ninety-five thousand dollars.

Ordnance department — To pay the salaries of the ordnance officers, allowed by law, and the laborers employed therein, including the pay of the ordnance sergeant at the Virginia military institute, and charges for rent and fuel, and for purchase and transportation of supplies, and for transportation of arms collected and distributed, one hundred thousand dollars.

Militia — To pay brigade inspectors, adjutants, clerks of regimental courts, musicians, and other lawful charges of the militia establishment, five thousand dollars.

Military contingent fund — To pay expenses chargeable to the military contingent fund, fifty thousand dollars.

Naval retired list — To pay salaries and allowances of naval officers on the retired list, seven thousand five hundred dollars.

Military expenses — To pay military expenses, to be allowed and certified by the auditing board, one thousand dollars.

To pay pensions allowed by law for military services, four hundred and thirty-two dollars. Pensions

Annuities and similar Claims.

To the Central lunatic asylum, to pay salaries of officers, nurses, transportation of patients, and all other incidental expenses for support of patients confined therein, one hundred and fifty-two thousand dollars; and in addition thereto, whatever sum may have been paid into the treasury arising from the pay patient fund. Central lunatic asylum

To pay expenses of lunatics confined in jail, or supported out of jail, by contract, in pursuance of law, and with which the state is chargeable, thirty thousand dollars. Lunatics in jail

To pay annuity to the Virginia military institute, thirteen thousand five hundred dollars. Virginia military institute

To pay the annuity allowed by law to the institution for the deaf, dumb and blind, fifty thousand dollars. Deaf, dumb and blind

Criminal Charges.

To pay for the arrest and support of prisoners, pay of jurors, witnesses and other charges allowed by law, five hundred and fifty thousand dollars. Criminal charges

To pay the salaries of the superintendent, surgeon and other officers of the penitentiary, and allowances to the interior guard thereof; to purchase supplies, clothing, subsistence and support of convicts; to pay sheriffs and other officers for the transportation of convicts to the penitentiary, and all other incidental expenses attending the management of said institution, allowed by law, one hundred thousand dollars; and to pay in addition thereto, all sums necessary to carry on said penitentiary, which may have been paid into the treasury by the superintendent. Penitentiary

To pay for slaves condemned and executed, or sentenced to or reprieved for sale and transportation, eighty thousand dollars. Slaves condemned, &c

To pay expenses of bringing condemned slaves to penitentiary, two thousand dollars. Transportation

2. Be it further enacted, that so much of the public revenue as may be received into the public treasury after the thirtieth day of September eighteen hundred and sixty-four, and the surplus of all other appropriations made prior to that date, unexpended within the fiscal year ending on the last day of September eighteen hundred and sixty-four, and all other moneys not otherwise appropriated by law, shall constitute a general fund to defray such expenses authorized by law as are not herein particularly provided for, and to defray the usual allowances to lunatic asylums, and other current expenses of the commonwealth, in the fiscal year which shall commence on the first day of October eighteen hundred and sixty-four and terminate on the thirtieth day of September eighteen hundred and sixty-five; and the auditor of public accounts is hereby authorized and required to issue his warrants in the same manner as if the same had been specifically mentioned, subject to such exceptions, limitations and conditions as the general assembly have prescribed, or may deem it proper to annex and prescribe by law: provided, that nothing in this act contained shall be so construed as to authorize the auditor of public accounts to issue his warrant or warrants in satisfaction of any judgment or decree of any court of law or equity against the commonwealth for a sum exceeding three hundred dollars, without a special appropriation by law. The payments of the military institute, for support, to the lunatic asylums, for support and transportation of patients, and to the institution for the education of the deaf, dumb and blind, shall be made one-fourth in advance, on the first day of October, one-half on the first day of January (if the visitors or directors so require), and the remaining one-fourth on the first day of April. General fund, how constituted; Duty of auditor; Limitations; Payments, how made

3. This act shall be in force from its passage. Commencement

CHAP. 3.—An ACT authorizing the Receipt of the Treasury Notes of the Confederate States in payment of Taxes and other Public Dues, and regulating when and how the same shall be received.

Passed March 2, 1864.

What confederate treasury notes receivable in payment of taxes. Notes issued prior to 1st April

1. Be it enacted by the general assembly, that the non-interest bearing treasury notes of the Confederate States, issued after the first day of April eighteen hundred and sixty-four, shall be received in payment of taxes and other public dues, and the non-interest bearing notes of the Confederate States, issued prior to the first day of April eighteen hundred and sixty-four, except the notes of the denomination of one hundred dollars, shall in like manner be received in payment of taxes and other public dues, after the first day of April eighteen hundred and sixty-four, and until the tenth of December eighteen hundred and sixty-four, but only at the rate of sixty-six and two-thirds cents for one dollar of such notes. No sheriff or other collecting officer shall have credit for the notes issued prior to the first day of April eighteen hundred and sixty-four, collected by him, unless he shall pay the same into the treasury on or before the twenty-fifth day of December eighteen hundred and sixty-four. Notes of a less denomination than five dollars, issued by said Confederate States, shall be received without abatement at any time.

Discount thereon. When paid into treasury

Notes issued prior to 1st April, how received

2. It shall be lawful for sheriffs and other collecting officers of taxes and other public dues to receive, without abatement, until the first day of April eighteen hundred and sixty-four, the non-interest bearing treasury notes of the Confederate States, issued prior to the first day of April eighteen hundred and sixty-four, in payment of taxes and other public dues due prior to the first day of April eighteen hundred and sixty-four. But no sheriff or other collecting officer shall receive credit, unless he shall pay the same into the treasury on or before the twenty-fifth day of June eighteen hundred and sixty-four, nor until he shall make oath that the notes offered in payment by him were severally and actually received by him in payment of taxes and other public dues, at the times and rates specified in this act.

When to be paid in. Oath of officer

Notes of the denomination of five dollars

3. The non-interest bearing treasury notes of the Confederate States of the denomination of five dollars, issued prior to the first day of April eighteen hundred and sixty-four, may be received without abatement in payment of taxes and other public dues until the tenth day of June eighteen hundred and sixty-four: provided the same shall be paid into the treasury on or before the twenty-fifth day of June eighteen hundred and sixty-four.

When to be paid in

Act of Sept. 14th repealed

4. The act passed September fourteenth, eighteen hundred and sixty-three, entitled an act amending and re-enacting the one hundred and ninth section of an act entitled an act imposing taxes for the support of government, passed March twenty-eighth, eighteen hundred and sixty-three, is hereby repealed.

Act to be published

5. It shall be the duty of the keeper of the rolls to cause this act to be published immediately after its passage, in at least five newspapers published in Richmond, for a period of four weeks.

Commencement

6. This act shall be in force from its passage.

CHAP. 4.—An ACT to authorize the Funding of certain Currency belonging to the State, in Confederate Bonds, and to authorize the Sale of such Bonds if necessary, and to authorize the Conversion of other Notes into other Issues.

Passed March 3, 1864.

Commission appointed

1. Be it enacted by the general assembly, that the governor, treasurer and auditor of public accounts be and they are hereby authorized, in their discretion, a majority of them concurring therein, to fund, at any time before the first day of January eighteen hundred

and sixty-five, any or all of the treasury notes of the Confederate States now owned by the state, in the six per centum bonds of the Confederate States; and in like manner to fund in said bonds any of such notes that may be received, without the abatement of the thirty-three and one-third cents, as provided by the act of the congress of the Confederate States to reduce the currency, and for other purposes. Notes, how funded

2. The governor, treasurer and auditor of public accounts, a majority of them concurring therein, may sell, for treasury notes of the confederate government, issued after the first of April eighteen hundred and sixty-four, from time to time, so many of said bonds as may be necessary to meet appropriations authorized by law and expenses of government, and pay the proceeds of sale into the treasury. Any sale of such bonds shall be made at public auction, after due notice. But no sale shall be made for less than the current market value, and no commissions shall be paid for the sale of such bonds. Bonds, how sold

3. Any of said notes that may be lawfully received with the abatement of the thirty-three and one-third per centum, shall be converted by the treasurer and auditor of public accounts into the issues of treasury notes of the Confederate States, issued after the first of April eighteen hundred and sixty-four, as authorized by act of Congress. When notes to be converted

4. It shall be the duty of the governor, treasurer and auditor of public accounts to report their proceedings under this act to the general assembly. Report of proceedings

5. This act shall be in force from its passage. Commencement

CHAP. 5.—An ACT to authorize the Transfer of certain Bonds of the State, held in trust by the Government of the United States for the Cherokee Tribe of Indians, and providing for the Payment of Interest thereon.

Passed February 9, 1864.

Whereas it is represented to the general assembly, by the commissioner of Indian affairs of the Confederate States of America, that the secretary of the interior of the United States government holds, in trust for the Cherokee tribe of Indians, the sum of ninety thousand dollars of the registered bonds of this state, upon which sixteen thousand two hundred dollars interest is now due: And it is further represented, that in the war now pending between the governments of the United States and of the Confederate States, the said tribe of Indians have united themselves with the confederate government; and that government having assumed the "protectorate of the several nations and tribes of Indians occupying the territory west of Arkansas and Missouri, south of Kansas, north of Texas and east of Texas and New Mexico," embracing the country inhabited by the said tribe of Cherokees; and the said commissioner of Indian affairs having applied to this general assembly for the payment of the said interest now due, and to become due hereafter: Therefore, Preamble

1. Be it enacted by the general assembly of Virginia, that the second auditor be and he is hereby required to transfer on the books of his office the said sum of ninety thousand dollars, standing in the name of the secretary of the interior of the United States, to the secretary of the treasury of the Confederate States, to be held by said secretary in trust for said tribe of Cherokee Indians, as provided by the treaty entered into by the authorities of said confederate government and of said tribe of Cherokee Indians; and thereupon the certificates of the registered bonds of this commonwealth, held by the said secretary of the interior of the United States, shall be deemed to be canceled and be void, and all payment of any interest due thereon, or to become due hereafter, shall be illegal. And it shall be the duty of the said auditor to issue like certificates of the registered debt of this state for the full amount so held by the said Bonds, how transferred Certificates canceled New certificates, how issued

secretary of the interior of the United States, to the said secretary of the treasury of the Confederate States, to be held by him in trust for said Cherokee tribe of Indians, the said certificates of debt, bearing date on the first day of January eighteen hundred and sixty-one. And the commissioners of the sinking fund of the state shall direct the said auditor to pay to said secretary of the treasury the semi-annual installments of interest due thereon the first day of July eighteen hundred and sixty-one; the first day of January eighteen hundred and sixty-two; the first day of July eighteen hundred and sixty-two; the first day of January eighteen hundred and sixty-three; the first day of July eighteen hundred and sixty-three, and the first day of January eighteen hundred and sixty-four, and that may hereafter accrue; to be disbursed according to the trust reposed in him; and thereafter to pay the principal and interest which may become due on said certificates of debt, as is now or may be hereafter prescribed for the payment of interest on the state debt.

Date

Interest, how paid

Principal and interest

Commencement

2. This act shall be in force as soon as the proper authorities of the Confederate States shall file with the second auditor an obligation, approved by the commissioners of the sinking fund, to indemnify the commonwealth against any loss or liability incurred by reason of this act.

CHAP. 6.—An ACT to authorize the Impressment of certain Salt Wells, Furnaces and other Property.

Passed March 8, 1864.

Impressment authorized

1. Be it enacted by the general assembly, that the superintendent of salt works, under the control of the board of supervisors, do proceed forthwith to impress and take possession of the three double furnaces at Saltville, known as the "Charles Scott furnaces," with the fixtures, equipments and implements used in connection with said furnaces, and all appurtenances to the same belonging; and also such sources of supply of fresh water as may be necessary and convenient in the manufacture of salt on said furnaces, together with all fixtures, conduits, rights of way and appurtenances incidental or pertaining thereto, and hold the same for the public use until the eighth day of June eighteen hundred and sixty-five; and also for the like use, to impress, take possession of and hold, until the said eighth day of June eighteen hundred and sixty-five, the salt well known as the "Preston well," and all fixtures, engines, equipments, implements and conduits used in procuring a supply of salt water from said well, and conducting the same to the said furnaces; and also such slaves, wagons, harness, horses and mules, sacks, provisions and supplies, forage, wood and other personal property provided, used in operating said furnaces and well, as shall be necessary or needful for successfully operating the same; and also for the like use, to impress, take possession of and hold, until the eighth day of June eighteen hundred and sixty-five, the dwelling house recently occupied by Williams and Leonard; the dwelling house at the river works now occupied by John N. Clarkson; such negro houses, store houses, wood yards, stables and appurtenances, and good and convenient access to and from the premises, as may be necessary and convenient for the proper working of said furnaces, and the conduct of the business of manufacturing and distributing salt among the people; also such meadow and other land in the vicinity of said furnaces as may afford proper facilities for the grazing of the mules, horses and stock used in conducting said business, and for the rearing of vegetables for the slaves and employees of the state: the said houses, offices, stables, lands and ways to be specified by the board of supervisors.

Time for which property is to be held

Slaves, &c

Dwelling houses &c

Land

Furnaces now leased to be impressed

2. That the superintendent, under the like control of the board of supervisors, do impress, prior to the eighth day of June eighteen

hundred and sixty-four, and continue the possession of, from and after that date, and hold for the public use, until the eighth day of June eighteen hundred and sixty-five, all the furnaces now leased and held by the state, except that operated by Thomas R. Friend, together with the fixtures, equipments and implements used in connection with said furnaces, together with all blocking water furnaces, and other appurtenances to the same belonging; and also such sources of supply of fresh water as may be necessary and convenient in the manufacture of salt on said furnaces, together with all fixtures, conduits, rights of way and appurtenances incidental or pertaining thereto; also so much of the salt water necessary to be supplied by other salt wells than the Preston well aforesaid, as may be sufficient to keep the said furnaces in continued operation to their full boiling capacity; said supply to be furnished in the cisterns of the said furnaces respectively, by the proprietors of said salt wells, prior to any other furnaces operated by any party whatsoever: and in case of failure of the supply of brine to said furnaces (which is to be determined by the board of supervisors), the superintendent, under the direction and control of the board of supervisors, shall take possession of the salt wells from which said furnaces derive their salt water, their fixtures, engines and equipments, conduits and appurtenances, and operate the same to the best advantage; and shall, after supplying the said furnaces with salt water sufficient to keep them in continued operation to their full boiling capacity, permit the remainder of the salt water to flow to such furnaces as the proprietors may direct. *All appurtenances* *Salt wells*

3. That for the purpose of ascertaining a just compensation for the property and privileges impressed in pursuance of the foregoing sections of this act, the board of supervisors shall appoint one assessor, and the owner or owners another assessor; and in case they fail so to do, or for any cause the assessor appointed by them fail to attend and enter upon the duties imposed upon him, the board of supervisors shall appoint such other assessor; and the two so appointed shall select a third assessor: and if any of said assessors should die or fail from any cause to render an award, another board of assessors, consisting of persons to be appointed in like manner, shall be convened; and said assessors, after being duly sworn faithfully to discharge the duties required of them under this act, shall, by concurrence or agreement of a majority of them, ascertain what will be a just compensation for the property, rights and privileges impressed in pursuance of the foregoing provisions of this act, and make report thereof in writing to the governor, to be filed by him in the office of the secretary of the commonwealth; and a copy thereof shall be forwarded by the secretary of the commonwealth to the owner or owners and the said board of supervisors; and thereupon the superintendent shall take possession of the property so assessed; and unless such owner or owners or the board of supervisors shall, within thirty days after such copy shall be delivered to them, refuse by written objections to accept the same, such assessment shall be deemed final. If the board of supervisors of salt, on behalf of the state, or any such owner or owners, within the said thirty days after such a copy shall have been delivered to them, refuse, by written objections filed with the secretary of the commonwealth, and in the office of the circuit court of the city of Richmond, an appeal shall lie from such assessment to said circuit court; and the proceeding thereon in said court shall be according to the provisions of chapter fifty-six of the Code of Virginia, so far as the same are applicable thereto, except that the commonwealth shall not be required to pay the compensation to the parties entitled thereto, nor into court, before the decision of the appeal. No order shall be made, nor any injunction awarded by any court or judge, to stay any proceedings authorized by this act. The said assessors shall be paid each the sum of ten dollars per day and actual expenses in traveling; to be paid out of the public treasury, by warrants to be issued upon the orders of the board of supervisors. *Compensation, how ascertained* *Assessors appointed* *Award* *Report of assessors* *Possession* *Appeal* *Injunction not to be awarded* *Pay of assessors*

Powers conferred by act of 30th March 1863

4. That in addition to the powers conferred on said superintendent by virtue of the act passed March thirtieth, eighteen hundred and sixty-three, entitled an act to provide for the production and distribution of salt, he is hereby empowered to impress, under the control of the board of supervisors, standing wood, in case he be unable to agree with the owner thereof upon the prices to be paid therefor; and the mode of ascertaining the value thereof, and of payment therefor, shall be the same as that provided in said act of thirtieth of March eighteen hundred and sixty-three: provided, however, that in making such impressments there shall be left on each farm at least one-fifth of the whole number of acres in the tract, in standing timber of average quality and value.

Proviso

Duty of governor to enforce impressments

5. That it shall be the duty of the governor of this commonwealth to enforce any impressment authorized to be made by the provisions of this act, and of the said act of thirtieth of March eighteen hundred and sixty-three, with the power of the county, and to place the said superintendent, or his duly authorized agent, in possession of the property so impressed; and it shall be lawful for said superintendent to make the impressments authorized by this act, through his agent duly constituted for that purpose.

Powers of act of 1863 conferred

6. That all the duties imposed and powers conferred upon the said superintendent and upon the board of supervisors over the property, rights and franchises of every kind specified in the act passed March the thirtieth, eighteen hundred and sixty-three, entitled an act to provide for the production and distribution of salt, be, and are hereby imposed and conferred upon said superintendent and board of supervisors over the property, rights and franchises of every kind that may be acquired for the use of the state by virtue of the provisions of this act, or any future act; and said superintendent, under the control of the board of supervisors, shall have like control of transportation on the several rail roads in the commonwealth, for the conveyance of supplies and distribution of salt, as is specified in the said act of thirtieth of March eighteen hundred and sixty-three.

Transportation

Transportation from other roads

7. The board of supervisors shall have plenary power, at their discretion, to procure transportation from other roads, by hiring engines or cars, and placing them on the Virginia and Tennessee rail road, and using the same for transportation of salt, or of wood for the manufacture of salt.

Salt to army of the Confederate States

8. The board of supervisors are hereby authorized to supply salt to the army of the Confederate States on such terms as may be agreed upon between the secretary of war and said board.

Appropriation

9. The sum of two millions of dollars is hereby appropriated to carry into effect the provisions of this act; to be paid out of any money in the treasury not otherwise appropriated; and such additional sums are hereby appropriated as may be paid into the treasury from time to time from the proceeds of the sale of salt, or so much thereof as may be necessary for the purposes of this act.

Commencement

10. This act shall be in force from its passage.

CHAP. 7.—An ACT to amend the fifth section of the act to provide for the Production and Distribution of Salt, passed March 30th, 1863.

Passed March 10, 1864.

Act of 1863 amended

1. Be it enacted by the general assembly, that the fifth section of an act passed March thirtieth, eighteen hundred and sixty-three, entitled an act to provide for the production and distribution of salt, be amended and re-enacted so as to read as follows:

Powers of superintendent

"§ 5. The superintendent shall have power to appoint, and remove at his discretion, the following assistants, to wit: two deputy managers, at a salary of thirty-five hundred dollars each; two clerks, at a salary of three thousand dollars each; one shipping clerk, at a salary of twenty-five hundred dollars; one clerk to issue supplies, at a salary of twenty-five hundred dollars. No officer or clerk created by this act shall be engaged directly or indirectly in the purchase or sale of salt for any purpose whatever other than for the state; and the said officers and clerks shall be paid in such funds as are receivable in payment of public dues. Any violation of this provision shall lead to the immediate dismissal of the officer or clerk so violating it." No officer or clerk to purchase or sell salt In what funds to be paid Penalty

2. Be it further enacted, that the eleventh section of the act passed March thirtieth, eighteen hundred and sixty-three, entitled an act to provide for the production and distribution of salt, as amended by the act passed September eighteen, eighteen hundred and sixty-three, entitled an act amending and re-enacting the sixth and eleventh sections, &c., and as further amended by the act passed October thirtieth, eighteen hundred and sixty-three, entitled an act to amend and re-enact the eleventh section, &c., be amended and re-enacted so as to read as follows: Act of 1863 amended

"The salt so manufactured shall be sold at cost, for cash, and be distributed to the different counties, cities and towns, through duly accredited agents, to be appointed by the county and corporation courts respectively, or where said courts cannot meet because of the presence or proximity of the public enemy, by the board of supervisors, on the recommendation of any three or more justices of said county, or of the senator and delegate or delegates representing such county in the general assembly; and in order to do so, it shall be the duty of the board of supervisors from time to time to ascertain as near as may be the actual cost of production and distribution, and fix the price accordingly, so as to cover such entire cost. But no agent of any county or corporation, hereafter appointed, shall be entitled to act as such until he shall have given bond, with sufficient sureties, in the penalty of not less than ten thousand nor more than thirty thousand dollars, conditioned for the faithful distribution of the salt received by him, among the people of his county or corporation. Said bonds shall be taken by the said courts when the appointments are made by them; and in all other cases, by the board of supervisors; and such agents shall distribute to refugees, and to persons temporarily sojourning in their counties, cities and towns, as well as to permanent citizens thereof: provided, however, that the said courts and the said board shall respectively have power to revoke any appointment of agent heretofore or hereafter made by them, whenever they deem it proper to do so; and shall in like manner appoint another agent in place of the one so removed: provided, that it shall not be lawful for any county or corporation court, or its agent, in any way to dispose of any salt, received for distribution, otherwise than by distributing the same among the citizens of such county or corporation, according to the provisions of this act, except in cases when, in the opinion of the said court or agent, it shall be necessary to dispose otherwise of the salt to prevent its falling into the hands of the public enemy, or where it may be impossible to distribute the salt among the people of the county." Salt, how sold and distributed Duty of supervisors Bond By whom taken Proviso Proviso

3. This act shall be in force from its passage. Commencement

CHAP. 8.—An ACT imposing Fines on Agents for failing to deliver Salt to persons entitled thereto.

Passed February 25, 1864.

1. Be it enacted by the general assembly, that if any agent having in his hands salt for distribution, by virtue of the several acts passed for the production and distribution of salt in this commonwealth, shall fail or refuse, when applied to, within the period fixed for delivery by said agent, to deliver to any person entitled thereto, the quantity such person has the right to demand, upon tendering in Fine for failure to deliver salt

currency the price thereof, shall be fined twenty dollars, to the use of the party injured; to be recovered by indictment, presentment or information, or upon ten days' notice before any court of record having jurisdiction thereof, or by warrant before a justice of the peace; and upon conviction thereof, shall be removed from office, and another appointed in his place, in the manner prescribed by law.

Proviso

2. Provided, however, that the agent shall not be liable to the penalties of this act, if the failure to deliver the salt is caused by no neglect or fault on his part; and the currency hereby authorized to be tendered shall be the same received in payment of public dues to the state, and shall be received upon the terms such currency may at the time be received for public dues.

Commencement

3. This act shall be in force from the passage thereof.

CHAP. 9.—An ACT amending and re-enacting chapter 213 of the Code of Virginia, reorganizing the Penitentiary.

Passed January 14, 1864.

Be it enacted by the general assembly, that chapter two hundred and thirteen of the Code of Virginia be amended and re-enacted so as to read as follows:

Property attached to penitentiary

1. The lot of twelve acres and fourteen square rods of land, on which the penitentiary is situated, and the lot numbered seven hundred and twenty-nine, being one-fourth of a square in the city of Richmond, between the southwest end of First street and the eastern boundary of the land aforesaid, and the square of land between Cary and Main and Jefferson and Madison streets, containing the penitentiary springs, with the pipes and fixtures for conveying water to that institution, shall be and remain the property of the commonwealth, for the use of the said penitentiary, and shall be under the control of the superintendent of the penitentiary. The superintendent shall have the custody of the property of the penitentiary, real, personal and mixed, and he shall, in the name of the commonwealth, have authority to institute and prosecute any suit, prosecution or proceeding for the recovery of any such property, or its value, or for any injury thereto, which may be proper to protect the rights of the state. He shall have authority to employ the prisoners in improving and cultivating any part of the lands aforesaid, or in repairing the water pipes and fixtures, or the roads from the penitentiary to proper points of intersection with the streets, or in taking out or bringing into the enclosure any necessary thing to or from the said city or James river canal.

In whose custody

When prisoners to be employed out of the penitentiary

Penitentiary continued

2. The public jail and penitentiary house shall continue under the name of "the penitentiary," to be appropriated to the confinement of convicts sentenced, according to law, to confinement therein by the courts of this commonwealth. Persons sentenced to imprisonment by a court of the Confederate States held in Virginia, for a term of three years or more, may also be confined therein, with the approbation of the superintendent and the governor, and be safely kept and employed, pursuant to the rules of the prison, so far as it is not inconsistent with such sentence, until discharged by due course of the laws of the Confederate States: provided, that before any other such prisoners shall be received in said penitentiary, the Confederate States shall pay the sums now due, or which shall be due for the confinement and support of their prisoners, and in future, pay half-yearly, at the rate of one dollar and twenty-five cents per day, for the imprisonment and support of every such prisoner now in prison, or hereafter so imprisoned, with proper medical charges. Annually its condition shall be examined and reported on by a committee of the general assembly.

Confederate States prisoners may be confined therein

Proviso

Committee of legislature to examine its condition and report annually

3. The governor may from time to time prescribe rules, not contrary to law, for the preservation of the property at, and the health of the convicts in the penitentiary, and the government of the interior thereof. Printed copies of such of the said rules as may relate to the government and punishment of the convicts, and of any provisions of law which the governor may direct, shall be posted up in at least six conspicuous places of the interior. The clerk of the penitentiary shall file and preserve the record of the trial and conviction of each convict, and keep a register describing him, the time of his confinement, for what offence, and when received into the institution.

Governor to prescribe rules

Printed copies to be posted in prison

Record of conviction and register to be kept

4. When a person, other than a married woman, is sentenced to confinement in the penitentiary for more than a year, the estate of such convict, if he have any, both real and personal, shall, on the motion of a party interested, be committed, by the court of the county or corporation in which his estate, or some part thereof, may be, to a person selected by the court, who, after giving bond before the said court, in such penalty as it may prescribe, shall have charge of the said estate until such convict is discharged from confinement.

Real and personal estate of convicts other than married women to be committed to a committee appointed by the court

Bond to be given

Penalty

5. Such committee may sue and be sued in respect to the debts due to or by such convict, and any other of the convict's estate, and shall have the privilege of an administrator as to the right of retaining for his own debt. He shall allow (subject to the claims of creditors) a sufficient maintenance out of the convict's estate for his wife and family, if any; the wife to be entitled, so long as he is confined, to the profits of such portion of his estate as she would have, had he died intestate.

Committee may sue and be sued

6. The committee shall render accounts of his trust, and may be made to account therefor, and shall be entitled to compensation for his services, and may forfeit his right thereto, in the same manner as if he were an administrator or guardian. Every such committee shall deliver such estate as he may be liable for at that time, to the convict on his discharge, or to his real and personal representatives, on his death before being discharged.

Committee to render accounts of his trust

His compensation

To deliver estate to convict on his discharge

7. If the person so appointed refuse the trust, or fail to give bond as aforesaid, the court, on like motion, shall commit the estate to the sheriff of the county, or sergeant of the corporation, who shall be the committee, and he and the sureties in his official bond shall be bound for the faithful performance of the trust.

If committee appointed refuse the trust or fail to give bond, court to commit estate to sheriff or sergeant

8. The real estate of such convict may be sold, when necessary for the payment of his debts, in the same manner as the real estate of an insane person in the hands of a committee.

When and how estate of convict to be sold

9. Every convict, when first brought to the penitentiary, shall be washed, cleaned and kept in a separate lodging until the surgeon certifies that he is fit to be put among the other prisoners; and the clothes he wore shall be either destroyed, or purified and preserved until he is discharged, and then returned to him, or they may be disposed of as the prisoner may desire, with the consent of the superintendent.

Personal treatment of new convicts

10. All money found on the person of a convict, and all money which may be lawfully and properly received after his committal, shall be charged to the penitentiary, and be paid to him out of the fund of the penitentiary when he shall be discharged, or for good cause, in the opinion of the superintendent, may be used for his or her benefit. Before any male prisoner shall be permitted to labor in the shops, or elsewhere out of his room, he shall make and subscribe such promise of obedience and fidelity to the rules and orders of the institution as shall be prescribed by the governor. And it shall be the duty of the superintendent, as far as practicable, to provide suitable employment in separate rooms for the refractory and obstinate, and for those of disordered minds, or who for any cause are unfit to be congregated in the shops.

How money of convict to be disposed of

Convict required to subscribe rules

How employed

How kept and clothed

11. The male and female convicts shall be kept separate from each other, and the males shall have their heads and beards close shaven or sheared once a fortnight, or oftener if need be. Every convict shall be clothed at public expense, in a distuctive uniform for each sex, made of coarse materials.

Labor of convicts

Social intercourse

12. The convicts shall be kept to the hardest labor suitable to their sex and fitness, and such of them as need it, instructed in some mechanic art. Social intercourse, conversation and acquaintance between the convicts, shall be prevented as far as may be, and silence constantly observed by them as far as possible.

Their diet

Accounts for diet, how certified

13. The convicts shall be fed on bread of Indian corn, or other coarse bread, and have one meal a day of coarse meat. The superintendent may change or regulate the diet for good cause. The account for purchases of diet for the prisoners shall be certified by the superintendent to the auditor of public accounts for payment. The superintendent may, when he may deem it necessary, or the physician shall so advise, change the diet, and adapt it to the health or condition of the prisoners, or any of them, or he may allow extra diet to those who need it. He shall cause the hospital and all the cells and rooms of the prison to be whitewashed (by prisoners qualified for the business) twice a year or oftener, and the floors to be washed as often only as may be necessary for health and comfort.

Washing and whitewashing

Governor to prescribe hours and time of labor

Time and conditions of visiting prison

14. The governor shall prescribe, by rules and regulations, the hours within which the prisoners shall be employed at the respective branches of business carried on in the institution, and the time they shall labor on each day, and also the times and conditions upon which persons may visit the interior of the penitentiary.

When allowed to walk or work in the yard

Where to be employed on public buildings and grounds

15. The superintendent may allow the prisoners, at stated times, to walk, for the benefit of their health, in the grounds of the penitentiary, and to work therein, but in either case, in the presence or in the view of the superintendent or proper guard. He shall, at the discretion and under the direction of the governor, employ them at Richmond, or within a mile thereof, in improving, repairing or working on public buildings, grounds and property.

To be locked in cells on Sunday and at night

16. Each convict shall be locked up during the night and every Sunday (except to attend religious service), and when the number of apartments will permit, each separately, unless in the hospital.

Punishment for misbehavior

17. A convict guilty of profanity, indecent behavior, idleness, neglect or willful mismanagement of work, insubordination, an assault not amounting to felony, or a violation of any of the rules prescribed by the governor, may, under the order of the superintendent, subject to the said rules, be punished by lower and coarser diet, the iron mask or gag, solitary confinement in a cell, or the dungeon, or by stripes. Under such orders, and subject to the said rules, the superintendent may, where a convict is charged with an offence for which he is to be tried under chapter two hundred and fourteen or two hundred and fifteen, confine him in a cell or dungeon until such trial.

What allowed prisoners on discharge

18. The superintendent, in his discretion, may allow a convict, on his discharge, not exceeding thirty dollars, and if he needs it, a suit of coarse clothing.

Duties of surgeon

19. The surgeon to the penitentiary shall visit the penitentiary once at least every day, and oftener when there are cases of sickness requiring it, or when he is called on to attend by the superintendent. Before leaving the city of Richmond at any time, he shall notify the superintendent of his intention, and the time he expects to be absent, and what physician may be called on to officiate for him in his absence.

20. The surgeon shall render to the convicts all surgical and medical aid which may be requisite or may be required by the superintendent.

Hospital

21. The room now kept for that purpose shall be continued to be used as a hospital. A sick convict shall be kept in it when the sur-

geon so prescribes. There shall be a book in which shall be entered the name of each convict put in the hospital, and the time that he goes in and comes out.

Book kept therein

22. The superintendent, with one of his assistants, shall once a week visit the hospital, and the two shall make a report of the treatment and condition of the sick, and the clerk shall record the same. The annual report of the superintendent shall show the condition of the health of the convicts. It shall state the number in the hospital every month from each ward, the disease of each person put in the hospital, and the number of deaths in each ward.

Report of condition of sick, &c

23. The governor, members of the general assembly, ministers of the gospel for performing religious services, and the officers and others having duties or business therein, may go into the interior of the penitentiary. Any other person, under rules and regulations to be prescribed by the governor, may also visit the same. There shall be no conversation between a visitor and a convict, unless special license therefor be given by the governor or superintendent.

Who allowed to visit the penitentiary

24. The superintendent may apply the means of the institution to repair and enlarge the shops, and increase the number of cells when required. He shall cause to be done in the penitentiary any work which can be done therein towards effecting the improvement or repairs mentioned in the fifteenth section. He shall direct the manufacturing operations, and have the goods manufactured and work done at the penitentiary (excepting as otherwise provided), and have an invoice made out weekly of the goods manufactured, with the prices thereon; one copy of which shall be filed with the clerk of the penitentiary, and one other copy delivered weekly to the secretary of the commonwealth. The superintendent and the clerk appointed by the governor, shall from time to time fix the prices of goods manufactured at the penitentiary; and the schedule of prices so fixed shall be recorded in a book to be kept for that purpose.

Superintendent authorized to repair and enlarge shops, and increase number of cells, when required

Superintendent and clerk to fix the prices of goods manufactured

25. When an investigation is ordered by the governor as to a matter concerning the penitentiary, or the conduct of persons connected therewith, it shall be his duty to constitute a commission of three intelligent gentlemen to make the investigation; and the clerk of the penitentiary, by order of said commission, may issue a summons, directed to the sheriff of any county, commanding him to summon any person to attend at the penitentiary on a certain day, to give evidence before the said commissioners, and may administer an oath to such person. The commissioners shall have like powers, under the twenty-third and twenty-fourth sections of chapter one hundred and seventy-six, as if it was a court whose clerk had issued the summons; and the clerk of the penitentiary shall make such entry as would be made under the thirty-fifth section of the same chapter, if the attendance were before a court, and made by the clerk thereof. The sum to which the witness is entitled shall be paid out of the funds of the institution. Testimony taken before the said commissioners shall not be read on the trial, by a court martial, of an officer or soldier of the public guard, but shall be delivered to the governor to take such action thereon as he may deem proper. The interior guard and all the officers of the penitentiary shall take the oaths prescribed by law for public officers.

Power of board investigating any matter ordered by the governor

Clerk to issue summons for witnesses

Compensation of witnesses, how paid

Interior guard and officers to take oaths prescribed for public officers

26. The soldiers of the public guard, while stationed at the penitentiary, shall attend to the outer gates as heretofore, and obey the orders of the superintendent in relation to the security of the prisoners and the protection of the property of the penitentiary; and it shall be lawful for any officer of the penitentiary, interior guard or soldier to carry sufficient weapons to prevent escapes, suppress rebellion and for self-defence, and to use the same against any prisoner for such purpose. No officer of the penitentiary or officer or soldier of the public guard shall be allowed to trade or traffic with convicts, on pain of being dismissed if an officer, or punished if a soldier.

Duties of soldiers of public guard to obey orders of the superintendent

Allowed to carry weapons to suppress rebellion and for self-defence

Trade and traffic with the convicts prohibited

And if any person bring into or carry out of the penitentiary any article or thing which may be prohibited by the rules and regulations thereof, he shall be deemed guilty of a misdemeanor, and upon conviction thereof shall be fined in a sum not exceeding one thousand dollars, and shall be confined in jail for a term not exceeding twelve months.

Clerk of penitentiary
His duties

27. The clerk of the penitentiary, who shall be appointed by the governor, shall keep the books thereof, enter all orders made at the penitentiary, and daily enter on one of the books of the penitentiary the cost of raw materials furnished to each ward, copies of the accounts of all sales for the penitentiary, reported to him by the superintendent, and a copy of entries in the receiving clerk's books of the sale of manufactured goods for the day, including all moneys received for the use of the penitentiary. It shall also be his duty to compare the books of the different ward masters with his own books and books of the receiving clerk, at least once a week, and enter on record the result of such comparison, and be subject to the orders of the superintendent.

Residence, &c. of superintendent allowed him

28. The superintendent may reside in the front building of the penitentiary, and be allowed his fuel and lights. He shall also be authorized to use a small piece or lot of the land for a garden to raise vegetables for his own family use. He shall be the chief executive officer of the penitentiary, and direct its internal police and management, subject to the orders of the governor. He shall, under rules and regulations to be prescribed by the governor, sell all surplus manufactured goods or other articles manufactured at the penitentiary, or the proceeds of the labor of convicts or transports elsewhere, and shall furnish accounts thereof to the clerk of the penitentiary for record.

Power to appoint assistants

He may, with the approval of the governor, appoint seven assistants, whose duties he shall prescribe, to be designated and stand in authority as "first, second, third, fourth, fifth and sixth ward masters;" and the seventh assistant shall be known and denominated as "the receiving and delivering clerk and gate keeper," and shall keep a book, in which an entry shall be made of all moneys received by him as gate keeper; and he shall also keep an account of the value of all manufactured articles sold outside of the penitentiary by the superintendent or any of his officers, and shall receive the money for all manufactured articles sold at the penitentiary, and pay over to the superintendent the same at the end of each week, or oftener if required by him, taking his receipt therefor in a receipt book kept for that purpose. The superintendent may require bond and security from said delivering clerk, for the faithful performance of the duties of his office, and may also prescribe the mode and manner of keeping and making entries in his books.

Delivering clerk and gate keeper

Acting superintendent to be designated

The superintendent shall at all times, when he is about to leave the penitentiary, designate which of his officers shall perform the duties of his office of superintendent during his absence.

Proceeds of sales to be paid into treasury monthly

Proviso

All money realized from the sale of manufactured goods or other articles, and from the labor of convicts and transports, shall be paid into the treasury monthly by the superintendent of the penitentiary: provided, that the superintendent shall be authorized to use the money received at the penitentiary during any one month, before he pays the money into the public treasury, for the necessary purchases of subsistence and raw materials, an account of which he shall render to the auditor of public accounts when he makes his deposits at the end of each month.

Auditor to report failure

Governor may suspend superintendent

Should the superintendent fail to make the payment into the treasury, directed by this section, for ten days after it becomes due, the auditor shall report the fact to the governor, who shall thereupon have authority to suspend the superintendent from the discharge of the duties of his office, and appoint temporarily a successor, who shall discharge the duties of the office, first executing such bond as the governor may deem proper. All expenditures for the purchases of raw materials and all other expenses of said institution shall be defrayed out of the treasury, upon the warrant of the auditor of public accounts. All accounts of purchases so made and of other expenses shall be approved by the said superintendent; and if it shall at any time become necessary to use money for purchases out of this state, the superintendent may, by the consent and authority of the governor, have a sum of money, not exceeding at any one time the sum of twenty thousand dollars, advanced to him out of the treasury for that purpose; but such advance of twenty thousand dollars shall not be made oftener than once in three months. The superintendent, for facilitating the procuring of supplies, may, if he deem it necessary and proper, appoint, with the approbation of the governor, an additional assistant, who shall be denominated a purchasing clerk, whose duty it shall be, under the direction of the superintendent, to purchase raw material and other supplies for the penitentiary, and do and perform such other duties as the superintendent may direct; and the superintendent may require, for his own safety, of said assistant, bond with security, in such penalty as he may deem proper, for the faithful performance of the duties assigned him by the superintendent: and it shall be the duty of the several rail road and other internal improvement companies to cause all materials so purchased to be promptly transported over their respective lines to the city of Richmond.

Advancement to superintendent

Superintendent may appoint an additional assistant

Duty of rail road companies

29. When the board of directors of either of the lunatic asylums desire to purchase, for the use thereof, cloth, clothing or shoes of the manufacture of the penitentiary, if they make requisitions in reasonable time, the superintendent of the penitentiary shall pack up the articles, forward them to the asylum at its cost, and charge the articles to the state. The prices of manufactured goods and other articles shall be regulated under the direction of the superintendent, and be sold by him, his purchasing clerk, or such other officer as he may direct.

To have work done for lunatic asylums

30. The superintendent shall, at the end of each fiscal year, furnish the auditor of public accounts with a receipt from an officer of the asylum for any articles so furnished within said year, and a statement of their prices, for which the penitentiary shall have credit, and the asylum be charged.

To furnish receipt to auditor

31. He shall, at the end of each fiscal year, state a general account between the state and the penitentiary for such year, charging the latter with the value of the tools, machinery, fixtures and materials on hand at the commencement of the year; the raw materials purchased during the year; the rations furnished for the convicts; the salaries of all the officers, and all the contingent expenses of the penitentiary, and crediting it with the work of the convicts done during the year; the work and repairs done by the convicts on the prison and other public property; clothing furnished the convicts, and the value of the tools, machinery, fixtures and materials on hand at the end of the year; amount of all sales of manufactured goods and other articles—with all other debts and credits necessary to show a true account with the institution and the state: which shall be made a part of his annual report.

To render annually a general account

32. It shall be the duty of the governor to appoint, at the end of each quarter, a commissioner, who, after being duly sworn, shall go to the penitentiary, and take an account of the manufacturing and financial operations of the penitentiary through the quarter just ended, and diligently enquire into the manner in which the superintendent, officers and guards have performed their duties, and make report to the governor: a copy of which report shall be recorded in the books of the penitentiary; and he shall be paid out of the civil contingent fund such sum as the governor may deem proper.

Governor to appoint a commissioner

Duties, &c

33. The force sent to the penitentiary from the public guard shall consist of a non-commissioned officer's command, and be in charge of

Force sent to penitentiary, how commanded, &c

such officer, and a chain of sentinels shall surround the penitentiary night and day.

Convicts employed outside to be attended with sufficient guard

34. While the convicts are employed in any work on the public grounds or property outside of the penitentiary, they shall be attended with a sufficient guard detailed by the captain of the public guard.

Interior guard, how appointed, dismissed and paid

35. The superintendent may employ a guard, not exceeding twelve persons, for the interior of the penitentiary, who shall perform such duties as the superintendent may direct. Any person so employed may be dismissed from service at the pleasure of the superintendent: and the superintendent may assign one of the said guard to superintend and cut out the leather in the shoe shop, and provide for its safe-keeping through the day, who shall be allowed such additional compensation as may, in the opinion of the governor, be just and proper.

Rewards for prisoners escaping, how paid

36. If any convict escape from the penitentiary, or from the custody of the superintendent, he may offer a reward for the apprehension and redelivery of such convict, not exceeding five hundred dollars; one-half thereof to be paid by the institution, and the other by the superintendent, his assistants and the interior guard, in proportion to the amount of their salaries; but none of said officers shall be entitled to such reward.

Superintendent to execute new bond

Penalty

37. The superintendent shall, within thirty days from the passage of this act, execute a new bond in the penalty of one hundred thousand dollars.

Commencement

38. This act shall take effect from its passage, and all acts and parts of acts coming in conflict with this act are hereby repealed.

CHAP. 10.—An ACT vacating the Commissions of Militia Officers of the Line.

Passed February 11, 1864.

Commissions vacated

1. Be it enacted by the general assembly, that from and after the passage of this act, the commissions of all major generals and brigadier generals, and their respective staffs, all colonels, lieutenant colonels, majors, captains and lieutenants of the militia of the line, be and the same are hereby vacated.

Proviso

2. Provided, that this act shall not be construed to apply to officers of the second class militia, nor to the officers of the nineteenth regiment of the militia of the line.

Commencement

3. This act shall be in force from its passage.

CHAP. 11.—An ACT disbanding the 179th Regiment of the Militia of the Line, and for the more efficient organization of the 19th Regiment of the Militia of the Line, and the 1st Regiment of the Second Class Militia.

Passed February 11, 1864.

Examining board, how appointed

1. Be it enacted by the general assembly, that whenever any field, staff or company officer of the militia of the line, or of the second class militia, shall be deemed by the governor inefficient or incompetent, he may appoint an examining board, who shall thoroughly examine into the qualification and fitness of such officer, and if their report be unfavorable to the officer, the governor shall have authority to remove such officer, and the vacancy shall be filled in such mode as may be prescribed by law: but no new officer shall be commissioned until he has in like manner been examined by the board, and found qualified and fit.

How composed

The board of examination for field officers shall be composed of the adjutant general of this state, and two commissioned military officers, to be associated with him by order of the governor; and for company officers, the board shall be composed of three officers of a grade not less than that of the officer to be examined.

2. Whenever any private or non-commissioned officer neglects, fails or refuses to perform the duties required of him, and disobeys the proper orders of his superior officers, it shall be lawful for the commandant of the regiment, battalion or company to have him arrested and promptly tried by a court martial; and upon conviction, he shall be fined not less than one hundred dollars, or be punished, as provided for in the case of enlisted men, by the rules and articles of war of the Confederate States. The fines imposed under this section shall be collected by the sheriff or sergeant of the county or corporation, as in other cases of militia fines, within sixty days from the time of their imposition. Penalty for neglect of duty. Fines

3. The one hundred and seventy-ninth regiment of the militia of the line is hereby disbanded, and the commissions of the officers composing the same are vacated, and the governor shall attach the persons liable to duty within the bounds of said regiment to the nineteenth regiment of the militia of the line and the first regiment of the second class militia, according to the class to which they respectively belong; and he is authorized to take such measures as he may deem proper to secure the enrollment of all persons liable to duty within the bounds of the nineteenth and one hundred and seventy-ninth regiments; and the governor may, in his discretion, organize the persons thus enrolled by companies, or he may attach them to existing organizations. Should the number of men justify it, a new regiment may be organized by the governor within the bounds above referred to. 179th regiment disbanded. Persons, how attached. New regiment, when formed

4. This act shall be in force from its passage. Commencement

CHAP. 12.—An ACT amendatory of the act passed October 27th, 1863, entitled an act to authorize the Arrest of Deserters by the Civil Authorities.

Passed January 20, 1864.

1. Be it enacted by the general assembly, that the first, second and third sections of the act passed October the twenty-seventh, eighteen hundred and sixty-three, entitled an act to authorize the arrest of deserters by the civil authorities, be amended and re-enacted so as to read as follows: Act of 1863 amended

"That all magistrates, sheriffs, sergeants and constables of the several counties and towns in this commonwealth be required to inform the nearest confederate officer of all deserters and other delinquents owing military service to the confederate government, who may be found in their respective counties, cities or towns, and to arrest and to aid in the arrest of all such delinquents, whether deserters, conscripts, or absentees without leave from the army or navy of the Confederate States; and they shall promptly notify the nearest confederate officer or adjutant general or the secretary of war of such arrest, and shall commit such deserter or other delinquent to some secure county or corporation jail until he can be delivered to the confederate authorities. Duty of magistrates and officers. Arrest of deserters. Deserter, how committed

2. The said officers may summon so many of the people of their county or corporation, or require the nearest commissioned officer of state forces to call out such portion of his command as may be sufficient for the purpose, to aid in arresting and safely guarding such delinquents until they can be secured in jail as aforesaid: and in making any arrest herein directed, the officers, whether civil or military, shall have the same powers and jurisdiction conferred in the twenty-fourth section, chapter forty-nine of the Code. State forces, how called out. Powers of officers

3. If any officer shall willfully fail or refuse to perform any duty herein required of him, and any citizen who shall fail or refuse to obey the summons provided for in the second section, or shall refuse, when called on by any officer authorized to arrest deserters and other military delinquents, to assist in making any arrest, or in securing Failure to discharge duty

When deemed a misdemeanor

and safely keeping any prisoner after his arrest, such officer or citizen shall be deemed guilty of a misdemeanor, and on conviction thereof, shall be fined by the jury not less than fifty nor more than five hundred dollars, and shall be imprisoned in the county or corporation jail not less than two nor more than six months: but if any such jail shall for any cause be insecure as a place of confinement, he shall be removed to the nearest county or corporation jail that may be deemed safe, upon the order of the court or presiding justice of the court in which he was convicted.

In case jail is insecure

Duty of presiding justice

4. Be it further enacted, that to facilitate the arrest and return of deserters and other delinquents from the army and navy of the Confederate States, it shall be the duty of the presiding justice of any county, city or town, whenever thereto requested by the governor of the state, the secretary of war of the Confederate States, or the commanding general of the district or department, and also when reliable information shall be brought to him that there are deserters or other delinquents as aforesaid lurking about or passing through his county, city or town, to convene immediately two other magistrates to act with him, and shall detail from the body of the county a sufficient patrol, under charge of an officer to be appointed by said court, who shall be required diligently to patrol and make search for deserters and other delinquents, and to arrest and dispose of the same as herein before prescribed: and the officer of said patrol shall have all the powers conferred in the first and second sections of this act. The court herein mentioned may meet at any convenient and safe point designated by the presiding justice.

To convene court

Patrol, how called out

Powers of officer of patrol

Orders of court, how certified

5. The orders of said court shall be certified by the presiding justice to the clerk of the county or corporation court, when the same shall not be held at the courthouse thereof, and shall be issued and executed as other orders of the court.

Neglect of duty

6. Any willful neglect or refusal to perform the duties prescribed in the last two preceding sections shall be deemed a misdemeanor, and subject the offender to the pains and penalties mentioned in the third section of this act.

Act to be given in charge

7. This act shall be specially given in charge to all grand juries, and shall, immediately after its passage, be published by proclamation of the governor.

Commencement

8. This act shall be in force from its passage.

CHAP. 13.—An ACT authorizing the Governor to cause sufficient Covering to be erected for the protection of the Artillery belonging to the State

Passed January 22, 1864.

Sheds to be erected

1. Be it enacted by the general assembly, that the sum of twenty-two thousand five hundred dollars be and is hereby appropriated for the purpose of erecting sheds or other suitable covering at or near the city of Richmond, and at the Virginia military institute, to protect the guns, caissons, gun carriages and artillery harness belonging to the state of Virginia.

Amount appropriated

2. The money hereby appropriated shall be expended under the direction of the governor; and the auditor of public accounts shall pay such amount of the sum hereby appropriated as may be expended, upon the order of the governor.

Commencement

3. This act shall be in force from its passage.

CHAP. 14.—An ACT to establish an Army Agency in the City of Richmond, for the relief of Soldiers, Seamen and Officers of Virginia in the Confederate Service, and to repeal the 1st, 2d and 3d sections of an act establishing such Agency, passed March 9th, 1863.

Passed March 4, 1864.

1. Be it enacted by the general assembly, that the governor shall appoint an army agent to superintend and conduct the agency hereby constituted for the relief and comfort of the soldiers, seamen and officers in the confederate service from the state of Virginia. Army agent, how appointed

2. It shall be the duty of such agent to receive and forward to the soldiers, seamen and officers aforesaid any contributions of clothing, shoes or other necessary and proper supplies which shall be furnished by their families or friends or by the state for that purpose; to receive and store all supplies, baggage and clothing of such soldiers, seamen and officers, and deliver the same when demanded by the owners or by the proper military authorities, and as far as practicable provide a place of lodging, and when necessary, food or rations for all indigent soldiers, seamen and officers of Virginia in transitu through the city of Richmond on furlough or sick leave. Such provisions for food and lodging may be limited and regulated in such manner as said agent shall find prudent and necessary, subject to the direction and control of the governor. The said agency shall be located in the city of Richmond; but said agent may appoint such sub-agents at such other points as he shall deem necessary for the proper discharge of the business of the agency. He shall receive and take care of all hospital stores that may be contributed or purchased for the sick or wounded soldiers and seamen of Virginia, and shall dispense the same on requisitions from their attending physicians or surgeons, or in such manner as the governor shall authorize. He may, under the direction and control of the governor, provide such supplies of clothing as may be obtained by contribution or by purchase, on such terms as he shall deem reasonable, and shall cause such clothing to be issued to the destitute soldiers and seamen of Virginia, under such regulations as the governor shall prescribe or approve. Duty of agent; Where agency located; Clothing, how supplied

3. Said agent shall provide a suitable place for the lodging of soldiers, as provided in the foregoing section, and for the safe-keeping of all goods which he shall procure, or which shall come to his care, until the same can be distributed, delivered or transported to the places of their destination. He shall make such arrangements as may be practicable with the quartermaster's department of the Confederate States, for the safe and speedy transportation of all goods to be transported; and he may hire means of transportation, and may employ such other agents as he shall find necessary to aid and superintend in the care and preservation and the safe and speedy transmission of goods in his custody. Lodging of soldiers, how provided for; Transportation of goods

4. The said agent shall from time to time, as he shall deem necessary, give such notice, by advertisement in the public press and otherwise, of the objects of the agency and the place of his location, as will in his judgment render the agency in the largest degree useful for the purposes designed; and he may invite and receive contributions from the public for such purposes. He may employ clerks, not exceeding two in number, to aid him in his office or otherwise, who shall receive such salary as the said agent shall deem reasonable and contract for, and the governor approve, not to exceed fifteen hundred dollars per annum. The said agent shall be entitled to compensation for his services, at such rate as the governor shall approve, not to exceed the sum of three thousand dollars per annum. He may, under the control of the governor, provide subsistence and lodging for all persons in the service of the agency; and for such period as they are so provided, they shall not receive any other compensation from the state for such services, unless the same be authorized by the Notice of objects of agency; Agent may employ clerks; Subsistence and lodging

governor, and then not exceeding the rate of two dollars per day: provided, that nothing herein contained shall prevent the detailing of soldiers unfit for field duty to act as sub-agents or clerks, whenever the consent of the Confederate States government can be obtained therefor. Before the said agent shall proceed to discharge the duties of his agency, he shall enter into bond with approved security, before the clerk of the circuit court of the city of Richmond, in the penalty of twenty thousand dollars, with condition for the faithful performance of his duties as such agent: and any party who may be injured by the willful default or negligence of said agent, may recover judgment against him, by motion, upon ten days' notice, before the circuit court of the city of Richmond.

Detailed soldiers

Bond of agent

5. In order to carry out the purposes of this act, the sum of one hundred thousand dollars is hereby appropriated.

Appropriation

6. The first, second and third sections of the act passed March ninth, eighteen hundred and sixty-three, entitled an act establishing an agency in the city of Richmond for receiving and forwarding clothing, shoes and other supplies to Virginia soldiers, are hereby repealed.

1st, 2d and 3d sections of act of 1863 repealed

7. This act shall be in force from its passage.

Commencement

CHAP. 15.—An ACT for the relief of Families of Soldiers living in Counties within the Lines or under the Control of the Enemy.

Passed February 20, 1864.

1. Be it enacted by the general assembly, that the sum of one million dollars be and the same is hereby appropriated for the relief of the needy families of soldiers and sailors in the confederate service from the state of Virginia, residing in counties within the lines or the power of the enemy, as herein after provided.

Amount appropriated

2. The auditor, second auditor and secretary of the commonwealth are hereby appointed commissioners, to act without compensation, to attend to the apportionment and expenditure of said money; and they are hereby authorized to appoint agents for the several counties, to expend such sums as the commissioners may allot to them, for the relief of the needy families of such soldiers and sailors residing in their respective counties or corporations, and for the needy families of those who have been disabled or honorably discharged, and of the needy widows and minor children of such as may have died or may hereafter die; and shall take bond and security from such agents, payable to the commonwealth, in a sufficient penalty, for the performance of the trust reposed in them; and shall require said agents to return an account of such expenditure, showing the amount expended for each family; and shall make such regulations as they may think proper, to prevent fraud, and secure a faithful, just and equitable distribution of said funds among the several counties, and among the families in each county: provided, that the widowed mother and her family shall be considered as the family of a son who has been killed or disabled, or who has died in the service: and provided further, that the provisions of this act shall also be extended to the classes of persons named therein who may not reside within the lines of the enemy, but upon neutral ground, or in such relation thereto as that in the opinion of said commissioners the county courts of the counties in which they reside cannot afford them relief under existing laws: and provided further, that the agents appointed for the several counties shall be residents of the county for which they are appointed, and are over forty-five years of age, or not subject to military service: and provided further, that where the money cannot be distributed on account of the enemy, it shall be retained in the hands of the proper agents until such time as it can be so distributed.

Commissioners appointed

To whom to be distributed

Bond, &c

Proviso

3. In order to raise funds available for the purposes of this act,

Funds, how raised

the said commissioners are hereby empowered to direct the issue of coupons or registered bonds of this commonwealth, bearing six per centum interest per annum, authenticated in the manner prescribed in the second section of the sixty-seventh chapter of the Code of Virginia (edition of eighteen hundred and sixty), to such an amount as may be necessary, not exceeding the sum of five hundred thousand dollars; and said commissioners are directed to effect an exchange of said bonds for at least an equal amount of the notes of the banks of this commonwealth, with said banks or others; and the notes thus obtained are to be applied exclusively to the support of needy families in those counties where, from the presence of the public enemy, confederate treasury notes cannot be used. The said commissioners shall use confederate or Virginia treasury notes wherever they can, and shall draw orders on the auditor of public accounts, who shall issue his warrant on the treasurer therefor: provided the whole amount of bonds issued and treasury notes paid shall not together exceed the amount appropriated in the first section of this act.

Notes of banks, how obtained

Payments, how made

4. The commissioners shall report their proceedings under this act to the next session of the general assembly.

Proceedings to be reported

5. This act shall be in force from its passage.

Commencement

CHAP. 16.—An ACT providing Compensation for Members of the General Assembly, Judges and other Officers of the Government, in lieu of the Compensation now allowed by law.

Passed December 16, 1863.

1. Be it enacted by the general assembly of Virginia, that the auditor of public accounts allow to the members of the general assembly, for their services for the past and present sessions, in lieu of the per diem compensation to which they are entitled by law, the sum of twelve dollars per day, in Virginia or Confederate treasury notes: and that the president of the senate and the speaker of the house of delegates each be paid, in lieu of their per diem compensation for the past and present sessions, the sum of twenty dollars per day, in like currency. To the governor of Virginia, ten thousand dollars for the years ending the thirty-first day of December eighteen hundred and sixty-three and the thirty-first day of December eighteen hundred and sixty-four, in like currency, in lieu of the compensation now allowed by law. To the judges of the supreme court of appeals, not residing in the lines of the enemy, in like currency, in lieu of the compensation now allowed by law, each the sum of five thousand dollars for the year ending the thirty-first day of December eighteen hundred and sixty-three, and the like sum of five thousand dollars for the year ending the thirty-first day of December eighteen hundred and sixty-four; to be paid quarter yearly. To the reporter of the supreme court of appeals, in like currency, in lieu of the compensation now allowed by law, the sum of three thousand five hundred dollars for the year ending the thirty-first day of December eighteen hundred and sixty-three, and the like sum of three thousand five hundred dollars for the year ending the thirty-first day of December eighteen hundred and sixty-four, payable quarter yearly. To the attorney general, in like currency, in lieu of the compensation now allowed by law, the sum of four thousand dollars for the year ending the thirty-first day of December eighteen hundred and sixty-three, and the like sum of four thousand dollars for the year ending the thirty-first day of December eighteen hundred and sixty-four, payable quarter yearly. To the clerk of the supreme court of appeals at Richmond and the clerk of the supreme court of appeals at Lewisburg, each the sum of two thousand dollars for the year ending the thirty-first day of December eighteen hundred and sixty-three, and the like sum of two thousand dollars each for the year

Compensation of members of the general assembly

Governor

Judges of court of appeals

Reporter

Attorney general

Clerks of court of appeals

ending the thirty-first day of December eighteen hundred and sixty-four, in lieu of the compensation now allowed them by law, payable quarter yearly. To the judges of the circuit courts not residing within the lines of the enemy, in like currency, in lieu of the compensation now allowed by law, each the sum of four thousand five hundred dollars for the year ending the thirty-first day of December eighteen hundred and sixty-three, and the like sum of four thousand five hundred dollars, payable quarter yearly, for the year ending the thirty-first day of December eighteen hundred and sixty-four.

Circuit judges

Commencement

2. This act shall be in force from its passage.

CHAP. 17.—An ACT amending and re-enacting an act passed October 13th, 1863, and an act amendatory thereof, passed October 26th, 1863, in relation to an Increase of the Salaries of certain Officers of Government.

Passed January 22, 1864.

Act allowing additional compensation to officers of the government amended

1. Be it enacted by the general assembly, that the act entitled an act to amend the first, second, third, fourth, fifth, thirteenth, fourteenth and sixteenth sections of chapter fourteen; the fourteenth section of chapter twenty-one; the twenty-seventh section of chapter twenty-three, and the tenth section of chapter sixty-six of the Code of Virginia (edition of eighteen hundred and sixty), so as to increase the salaries of certain officers of the government, passed October thirteenth, eighteen hundred and sixty-three, and an act amendatory thereof, entitled an act to amend and re-enact the fourteenth section of chapter fourteen of the Code of Virginia, as amended and re-enacted by an act entitled an act to amend the first, second, third, fourth, fifth, thirteenth, fourteenth and sixteenth sections of chapter fourteen; the fourteenth section of chapter twenty-one; the twenty-seventh section of chapter twenty-three, and the tenth section of chapter sixty-six, of the Code of Virginia (edition of eighteen hundred and sixty), so as to increase the salaries of certain officers of the government (passed October thirteenth, eighteen hundred and sixty-three), passed October twenty-sixth, eighteen hundred and sixty-three, be amended and re-enacted so as to read as follows:

2. The several officers herein after mentioned shall receive annually from the public treasury the following sums; that is to say:

In the executive department.

Officers in executive department

The secretary of the commonwealth, five thousand two hundred dollars, including all fees and perquisites received by him as secretary of the commonwealth and librarian; the assistant clerk, two thousand six hundred and twenty-five dollars; and the copying clerk, two thousand two hundred and fifty dollars.

In the office of the auditor of public accounts.

Auditor of public accounts and his clerks

3. The auditor of public accounts shall receive the sum of five thousand two hundred dollars; the clerk of accounts, three thousand seven hundred and fifty dollars; the first clerk, two thousand six hundred and twenty-five dollars; and the second, third, fourth, fifth, sixth and seventh clerks, each the sum of two thousand two hundred and fifty dollars.

In the second auditor's office.

Second auditor and his clerks

4. The second auditor shall receive the sum of four thousand five hundred and fifty dollars; the first clerk, two thousand six hundred and twenty-five dollars; and the second, third and fourth clerks, each the sum of two thousand two hundred and fifty dollars.

In the treasurer's office.

Treasurer and his clerks

5. The treasurer shall receive the sum of four thousand five hundred and fifty dollars; the first clerk, the sum of two thousand six

hundred and twenty-five dollars; the second clerk, two thousand two hundred and fifty dollars; and the third clerk, to be denominated clerk of the banking department, the sum of two thousand two hundred and fifty dollars; to be paid as heretofore.

In the land office.

6. The register of the land office shall receive the sum of four thousand five hundred and fifty dollars; the first clerk, two thousand six hundred and twenty-five dollars; and the second clerk, the sum of two thousand two hundred and fifty dollars. Register and his clerks

7. The clerk of the senate, who is required to prepare an index to the Journal of the Senate and the Documents printed by its order, shall receive an annual salary of four thousand one hundred dollars. The clerk of the house of delegates, who is hereby required to keep the rolls, to prepare an index to the Journal of the House of Delegates and the Documents; to prepare tables of the places of holding separate elections, and of the terms of the courts, as required by the sixteenth chapter, shall receive an annual salary of four thousand five hundred and fifty dollars. The further sum of eighty-four dollars per week during the session of the general assembly shall be allowed to the clerk of the senate, and the same sum to the clerk of the house of delegates, to enable each of said clerks to employ one assistant. Hereafter, at the expiration of each annual session of the general assembly, it shall be the duty of the clerk of the house of delegates to prepare for publication a sketch or synopsis of the several acts and joint resolutions passed during the session. Clerk of senate. Clerk of the house of delegates. To employ assistants. Clerk of house to prepare sketches of acts, &c.

8. The sergeant at arms of the senate and the sergeant at arms of the house of delegates shall each receive the sum of eighty-four dollars per week during the session of the general assembly. Each of said sergeants shall be allowed for taking any person into custody, by order of the house, two dollars; for every day he detains such person in custody, two dollars; and for the travel of himself or a messenger, to take any person into custody by such order, eight cents per mile going, and the same returning. The doorkeepers of both houses shall receive the sum of eighty-four dollars each week during the session of the general assembly. The clerks of the several standing committees of each house shall be allowed for their services eighty-four dollars per week until discharged; that is to say: In the senate, the clerk of the committee on roads and internal navigation; the clerk of the committees on general laws and confederate relations; the clerk of the committees for courts of justice and of finance; the clerk of the committees on public institutions, of privileges and elections and on banks: and in the house of delegates, the clerk of the committees for courts of justice and of schools and colleges; the clerk of the committees of propositions and of claims; the clerk of the committee on finance; the clerk of the committees of privileges and elections and on agriculture and manufactures; the clerk of the committees on banks and on military affairs: and the clerk of the committee of roads and internal navigation. The said clerks shall be appointed by the clerk of the senate and the clerk of the house of delegates respectively, and shall perform the duties of clerks of any other committees in their respective houses, and any similar services that may be required of them, without additional compensation. Sergeant at arms. Doorkeepers. Clerks of committees in senate. Clerks of committees in house of delegates.

9. The superintendent of the penitentiary shall receive annually the sum of three thousand seven hundred and fifty dollars; the first, second, third, fourth, fifth, sixth, seventh and eighth assistant keepers, each fifteen hundred dollars; and at the end of each fiscal year the superintendent may receive an additional sum of one thousand dollars, and each assistant keeper an additional sum of five hundred dollars, if the net profits of the said penitentiary shall amount to a sum equal thereto; but if the profits shall not be sufficient to pay Superintendent of penitentiary. Assistant keepers of the penitentiary.

the superintendent and assistant keepers the sums aforesaid, they shall be paid pro rata. The clerk of the penitentiary shall receive the sum of two thousand dollars. The surgeon of the penitentiary and public guard shall receive the sum of two thousand dollars. The interior guard of the penitentiary shall receive each four dollars per day.

Superintendent of public buildings

10. The superintendent of public buildings shall receive annually out of the treasury a salary of fifteen hundred dollars, payable as other salaries are paid. He shall also receive annually out of the treasury a reasonable sum, to be appropriated thereto, not to exceed twelve hundred dollars, payable monthly out of the civil contingent fund, to enable him to pay the servants and assistants he may have to employ.

Adjutant general and his clerk

11. The adjutant general shall receive for his services four thousand five hundred and fifty dollars, payable as other salaries are paid. He shall appoint one clerk in his office, who shall receive a salary of two thousand six hundred and twenty-five dollars, to be paid as other salaries are paid. He shall reside at or near, and shall keep his office at the seat of government; but when the public service shall render it expedient, the governor may direct him to remove with his office to any other place within the state.

Board of public works to appoint secretary

12. The board of public works shall have power to appoint a secretary, whose salary shall be annually three thousand three hundred and seventy-five dollars. He shall keep a record of the official acts of the board, and shall discharge such other duties as may be prescribed by the board. The proceedings of each day shall be signed by the person presiding on that day. The said proceedings shall be at all times open to inspection.

Not to apply to officers not now in office

13. The salary of each of the officers mentioned in the preceding sections of this act shall commence on, and be computed from the first day of October eighteen hundred and sixty-three: provided, that this section shall not be construed to apply to persons not now in office; and said salaries shall be payable in currency receivable by the state for public dues at the times when such salaries shall become due.

Officer not to receive from treasury other compensation than his salary

14. No officer, whose salary is hereby increased, shall receive from the treasury any other compensation for services hereafter rendered, by virtue of his office aforesaid. than the salary aforesaid; and the fees and other perquisites hereafter accruing and now allowed by law to any such officer, shall be paid by him into the public treasury.

Commencement and duration

15. This act shall be in force from its passage, and shall continue in force for six months after the ratification of a treaty of peace between the United States and the Confederate States of America, unless sooner altered or repealed by the general assembly.

Chap. 18.—An ACT providing Compensation for the Pages and Porters of the Senate and House of Delegates, and for the Clerk of the Joint Committee on Salt, and the Engineer employed to examine the Condition and Capacities of the Salt Works, &c.

Passed February 15, 1864.

Pages

1. Be it enacted by the general assembly, that the pages of the senate and of the house of delegates shall each receive the sum of six dollars per day for their services during the session of the general assembly; to be paid on the certificate of the clerk of the senate and of the clerk of the house of delegates respectively.

Porters

2. The porter of the senate and the porter of the house of delegates shall each receive for their services, during the session of the general assembly, the sum of six dollars per day; to be paid on the certificate of the clerk of the senate and of the clerk of the house of delegates respectively.

3. The clerk of the joint committee on salt shall receive for his services as such, at the late extra session, the sum of ten dollars per day for such number of days as he was actually engaged as such; to be paid on the certificate of the clerk of either house of the general assembly. The engineer employed by the joint committee on salt to examine and report on the condition and capacities of the salt wells, et cetera, shall receive the sum of two hundred dollars; to be paid on the certificate of either chairman of said committee: provided, that the several sums herein named shall be paid in such currency as is received by the state in payment of her public dues.

Clerk of joint committee on salt

Engineer

4. This act shall take effect from the seventh day of September eighteen hundred and sixty-three, and continue in force during the present war.

Commencement

CHAP. 19.—An ACT amending and re-enacting the 7th section of chapter 165 of the Code of Virginia, as amended by the act passed March 28th, 1861, entitled an act to increase the Pay of the Commonwealth's Attorney for the Circuit Court of Ohio County.

Passed February 12, 1864.

1. Be it enacted by the general assembly, that the seventh section of the one hundred and sixty-fifth chapter of the Code of Virginia be amended and re-enacted so as to read as follows:

Code amended

"§ 7. Such attorney in any county or corporation court shall be allowed by the court such sum as it deems reasonable, for public services (for which no other fee or reward is allowed by law), which shall be chargeable to such county or corporation; and in the circuit court, shall be allowed by it, when the attorney has no annual salary, such sum as it deems reasonable, not exceeding in one year three hundred dollars: except that the attorney for the circuit court of Richmond city shall hereafter receive annually the sum of three thousand dollars; and except that the attorney for the circuit court of the city of Lynchburg shall hereafter receive annually the sum of fifteen hundred dollars; and except that the attorney for the circuit court of the city of Petersburg shall hereafter receive annually the sum of fifteen hundred dollars.

Allowance to commonwealth's attorneys.

In Richmond city

Lynchburg and Petersburg

2. This act shall be in force from its passage, and shall continue in force until the expiration of six months after the ratification of a treaty of peace between the Confederate States and the United States, unless sooner altered or repealed by the general assembly.

Commencement

CHAP. 20.—An ACT authorizing an Increase of the Salaries of the Professors of the University, and providing for the Education of Persons disabled by Wounds received in the Public Service.

Passed March 4, 1864.

1. Be it enacted by the general assembly, that in lieu of the annuity provided for in the fourth section of chapter seventy-nine of the Code of eighteen hundred and sixty, there shall be appropriated annually to the university of Virginia, out of the revenues of the literary fund, the sum of thirty-seven thousand and five hundred dollars, in currency receivable at the treasury in payment of public dues.

Appropriation

2. Be it further enacted, that in lieu of the stated salary prescribed in the tenth section of the eighty-third chapter of the Code of eighteen hundred and sixty, and in addition to the fees of tuition to which he is now entitled by law, each professor of the university shall receive, out of said annual appropriation, a sum not exceeding three thousand dollars.

Salaries of professors

3. Any citizen of Virginia, who shall have been discharged from the military service of the state or of the Confederate States on

Education of disabled soldiers

account of wounds in battle, and who shall satisfy the authorities of the university that he is a man of suitable character and capacity (and that he is unable to pay the fees and charges), shall be entitled to the full course of instruction at the university, without charge for tuition, use of laboratories, lecture rooms, public halls or dormitories.

Commencement and duration

4. The first and second sections of this act shall take effect from the first day of October eighteen hundred and sixty-three, and shall continue in force for two years from that period, unless the present war with the United States terminates before that time; in which event, the provisions of those sections shall continue in force until the end of the session thereafter, and no longer; and the residue of this act shall be in force from its passage.

CHAP. 21.—An ACT to amend and re-enact section 15 of chapter 14 of the Code of Virginia (edition of 1860), so as to increase the Salary of the Printer of the Senate.

Passed March 4, 1864.

Code amended

1. Be it enacted by the general assembly, that the fifteenth section of chapter fourteen of the Code of Virginia (edition of eighteen hundred and sixty), be amended and re-enacted so as to read as follows:

Salary

"§ 15. The printer of the senate shall receive annually the sum of twenty-four hundred dollars, payable in the currency receivable, at the time the said salary is due, in payment of taxes and other public dues."

Commencement

2. This act shall take effect on the first day of October eighteen hundred and sixty-three, and continue in force during the present war.

CHAP. 22.—An ACT to increase the Compensation of the Clerk of the Circuit Court of the City of Richmond.

Passed March 10, 1864.

Salary increased

1. Be it enacted by the general assembly, that in lieu of the salary now allowed by law to the clerk of the circuit court of the city of Richmond, he shall receive a salary of seven hundred and fifty dollars per annum for the years eighteen hundred and sixty-three and eighteen hundred and sixty-four.

Commencement

2. This act shall be in force from its passage.

CHAP. 23.—An ACT to amend and re-enact section 44 of chapter 49 of the Code, so as to increase the Allowance to Sheriffs and Sergeants for Services to the Public.

Passed February 24, 1864.

Code amended

1. Be it enacted by the general assembly, that the forty-fourth section of chapter forty-nine of the Code of Virginia be amended and re-enacted so as to read as follows:

Allowance

"§ 44. There shall be chargeable in every county or corporation such sum as the court thereof may, for services to the public of the county or corporation, allow the sheriff or sergeant attending it, not exceeding for one year two hundred dollars; except that the corporation court of Richmond city may make such allowance as it may deem proper to its sergeant, for services for which no other compensation is made by law."

Exception as to Richmond

Commencement

2. This act shall be in force from its passage, and shall continue in force during the present war.

CHAP. 24.—An ACT to authorize Clerks of Courts, for certain services, to charge double the sums specified in the act passed March 24, 1863, entitled an act to amend and re-enact an act entitled an act increasing the Compensation of Clerks of Courts during the existing war.

Passed February 15, 1864.

1. Be it enacted by the general assembly, that in addition to the fees now authorized by an act passed March twenty-fourth, eighteen hundred and sixty-three, entitled an act to amend and re-enact an act increasing the compensation of clerks of courts during the existing war, the said clerks are hereby empowered to charge and receive as much more for each item of service therein mentioned as is therein specified, so that the entire charge shall be double the sums specified in said act for said services, payable in any currency receivable by the state for taxes or other public dues. Fees of clerks of courts increased

2. This act shall be in force from its passage, and continue in force until the expiration of six months after the ratification of a treaty of peace between the Confederate States and the United States, unless sooner modified or repealed; whereupon, the laws in force before the passage of this act and that of twenty-fourth March eighteen hundred and sixty-three, regulating the fees of clerks of courts, shall be deemed to be in full force. Commencement and duration

---

CHAP. 25.—An ACT to amend sections 31 and 32 of chapter 184 of the Code, so as to increase the Fees of Clerks of Courts for certain services.

Passed February 11, 1864.

1. Be it enacted by the general assembly, that the thirty-first and thirty-second sections of chapter one hundred and eighty-four of the Code of Virginia be amended and re-enacted so as to read as follows: Code amended

"§ 31. When the court is sitting for the examination of a person charged with felony, or for the trial of a negro, ten dollars, to be charged but once in the same case, whether the court sit therein more than one day or not. Felony case or trial of negro

"§ 32. For services rendered the commonwealth in a civil case, such fees as would be charged for the like services rendered to an individual; and for other public services, unless he receives an annual salary, such sum as the court may allow him, not exceeding one hundred dollars for one year." Services to public. Allowance by court

2. This act shall be in force from its passage, and until six months after the ratification of a treaty of peace between the Confederate States and the United States. Commencement

---

CHAP. 26.—An ACT to amend and re-enact the 13th, 33d, 34th and 36th sections of chapter 184 of the Code of Virginia, so as to increase the Fees and Compensation of Sheriffs and Sergeants.

Passed March 10, 1864.

1. Be it enacted by the general assembly, that the thirteenth, thirty-third, thirty-fourth and thirty-sixth sections of chapter one hundred and eighty-four of the Code of Virginia be amended and re-enacted so as to read as follows: Code amended

"§ 13. For serving on any person a declaration in ejectment, or an order, notice, summons or other process, where the body is not taken, and making return thereof, one dollar; except that the fee for summoning a witness shall only be fifty cents. For serving on any person an attachment or other process under which the body is taken, one dollar and fifty cents. For receiving a person in jail, seventy-five cents; and the like sum for discharging him therefrom. For carrying a prisoner to or from jail, for each mile of necessary travel either in going or returning, twenty cents. For taking any bond, Fees of sheriffs. For conveying prisoner to jail. Taking bond

Impanneling jury — one dollar. Where a jury is sworn in any court, for summoning and impanneling such jury, three dollars. Where a jury is summoned

Writ of elegit — upon a writ of elegit or ad quod damnum, or any inquest in vacation, for summoning them, three dollars; and for attending at the place of

Inquisition — their meeting, three dollars; and if the jury attend there, and an inquisition be found and returned, five dollars. For serving a writ of

Distringas — possession, three dollars. For serving a writ of distringas on a judgment or decree for personal property, if the specific thing be

Support of prisoners — taken, three dollars. For keeping and supporting any slave or other person confined in jail, for each day, one dollar; and a fair proportion

Rate to be prescribed by county court — of said sum for any time less than twenty-four hours: provided, that the county and corporation courts of the commonwealth may establish in their discretion a different rate, not less than fifty cents nor more

For stock — than four dollars per diem. For keeping and supporting any horse or live stock distrained or levied on, three dollars per day for each horse, mule or mare; and if the mare have a suckling colt, no more; one dollar per day for each hog or head of horned cattle, and fifty

Powers of courts — cents per day for every sheep or goat. The court of any county or corporation may at any time, when the acting justices have been summoned to consider the subject, and a majority thereof is present, fix or alter the rates to be thenceforth paid in such county or corporation for keeping and supporting any person in jail, or any horse or live stock; but the rates, as fixed or altered, shall never exceed those

Keeping property — herein before mentioned. The officer shall be repaid any necessary expense incurred by him in keeping property not before mentioned,

How, as to commissions — or in removing any property; and when, after distraining or levying, he neither sells nor receives payment, and either takes no forthcoming bond, or takes one which is not forfeited, he shall, if in no default, have (in addition to the one dollar for a bond, if one is taken) a fee of three dollars, unless this be more than the half of what his commission would have amounted to if he had received payment; in which case, he shall (whether a bond was taken or not) have a fee of sixty cents at the least, and so much more as is necessary to make the said half. The commission, to be included in a forthcoming bond (when one is taken), shall be five per centum on the first three hundred dollars of the money for which the distress or levy is, and two per centum on the residue of said money; but such commission shall not be received, unless the bond be forfeited, or the amount (including

Commission for selling goods — the commission) be paid to the plaintiff. An officer receiving payment in money on selling goods, shall have the like commission of five per centum on the first three hundred dollars of the money paid

On forthcoming bond — or proceeding from the sale, and two per centum on the residue; except that when such payment or sale is on an execution on a forthcoming bond, his commission shall be only half what it would be if the execution were not on such bond."

Code amended — 2. The thirty-third section of chapter one hundred and eighty-four is hereby amended and re-enacted so as to read as follows:

Conveying prisoner to jail or penitentiary — "§ 33. For an arrest for felony, two dollars and fifty cents; and for conveying any person charged with or convicted of felony to jail, or from one jail to another, or to the penitentiary, for each mile in

Expenses to be allowed — going and returning, twenty cents. The officer shall also be allowed for the support of the prisoner during the removal, and for assistance to make the arrest or effect the removal, such charge as may have been necessarily incurred by him, to be shown by his own affidavit: and where he has assistance, by the affidavit also of each person employed by him; such charge for assistance not to exceed, where it is in making an arrest, two dollars per day for each person employed to assist him, and not to exceed, where it is in conveying a prisoner, twenty cents per mile going and returning, for each guard."

Code amended — 3. The thirty-fourth section of chapter one hundred and eighty-four is hereby amended and re-enacted so as to read as follows:

Venire facias — "§ 34. For executing a writ of venire facias, four dollars; for whipping a free person, by order of a court or justice, one dollar; and for executing a sentence of death, ten dollars, in addition to the expenses actually incurred by the officer in its execution." Whipping Sentence of death

4. The thirty-sixth section of chapter one hundred and eighty-four is hereby amended and re-enacted so as to read as follows: Code amended

"§ 36. For attending any circuit court, and for all services for the commonwealth, not otherwise provided for, such sum as the said court may allow him, not exceeding two hundred dollars for one year." Attendance on circuit courts

5. This act shall be in force from its passage, and shall continue in force during the present war. Commencement

---

CHAP. 27.—An ACT concerning Jailors' Fees.

Passed February 27, 1864.

1. Be it enacted by the general assembly, that in all cases where the court of a county or corporation may have, since the second day of October eighteen hundred and sixty-three, and prior to the passage of this act, fixed a jailor's fees for keeping and supporting prisoners, under the act passed October second, eighteen hundred and sixty-three, entitled an act to increase jailors' fees for keeping and supporting prisoners, the fees so fixed by the court shall be paid from the time fixed by the court: provided the time is fixed on or subsequent to the second day of October eighteen hundred and sixty-three; and if the time has not been fixed by the court, the fees fixed by the court shall be paid for the time of imprisonment of such prisoner: provided such fees shall not be paid for any time of imprisonment prior to said second day of October eighteen hundred and sixty-three. Nothing herein contained shall be so construed as to repeal, modify or alter said act of October second, eighteen hundred and sixty-three, or abridge the power of the court given by said act. Jailor's fees, how fixed by court From what time to be paid Proviso Act of 1863 continued

2. This act shall be in force from its passage. Commencement

CHAP. 28.—An ACT to provide for the Purchase and Distribution among the People of the State, of Cotton, Cotton Yarns, Cotton Cloths and Hand Cards.

Passed March 9, 1864.

1. Be it enacted by the general assembly, that the governor is hereby authorized and required to establish a state agency in the city of Richmond, for the purpose of purchasing for and selling to the people of this state, raw cotton, cotton yarns, cotton cloths, cotton and woolen cards; and to this end, he shall appoint an agent, to be known by the name and style of The Commercial Agent of Virginia; who shall, before entering upon the discharge of the duties of his office, execute a bond with sufficient sureties, before the governor, to be approved by him, in the penalty of three hundred thousand dollars, conditioned for the faithful discharge of his duties under this or any future act. In case such agent shall fail to execute said bond as required, or if from any cause a vacancy may occur, another shall be appointed by the governor, subject to the same terms and conditions. And whenever such agent shall become interested, directly or indirectly, in the purchase and sale of raw cotton, cotton yarns, cotton cloths, cotton and woolen cards, or either of such articles, his office shall be declared vacant; and he may moreover at any time be removed by the governor. State agency Commercial agent Bond Agent not to be interested

2. Such agent, with the approval of the governor, is authorized to select and rent a suitable building or buildings in the city of Richmond, for a state storehouse, and to employ one or more clerks and Storehouse

such laborers as may be necessary to aid and assist him in the discharge of his duties under this act.

Requisition on factories

3. The governor is hereby authorized and required to make requisitions upon the president and directors of the several incorporated cotton factories within this commonwealth, and the owners or lessees of such as are not incorporated, to manufacture raw cotton, to be furnished by the state agent, into cotton yarns, from numbers four to twelve, both numbers inclusive, or cotton cloth, plain and unbleached. The gross amount of such requisitions shall be apportioned among the several factories referred to, according to their respective capacities to produce such yarns and cloths. The compensation of each of such factories, for the yarns and cloths so manufactured on state account, shall not exceed the price paid for the manufacture of similar goods by the confederate government, deducting therefrom the cost of the raw material furnished by the state. But the proceeds and labor of said factories shall not be required for the use of the state, so as to interfere with or impede the operations of the same for the confederate government.

Penalties

4. If any such cotton factory shall fail or refuse to comply with the requisition of the governor or the provisions of this act, such company shall be deemed guilty of a misdemeanor, and shall forfeit to the state, for each offence, the sum of five thousand dollars; to be recovered by motion in the circuit court of the city of Richmond, and paid into the public treasury; and it shall be the duty of the governor to inform the auditor of public accounts of every violation of this act, who shall forthwith proceed to enforce the collection of the penalty hereby imposed.

Duties of agent

5. It shall be the duty of such agent, subject to the control of the governor, to purchase, for cash, raw cotton, cotton yarns, cotton cloths, cotton and woolen cards in this or any other of the states of this Confederacy, and have the same deposited in the state storehouse.

Goods, how sold

The said raw cotton, cotton yarns, cotton cloths, cotton and woolen cards shall be sold by such agent at cost and charges, including interest on advances, and all expenses of the agency, to the different counties, cities and towns, through duly accredited agents, to be appointed by the county and corporation courts respectively; or when said courts cannot meet because of the presence or proximity of the public enemy, by the governor, on the recommendation of three or more justices of said county, or of the senator and delegate or delegates representing such county in the general assembly. But no agent of any county or corporation shall be entitled to act as such until he shall have given bond, with sufficient sureties, in a penalty to be fixed by the county and corporation courts, for the faithful discharge of his duties. Said bonds shall be taken and approved by said courts, when the appointments are made by them, and by the governor, when the appointment is made by him. Any county agent shall pay cash for all purchases authorized to be made by him. Such counties, cities or towns, through their agents, may demand and receive from the state agent raw cotton, cotton yarns, cotton cloths, cotton and woolen cards, in a proportion corresponding to the population of such county, city or town, including refugees and sojourners who are citizens of this state; and such agents shall sell to refugees and to persons temporarily sojourning in their counties, cities and towns, as well as to permanent citizens thereof, for their own and for family use, and not to speculators or retailers: provided, however, that the said courts and the governor shall respectively have power to revoke any appointment of agent made by them, whenever they deem it proper to do so, and shall in like manner appoint another agent in place of the one so removed. All the money arising from such sales shall be paid, on the last day of every month, into the public treasury, by the agent.

Agents of county courts. In case of presence of enemy

Bonds required

What counties may receive

Powers of agents, how revoked

Moneys, how paid in

Appropriation

6. For the purpose of carrying the provisions of this act into effect,

the sum of five hundred thousand dollars, or so much thereof as may be necessary, is hereby appropriated out of any money in the treasury not otherwise appropriated; to be paid from time to time on the order of the agent, approved by the governor. And the said sum, or part thereof, may in like manner be redrawn from the treasury, if the said agent shall in the interim have repaid into the treasury the amount theretofore drawn, or part thereof; but at no time shall such redraft be made for an amount greater than what said agent has paid into the treasury; so that at no time shall he have in his hands, in money and goods, more than three hundred thousand dollars in value. And all such sums so paid into the treasury by the agent are hereby reappropriated for the purposes of this act.

When may be withdrawn

Limitation of amount in hands of agent

7. The said agent shall report to the governor, on the first day of January, April, July and October in each year, a full statement of his transactions, showing accounts of his purchases and his sales, and of the expenses of the agency; and the governor shall, at the times aforesaid, and oftener, if he deems it proper so to do, appoint a commissioner, who shall, after being duly sworn, go into the state storehouse and examine the agent's books, vouchers and papers, and take an account of the operations of the agency, and make to the governor, without delay, a full, faithful and true report thereof. He shall also examine the agent's bond, and report whether it conforms to law; and whether the sureties thereto are good and sufficient. The agent shall also preserve vouchers for all his transactions, for examination by any commissioner which the general assembly or other authority may from time to time appoint for the purpose.

Reports of agent

Commissioner to examine affairs of state agency

8. The agent shall be allowed an annual salary of five thousand dollars, payable quarter yearly, and actual necessary traveling expenses incurred by him or his clerk in making purchases for this agency; and the clerk or clerks shall be allowed such compensation as the said agent may deem reasonable, not to exceed the sum of twenty-two hundred and fifty dollars each per annum.

Salary of agent

Of clerks

9. This act shall be in force from its passage, and shall continue in force during the present war.

Commencement

CHAP. 29.—An ACT to authorize the Board of Public Works to increase the Rates of Toll to be charged by Rail Road and other Companies, and declaring certain Duties and Liabilities of Rail Road, Express and other Companies.

Passed March 10, 1864.

1. Be it enacted by the general assembly, that whenever any rail road, turnpike, toll bridge, canal or navigation company in this state, whose rates of toll are limited by its charter or by any provision of law, shall desire to increase the same, such company shall prepare a tariff of the tolls proposed to be charged, and shall submit the same to the board of public works, for their revision; and such company shall, at least once in every three months thereafter, in like manner prepare and submit to said board a tariff of tolls, for like revision. The said board shall have authority to make any change therein, deemed by them to be proper; and said tariffs, so revised and corrected, shall thereafter be the lawful rate of toll to be charged by said company, and shall continue as such until changed upon like submission and revision: provided, that for express freight on packages not weighing more than two hundred and twenty-five pounds, carried by any rail road company on its own account, the said rail road company may increase the rates of transportation one hundred per centum over the rates for first class freight, and if carried for express companies, not over seventy-five per centum: provided, that no such rail road, canal or navigation company shall be entitled to the privileges of this act, unless such company shall provide its cars

Rates of toll, how increased

Tariff of tolls

How revised

Power of board of public works

Rate of charge

Duties of company as to fire, light, water, &c

and boats intended for the conveyance of passengers, with an ample supply of fuel, light and water, and shall keep the same clean and neat for the comfort of persons traveling therein: and on complaint to the board of public works, by any such traveler, that any such company has failed to supply such comforts, they shall examine into the case; and if the truth of the complaint be established, then the rates of toll to be charged by the company so failing shall thereafter be the rates heretofore provided by law; but if it shall be found, upon investigation, that the officers of said road, canal or navigation company used due diligence to furnish these articles, and that the default was in consequence of the failure of some of their subordinate officers, in violation of their orders or rules, that they may be excused, upon discharging from their employment the party so violating their orders and rules; and the officer so discharged shall not be reinstated in his place during the present war.

Penalties for failure

As to officers

Ticket offices and baggage cars

2. It shall also be the duty of the rail road companies to have their ticket offices opened, and their agents for the sale of tickets in attendance, and at the termini of such road the passenger cars open for the admission of passengers, and baggage cars for the reception of baggage, at least one hour before the advertised hour of departure of such train.

Connecting roads

Powers of board of public works

Exigencies of military service

Through tickets and checks

3. It shall be the duty of rail road companies whose roads connect, to run their trains in connection, unless the board of public works, for good and sufficient reasons, to be reported to the general assembly, shall release them from this obligation; and if said companies shall fail to run in connection, or shall be unable to agree upon a time table for running their several trains, so as to connect as aforesaid, the board of public works shall prescribe the regulations for running the several trains, and said companies shall conform thereto: provided, that the exigencies of the military service or wants of the confederate government interrupting said schedule at any time, shall exempt any rail road or canal or navigation company from all blame or penalties under this act. It shall also be the duty of said companies, when any passenger may desire a through ticket from any terminus of any of said roads, or from any station at or near a town or courthouse, or at which a stage regularly runs to any terminus, or to any such station or depot along said connecting roads, to deliver to him, on payment of fare, a ticket and a check for his baggage, specifying on the face of the ticket the points from and to which such passenger is to be conveyed; and said companies shall deliver to any passenger who may get on such trains at any other depot or station than those before mentioned, a check for his baggage to and from any depot or station on such roads; and said companies shall receive and transport such passenger and baggage to the point of destination, and shall settle between themselves the compensation each is to receive for such service; and if they cannot agree in regard thereto, the board of public works are hereby authorized to fix such compensation, and to revise and fix the tariff of charges for such through service. In the event of any loss of baggage thus transported, the owner thereof may maintain an action for the recovery of damages jointly against all or against either of the rail road companies respectively, whose lines of road are embraced within the route over which such passenger and baggage are to be conveyed, in which action such ticket and check shall be evidence, and obtain a joint or several judgment and execution for the amount of said recovery in the courts of any counties in which either of said companies are now liable to be sued: provided, however, that in order to fix the final liability on the company really delinquent in said loss, either one or more of the companies against whom such recovery may be had, shall, after satisfying the same, have a right of action in like manner over against either of the companies embraced, liable as aforesaid. Any rail road company failing to deliver a check or ticket when re-

Loss of baggage

Liability of company

Fines

quested as aforesaid, shall, in addition to the recovery provided in the preceding section, be liable to a fine of not less than fifty nor more than one thousand dollars; to be recovered, for the benefit of the commonwealth, by motion, after twenty days' notice, in any of the courts aforesaid.

4. If any company shall be dissatisfied with the rate so prescribed, and shall refuse to abide by the decision of said board, the tolls established by their charters and by the provisions of law, shall continue to be the rates to be charged by said company. How, if company dissatisfied

5. That it shall not be lawful for any express company to charge a higher rate of compensation for express freight carried over any rail road than fifty per centum on the amount the said rail road company is authorized to charge for like freight. As to express companies, rate of charge

6. All packages of two hundred pounds or less, intended for soldiers in camp or hospitals, shall be transported in turn, at one-half the tariff charges allowed for the transportation of similar packages. Packages for soldiers

7. Every express company shall, upon the payment or tender of the lawful rates of toll, transport to, and deliver at their proper destination on the line, or at the terminus of the line of such company, to be indicated by the owner, such articles as shall be delivered or offered at its office, or other receiving place, in proper condition to be transported. The property of all persons shall, as far as practicable, be transported in the order of time in which it shall be delivered and offered, and the tolls paid or tendered. Duties of express companies

8. If any express company shall, after payment or tender of the lawful tolls, fail to receive or to transport, or to deliver in a reasonable time any property so delivered or offered, or if the said company shall demand and receive more than is lawful, it shall forfeit and pay to the injured party a sum (to be recovered by motion or action) of not less than fifty nor more than five hundred dollars; and a recovery under this section shall not prejudice any claim or action against such company independent of this section. Fines for failures

9. The liability of a rail road or express company, as a common carrier, shall not be diminished or removed by any notice or by any contract, unless the same be in writing, signed by the parties. Liability as a common carrier

10. This act shall be in force from its passage, and shall continue in force during the continuance of the present war, and for one year thereafter, and no longer. Commencement

---

CHAP. 30.—An ACT authorizing Rail Road Companies and other Corporations to pay their Indebtedness to the Commonwealth in a certain manner.

Passed January 25, 1864.

1. Be it enacted by the general assembly of Virginia, that it shall be lawful for any rail road or other corporation indebted to this state, where the debt is not due, to pay said indebtedness into the treasury before maturity thereof. But all such payments shall be made in the registered or coupon bonds of this state; which the second auditor is directed and required to receive at par from such corporation. Any bonds so obtained by such sale shall constitute a part of the sinking fund. Indebtedness may be paid; How paid

2. This act shall be in force from its passage, and shall continue in force until six months after the ratification of a treaty of peace between the Confederate States and the United States, unless sooner altered or repealed by the general assembly of Virginia. Commencement

CHAP. 31.—An ACT authorizing the increase of the Capital Stock of the Virginia and Tennessee Rail Road Company.

Passed December 17, 1863.

Capital increased

1. Be it enacted by the general assembly, that it shall be lawful for the stockholders of the Virginia and Tennessee rail road company, at any general or special meeting thereof, to increase the capital stock of the company, so that such increase, added to the original capital stock, shall not exceed the amount of seven millions of dollars, by issuing to each of its stockholders certificates for additional amounts of stock therein, ratably, not exceeding the amounts of stock at present held by them respectively: provided, that such increase of issues of stock shall not exceed in the aggregate the amount of principal actually paid in, either from the earnings of said road, or loans, in addition to the original capital stock, and expended in construction.

How increased

Commencement

2. This act shall be in force from its passage.

CHAP. 32.—An ACT requiring Rail Road and Canal Companies to transport Troops and Munitions of War, without the right to demand prepayment of Fare.

Passed February 19, 1864.

Duty as to transportation of troops

1. Be it enacted by the general assembly, that in time of war, invasion or insurrection, it shall be the duty of rail road and canal companies within this commonwealth, and all common carriers engaged in the business of transportation upon the rail roads, rivers and canals therein, promptly to receive and transport all troops in the military or naval service of the state, with their baggage, and all arms and munitions of war, when such transportation is demanded by the proper authorities as immediately necessary, without having the right to require the payment of the legal fare therefor in advance.

Penalty

2. Any corporation or common carrier violating the provisions of the foregoing section, shall be fined, on conviction thereof, not exceeding ten thousand dollars.

As to arms, ammunition, &c

3. All arms, munitions or baggage belonging to troops or persons in the military or naval service of the state or confederate government, shall be transported upon any rail road subject to the authority of the state, upon the terms stated in the twenty-fifth section of the sixty-first chapter of the Code (edition of eighteen hundred and sixty), whether the said arms, munitions or baggage shall be transported upon the same trains and at the same time with the said troops or persons, or at any other time.

Commencement

4. This act shall be in force from its passage.

CHAP. 33.—An ACT requiring the Board of Public Works to suspend the payment of any subscription on the part of the State to certain Internal Improvement Companies.

Passed February 24, 1864.

Subscription suspended

1. Be it enacted by the general assembly, that the board of public works be and they are hereby required to suspend, until otherwise provided by law, making or carrying into effect any subscription on the part of the state to internal improvement companies authorized by existing acts, passed before the commencement of the present war between the Confederate States and the United States, in which companies the private stockholders have not, prior to the first day of July eighteen hundred and sixty-one, paid to the respective treasurers of said companies the amount of their respective subscriptions, and caused the same to be certified to the board of public works according to law; and in no case shall any further payment, on account of sub-

In what cases

Proviso as to

scriptions made by the state to any internal improvement company, be hereafter made, in bonds or certificates of debt of the state, but such payments shall be made in the currency received at the time by the state for taxes. Manner of payment

2. This act shall be in force from its passage. Commencement

CHAP. 34.—An ACT to authorize the James River and Kanawha Company and all other Navigation Companies to regulate all Charges by Boats and Boat Owners using the Works and Improvements of the said Companies.

Passed March 10, 1864.

1. Be it enacted, that the James river and Kanawha company and all other navigation companies in this state be and they are hereby authorized to prescribe a tariff of charges, with the approval of the board of public works, for freights and transportation of every kind upon their lines of improvement, and also to prescribe the rates of fare upon the packet boats using said lines and carrying passengers, and to make such regulations for the conduct and management of the said packet boats and freight boats as they may deem proper. Tariff of charges, how prescribed

2. The board of public works shall prescribe and publish such penalties for the violation of the regulations herein before provided for, as they may deem proper, which shall be a charge upon the delinquent boat as well as the owner thereof; and they may prohibit such delinquent boat from using any such line of improvement until the penalty incurred by it has been paid. All penalties incurred under this act shall be recoverable according to the provisions of the first section of chapter forty of the Code (edition of eighteen hundred and sixty). Penalties, how imposed How recovered

3. This act shall be in force from its passage, and until the expiration of six months after peace between the United States and the Confederate States shall have been established. Commencement

---

CHAP. 35.—An ACT more effectually to suppress unlawful Trading on Boats plying the Rivers and Canals of the Commonwealth.

Passed February 11, 1864.

1. Be it enacted by the general assembly, that if the master or other person in charge of any canal boat, batteau or other boat plying on the canals or rivers of this state, permit any article to be bought from, or sold to, or exchanged on board of his boat or batteau, with any free negro not having such certificate as is described in the thirty-seventh section of chapter one hundred and ninety-eight of the Code of Virginia, or with a slave not having the written permission of his master, by any person connected with his boat or batteau, and under his charge, other than a free white passenger, he shall be fined not less than twenty-five dollars nor more than five hundred dollars; and if a free negro, be also punished with stripes. Articles not to be bought from or sold to slaves or free negroes

2. And if such master or other person in charge of any such boat or batteau, permit any article bought or received from a free negro not having such certificate, or from a slave not having such permission, to be brought upon his boat or batteau by any person connected with such boat or batteau, and under his charge, other than a free white passenger, he shall be fined not less than twenty-five dollars nor more than five hundred dollars; and if a free negro, be also punished with stripes. When master liable to fine

3. If such master or other person in charge of any such canal boat, batteau or other boat, permit any free negro or slave serving as a hand on his boat, or under his charge, to transport on his boat or batteau, any agricultural products, fowls, meats or other commodity, from one place to another, for the purpose of selling the same, Trading by boat hands prohibited

or trading therewith, or of placing them with any other person for sale, he shall be fined not less than twenty-five dollars nor more than five hundred dollars; and the free negro or slave, on whose account any such commodity is transported, shall be punished with stripes.

In case of second conviction

4. In case of a second conviction of a master or other person having charge of such boat, under either of the three preceding sections, the person for whose benefit said boat is run shall be responsible for the fine imposed and costs, if not paid by the offender; and the same may be recovered, in the court in which the conviction was had, by motion, on ten days' notice, to be instituted by the attorney for the commonwealth in such court.

Inspectors, how appointed

5. It shall be lawful for the court of any county lying on any canal or navigable stream, to appoint one or more discreet persons as inspectors of boats, who shall be paid by county levy, and who shall be clothed with full power and authority, upon exhibiting the order appointing them, to examine and search, within their respective counties, all boats engaged in transportation on any such canal or navigable stream, for the detection of stolen property, and to require of the master of any boat a true account of every article found thereon.

Penalty for failure

If any master fail to render such true account, when required under this section, he shall be fined, in the discretion of a jury, not less than one hundred dollars, and in default of payment, be imprisoned not exceeding six months; and if a free negro, he shall be also punished with stripes. Any person who shall refuse to admit upon his boat, or shall obstruct or resist any inspector duly exhibiting his authority, in the discharge of his duty, shall be deemed guilty of a misdemeanor.

Inspector, how removed

The court may at any time, after summons to show cause against it, remove any such inspector, and may appoint another in his stead.

Commencement

6. This act shall be in force from its passage.

CHAP. 36.—An ACT to prevent the unlawful carrying of Slaves on Boats

Passed February 15, 1861.

Penalty for transporting slaves

1. Be it enacted by the general assembly, that if the master or any other person having charge of a canal boat, batteau or other boat plying on the canals or rivers of the state, shall carry any slave upon the same from one place to another within the state, without the consent of his owner, or of the guardian or committee of the owner, and without using due efforts to arrest such slave and lodge him in lawful custody, he shall, if a free person, be prosecuted therefor in the county in which the offence has been committed, and shall be fined not less than twenty-five dollars nor more than five hundred dollars; and shall moreover, in case the slave is not regained, forfeit and pay to the owner, guardian or committee of such owner, the value of said slave, and the reasonable expenses incurred

Owner of boat, when responsible

by him in attempting to regain said slave; and in case the slave is regained, then he shall forfeit and pay to the owner, guardian or committee of such owner, twice the amount of such reasonable expenses incurred by him in regaining said slave; to be ascertained by the jury sitting on the trial of the case.

Penalty on slave

2. If a slave violate the preceding section, he shall be punished with stripes, at the discretion of a justice.

Commencement

3. This act shall be in force from its passage.

CHAP. 37.—An ACT to amend the 1st section of an act passed April 12th, 1852, entitled an act to authorize the construction of the Wytheville and Grayson Turnpike, and to make Branches thereof to the Lead Mines of Wythe County, and Hillsville, in Grayson County.

Passed March 7, 1864.

1. Be it enacted by the general assembly of Virginia, that the first section of the act passed April twelfth, eighteen hundred and fifty-two, entitled an act to authorize the construction of the Wytheville and Grayson turnpike, and to make branches thereof to the lead mines in Wythe county, and to Hillsville, in Carroll county, be and the same is hereby so amended and re-enacted as to read as follows: Act amended

"§ 1. That it shall be lawful for Andrew Fulton, Ephraim McGavock, Robert Kent, Gustavus Crockett, Thomas J. Boyd, Alfred C. Moore, Alexander Pierce, George Kincannon, Guy F. S. Trigg, James Kincannon, Francis E. Kincannon, William Chaswell, Robert Holliday, Samuel McCamant, James Anderson, junior, Francis A. Crockett, William Dickenson, James Waugh, Ezra Nuckolls, Fielding L. Hale, John B. Mitchell, Robert Johnson, William Lindsey, William H. Cook, Madison Carter, Charles J. Davison and William C. Thornton, and such other persons as any three of the above named persons shall appoint, each to open books at such times and places as each of them may think proper, for the purpose of receiving subscriptions to a joint capital stock not exceeding in the whole the sum of thirty-three thousand dollars, to be divided into shares of twenty-five dollars each, for the construction of a turnpike road from a point at or near Wytheville, in Wythe county, by the Grayson sulphur springs and the old courthouse of Grayson county, to the North Carolina line, at or near Fisher's gap, in Grayson county." Corporators

2. And be it further enacted, that the board of public works be directed to subscribe for three-fifths of thirteen thousand dollars of the capital stock hereby authorized, that being the actual increase of the capital stock made by this act. The amount so subscribed by the said board shall be paid by the treasurer, upon the order of the board of public works, out of any money in the treasury not otherwise appropriated; but payments shall be made by said board only ratably with payments by others than the commonwealth, who shall subscribe for the remaining two-fifths of said increased capital stock. Board of public works to subscribe

3. This act shall be in force from its passage. Commencement

CHAP. 38.—An ACT to amend and re-enact an act entitled an act to extend the Time for the exercise of certain Rights and Remedies, passed March 14th, 1862.

Passed February 23, 1864.

1. Be it enacted by the general assembly, that the act passed on the fourteenth day of March eighteen hundred and sixty-two, entitled an act to extend the time for the exercise of certain civil rights and remedies, be amended and re-enacted so as to read as follows: Act amended

"Be it enacted by the general assembly, that the period between the seventeenth day of April, Anno Domini eighteen hundred and sixty-one, and four months after the ratification of a treaty of peace between the Confederate States of America and the United States of America, shall be excluded from the computation of the time within which, by the terms or operation of any statute or rule of law, it may be necessary to do any act or to commence any action or other proceeding to preserve or to prevent the loss of any civil right or remedy, or on account of the lapse of which any franchise or other right might otherwise be forfeited." Limitation

2. This act shall be in force from its passage. Commencement

CHAP. 39.—An ACT to authorize the admission of Wills to record, upon proof of the Handwriting of the Attesting Witnesses in certain cases.

Passed January 13, 1864.

Proof of handwriting allowed

1. Be it enacted by the general assembly, that whenever the attesting witnesses (or any of them) to a will may be within the lines or power of the enemy, so that the attendance of the requisite number of such witnesses cannot be enforced by summons, it shall be lawful for the court having jurisdiction thereof to admit such will to probate, upon proof of the handwriting of two of the attesting witnesses thereto whose attendance cannot be enforced, or of one of them, together with the evidence of the attesting witnesses whose attendance can be obtained.

Reservation of rights

2. Be it further enacted, that in all cases of wills admitted to record under the preceding section of this act, there shall be reserved to the parties all rights which they would have under the thirty-fourth, thirty-fifth and thirty-sixth sections of chapter one hundred and twenty-two of the Code of Virginia, if the will had been admitted to record under the provisions of that chapter.

Commencement

3. This act shall be in force from its passage.

CHAP. 40.—An ACT authorizing, in certain cases, the settlement of Fiduciaries' Accounts before Commissioners in Chancery of Courts other than those in which such Fiduciaries have been appointed, or in which the Instruments creating their authority have been recorded.

Passed February 25, 1864.

Fiduciaries' accounts, how settled in counties in power of enemy

1. Be it enacted by the general assembly, that whenever any county or corporation in this state shall be in possession of the enemy, or shall be so threatened with invasion as to render it probable that the jurisdiction of the courts cannot be safely and regularly exercised therein, it shall be lawful for a commissioner of the court of any county not in possession of the public enemy, or threatened with invasion, most convenient to that where the order was made or the instrument recorded conferring authority on any one as fiduciary, as specified in the one hundred and thirty-second chapter of the Code of Virginia (edition of eighteen hundred and sixty), or of any county wherein a majority in interest of the parties interested are for the time resident, to exercise the like authority and power in stating, settling and adjusting the accounts of such fiduciary, as if said fiduciary accounts had been laid before a commissioner of the court of the county wherein the order was made conferring on the fiduciary his authority: provided, that said commissioner shall, instead of posting a notice of the time and place of said settlement, as required by said chapter of the Code, cause a notice of the same to be published at least four weeks in some newspaper published in or nearest to the county, city or town in which the appointment of such fiduciary was made, or in the event of the removal of the parties in interest therefrom, in or nearest to which the majority of them may reside, and in the city of Richmond.

Publication

Jurisdiction of courts

2. The courts of the counties where settlements are made under this act, and those in which the same are required thereby to be subsequently recorded, shall exercise the same power and jurisdiction over the same, and the reports of the commissioners and the said settlements and reports shall have the same force and effect, and shall be subject to the same liability to be surcharged or falsified, as set forth and provided in regard to the settlements of fiduciaries in said one hundred and thirty-second chapter of the Code of eighteen hundred and sixty: provided, however, that in no case shall said court make any order directing the payment or distribution of any fund ascertained to be in the hands of such fiduciary.

What in cases of

3. Be it further enacted, that in cases where, by reason of the

presence or fear of the enemy, under acts of the general assembly, fiduciaries have qualified, and instruments creating trusts have been recorded, or may hereafter qualify, and instruments be hereafter recorded in other counties than those that would have taken jurisdiction but for such presence or fear of the enemy, it shall be lawful for such fiduciary to have his accounts settled, when practicable, before a commissioner of the county where the order would have been made or the instrument recorded but for the presence or fear of said enemy; which settlement shall be made and reported by said court to the court wherein such order was made, or such instrument recorded; and the same subsequent proceedings shall be had touching the same as if made by a commissioner of said court. Instruments recorded. How accounts may be settled.

4. Within six months after jurisdiction has been resumed and continued over the counties referred to in the first section hereof, the fiduciary whose accounts have been settled and recorded under this act, shall cause a copy of the same to be returned to, and recorded in the county where the same should have been settled but for the presence or fear of the enemy; and if he fail to do so, he shall derive no benefit whatever from the settlement made pursuant to this act. Where to be returned and recorded. Penalty.

5. If any such fiduciary shall fail to cause a copy of any settlement made under this act to be returned and recorded as provided in the fourth section, it shall be the duty of the clerk of the court in which the same is recorded to do so at the cost of such fiduciary. Duty of clerk in case of failure by fiduciary.

6. This act shall take effect from its passage, and shall continue in force until the ratification of a treaty of peace between the Confederate States and the United States, and no longer. Commencement.

CHAP. 41.—An ACT prescribing the mode of serving Notices in certain cases.

Passed February 12, 1864.

1. Be it enacted by the general assembly, that a notice of any motion which may be made under the act entitled an act authorizing the recovery of money stolen from the Exchange Bank of Virginia at Weston, passed March fourteenth, eighteen hundred and sixty-two, may be served by the publication thereof, once a week for four successive weeks, in a newspaper printed in the city of Richmond. Motion, how made.

2. This act shall be in force from its passage. Commencement.

CHAP. 42.—An ACT to amend the 1st and 2d sections of an act to suppress Gaming, passed October 16th, 1863.

Passed March 10, 1864.

1. Be it enacted by the general assembly, that the first and second sections of chapter one hundred and ninety-eight of the Code of Virginia (edition of eighteen hundred and sixty), as amended by an act to suppress gaming, passed October sixteenth, eighteen hundred and sixty-three, be further amended and re-enacted so as to read as follows: Act of 1863 amended.

"§ 1. A free person who shall keep or exhibit a gaming table, commonly called A B C, or E O table, or faro bank, or table of like kind, under any denomination, whether the game or table be played with cards, or any evasive substitute for cards, dice, or otherwise, or who shall be a partner, or concerned in interest, or employed or engaged in any manner in the keeping or exhibiting such table or bank, or who shall permit the keeping or exhibition of such table or bank in any room or apartment of his house or premises, shall, upon conviction thereof, be deemed to be guilty of an infamous offence, in the meaning of the constitution of this state, and shall be confined in jail not less than two nor more than twelve months, and be fined not less Penalty for exhibiting faro, &c. Infamous offence.

May be whipped than one hundred dollars nor more than one thousand dollars, and may, at the discretion of the court, be subjected to stripes on his bare back, not exceeding thirty-nine; and all the right, title and interest, legal or equitable, of such person in any real property, including the lot and premises thereto attached, in or upon which such gaming may be carried on, shall be absolutely forfeited to and vest in the commonwealth. Any such table or faro bank, and all money found thereon, or other property staked or exhibited to allure persons to bet at such table, and all household and other personal property, including slaves, used or employed in such gaming house, may, as to whatever title or interest the keeper or exhibitor of such gaming table shall have therein, be seized by order of a court, or under warrant of a justice, mayor of a city or town, or judge in vacation; and the property so seized, including said money, whether belonging to the said keeper or any better, shall be forfeited; and after deducting one-half the value or proceeds thereof for the person or persons making the seizure, and the costs and other expenses attending the safe-keeping and disposal thereof, shall be appropriated as provided in the twenty-fourth section of chapter fifty-one of the Code (edition of eighteen hundred and sixty), in respect to the forfeiture declared by said chapter: provided, that twenty per centum of the entire value of the property forfeited shall, in each case of conviction, be payable to the commonwealth's attorney, who prosecuted the case: and provided further, that the implements used or intended for such unlawful game shall be burnt.

Forfeiture of property

Seizure, how made

Proceeds, how distributed

Commonwealth's attorney

Penalty for renting property or hiring slave "§ 2. Be it further enacted, that any person who shall knowingly rent to any person any real property for such unlawful gaming, with intention to allow the use of the same for the purpose aforesaid; or any person who shall knowingly hire any slave to any such person, with intention to allow such slave to be employed in any service connected with such gaming, shall be fined not less than one hundred dollars nor more than one thousand dollars; and upon conviction, all their right, title and interest, legal or equitable, in any such real estate, and their right to such slave, shall be absolutely forfeited to and vest in the commonwealth. And the court in which any proceedings shall be commenced, or conviction had, either under this or the next preceding section, may make all proper orders for the safe-keeping and forthcoming of the property liable to forfeiture as aforesaid, and for the proper disposal thereof: provided, however, that as to any slave so seized under the provisions of this act, the owner or claimant thereof may have such slave released from custody, by executing, at any stage of the proceedings, bond with good security, in a penalty equal at least to the full value of the said slave or slaves, conditioned to have the same forthcoming to abide the orders of the court; and upon forfeiture of the condition of any such bond, judgment may be recovered thereon, upon ten days' notice to the obligors, in like manner as upon a forthcoming bond."

Forfeiture

Safe-keeping of property

Bond for release of slave

Witnesses, how attached 2. Any mayor or justice, or other officer authorized to issue a warrant for a search or arrest under this act, or the act passed on the sixteenth day of October eighteen hundred and sixty-three, entitled an act to suppress gaming, shall have power to issue at any time an attachment to compel the attendance of witnesses, without previous summons or other process.

Commencement 3. This act shall be in force from its passage.

CHAP. 43.—An ACT to authorize Sheriffs to summon the Posse Comitatus to aid in enforcing Impressments in certain cases.

Passed March 8, 1864.

When property impressed 1. Be it enacted by the general assembly, that should any person whose property has been or may hereafter be impressed under the provisions of an act entitled an act for the relief of the indigent soldiers and sailors of the state of Virginia, who have been or may be disabled in the military service, and the widows and minor children of soldiers and sailors who have died or may hereafter die in said service, and of the indigent families of those now in the service, passed October thirty-first, eighteen hundred and sixty-three, refuse to deliver the same to the impressing agent, it shall be the duty of the sheriff of the county, whenever notified of the fact by the said agent, on oath, to seize the property so impressed, and deliver it to the said agent; and he is authorized, if necessary for that purpose, to summon the posse comitatus. Posse comitatus

2. Be it further enacted, that all the costs attending the seizure of property as herein provided, shall be paid by the party refusing to deliver it. Costs

3. This act shall be in force from its passage. Commencement

Chap. 44.—An ACT to amend and re-enact an act authorizing the Court of Appeals to hold its Sessions at other places than at Lewisburg, passed March 12th, 1863.

Passed March 5, 1864.

1. Be it enacted by the general assembly, that the act entitled an act to authorize the court of appeals to hold its sessions at other places than Lewisburg, passed twelfth March eighteen hundred and sixty-three, be amended and re-enacted so as to read as follows: Act amended

"§ 1. That the annual sessions of the supreme court of appeals, provided by law to be held at Lewisburg, in the county of Greenbrier, shall be held at the town of Christiansburg, in Montgomery county, or at such other place as the said court, or a majority of the judges thereof in vacation, may from time to time direct and appoint; of which change due notice shall be given by publication thereof in one or more newspapers printed in the city of Richmond; and all laws now in force applicable to the said court when its sessions are held at Lewisburg, shall apply in like manner to said court and its sessions when held at any other place, under the provisions of this act. Court, where held

"§ 2. The said court, or a majority of the judges thereof in vacation, may order the removal of the library and records of said court at Lewisburg to such place as the said court may, under the provisions of this act, appoint for its sessions; and a sum not exceeding one thousand dollars is hereby appropriated for the purposes of such removal and for the procurement of a suitable house to keep said library and books in, to be paid, upon the order of said court, out of any moneys in the treasury not otherwise appropriated." Library may be removed Appropriation

2. This act shall be in force from its passage. Commencement

Chap. 45.—An ACT extending the jurisdiction of the Circuit Court of the Town of Danville.

Passed January 30, 1864.

1. Be it enacted by the general assembly, that the act passed March first, eighteen hundred and sixty-one, entitled an act changing the time of holding the circuit court in the town of Danville, be amended and re-enacted so as to read as follows: Act amended

"Be it enacted by the general assembly, that there shall be held in the town of Danville, twice in each year, a circuit court for said town, the jurisdiction whereof shall extend to all cases arising within the corporate limits of said town, over which the circuit court of the county of Pittsylvania now has jurisdiction, and also to all cases arising within one mile of the corporate limits of said town, whereof Court established. Its powers

Criminal jurisdiction — the circuit court of said county now has jurisdiction. And any person or persons charged with having committed any crime or crimes within one mile of the corporate limits of said town of Danville, and who may have been sent on to the jail of the county of Pittsylvania by the hustings court of Danville, to be tried in the circuit court of Pittsylvania, shall be remanded by the county court of the county of Pittsylvania, to be tried in the circuit court of Danville; Terms of court — and the said court shall be held on the twenty-fifth day of March and on the twenty-fifth day of August, by the judge of the fourth judicial circuit."

Commencement — 2. This act shall be in force from its passage.

CHAP. 46.—An ACT to authorize the County Courts to change the places of holding their Sessions, and to enlarge their Powers in certain cases.

Passed March 1, 1864.

How place of holding courts changed — 1. Be it enacted by the general assembly, that during the existing war it shall be lawful for the county court of any county, either where partially occupied by the public enemy, or where the regular sittings of the courts of such counties, at the respective courthouses thereof, shall be prevented by apprehended danger from the enemy, or from any other cause growing out of the war, to hold their sessions at such other place or places in such counties as may be agreed on and designated by the court, or by such number of justices as are required by law to constitute a court: provided, that in the latter case the justices so ordering a change of the place of holding the courts, shall certify their action in writing to the clerks of such courts, at least ten days before the time of holding the first term at such changed place of holding the same: and provided further, that no motion, action at law or suit in chancery shall be tried at said court when the place of meeting has been changed, unless by consent of parties.

Provision for poor — 2. In any of the counties so situated, as mentioned in the first section, it shall be lawful for the county courts, during the present war, to provide for the poor of such counties, by loans to be made in the same manner in all respects as provided in the act of the general assembly entitled an act to authorize the county courts and any incorporated city or town to arm the militia of their respective counties, cities and towns, and to provide means therefor, passed January nineteenth, eighteen hundred and sixty-one.

Commencement — 3. This act shall be in force from its passage.

CHAP. 47.—An ACT authorizing County and Corporation Courts to ratify and confirm the issue and sale of Bonds and other Securities in certain cases.

Passed March 10, 1864.

Justices to be summoned — 1. Be it enacted by the general assembly, that it shall be lawful for the court of any county or corporation, all the acting justices thereof having been summoned for the purpose of considering the subject, and a majority of them being present, Order to be entered ratifying and confirming issue and sale of bonds — to enter upon the records of the court an order ratifying and confirming the issue and sale of any bonds or other securities issued or sold before the date of such order, by the court of such county or corporation, or under its order, Under what acts of assembly — and for the purpose of carrying into effect the provisions of the act passed October thirty-first, eighteen hundred and sixty-three, entitled an act for the relief of the indigent soldiers and sailors of the state of Virginia, who may have been or may be disabled in the military service, and the widows and minor children of soldiers and sailors who have died or may hereafter die in said service, and of the indigent families of those now in service; or of the act passed January nineteenth, eighteen hundred and sixty-one, entitled an act to authorize the county courts and any incorporated city or town to arm the militia of their respective counties, cities and towns, and to provide means therefor; or of the ordinance of the convention, passed June eighteenth, eighteen hundred and sixty-one, entitled an ordinance to make provisions for the maintenance of families of soldiers in the actual service of the state or the Confederate States, and for other purposes; or of the act passed March tenth, eighteen hundred and sixty-two, entitled an act for the relief of the indigent soldiers who have been or may be disabled in the military service of the state, and the widows or minor children of soldiers who have died or may hereafter die in the service. And such ratification and confirmation shall be held to relate back to the time of the issue and sale of such bonds or other securities, and the proceedings upon which such issue and sale was made, and to cure all irregularities in such issue, sale and proceedings, and to make such bonds or other securities in all respects a lawful and binding charge upon such county or corporation, as if the issue and sale thereof, and the proceedings upon which such issue and sale was made, had been in strict conformity with law.

Ratification to relate back

2. This act shall be in force from its passage.

Commencement

CHAP. 48.—An ACT to prohibit the granting of Ordinary License at certain specified places in the Commonwealth.

Passed March 10, 1864.

1. Be it enacted by the general assembly, that it shall not be lawful for any court of this commonwealth to grant a license to keep an ordinary to any person within a city or town, or within five miles of the limits thereof, or at any depot, station or other point on any rail road.

License not to be granted

2. Any person who shall, without having first obtained an ordinary license, sell, by retail, wine, ardent spirits, or a mixture thereof, ale, porter or beer, or such like drinks, to be drank in or at the place of sale, he shall, in addition to the penalty now prescribed by law, forfeit the tenement where the sale is made, if he is the owner thereof, or such interest as he may have therein, if he is the lessee, and shall moreover forfeit the stock of liquors on hand, and all the personal property used in such business: and the court before which a conviction shall be had shall take such steps as it may deem proper for the confiscation and sale of the property forfeited by this act.

Forfeiture

Confiscation and sale

3. This act shall be in force from its passage.

Commencement

CHAP. 49.—An ACT providing an additional Appropriation to the Virginia Military Institute.

Passed January 22, 1864.

1. Be it enacted by the general assembly, that for the purpose of supplying the estimated deficiency in the fund for the support of the state cadets in the Virginia military institute, the additional sum of twenty thousand dollars is hereby appropriated for the fiscal year ending on the thirtieth day of June eighteen hundred and sixty-four; and the auditor of public accounts is hereby authorized and required to issue his warrant or warrants on the treasury for the same, in the manner that other warrants to the said institute have been heretofore issued: provided, however, that the auditor of public accounts shall not issue his warrant for the money hereby appropriated, until satisfactory evidence is furnished his office that the number of state cadets authorized by law have been appointed (within the ages and manner prescribed by law); if the whole number so appointed at the last

Amount appropriated

Duty of auditor

annual meeting of the board of visitors shall not have elected to enter the school, the auditor of public accounts may issue his warrant for a pro rata proportion of the sum hereby appropriated, to defray the expense of new state cadets so appointed and in actual attendance.

Commencement 2. This act shall be in force from its passage.

CHAP. 50.—An ACT to authorize the Governor to lease a portion of Land adjoining the Armory.

Passed March 8, 1864.

Lease authorized 1. Be it enacted by the general assembly, that the governor of this commonwealth be and he is hereby authorized to lease, for the benefit of the commonwealth, to R. Archer, R. S. Archer and A. D. Townes, for an additional term of ten years from and after the expiration of the present lease to R. Archer and Company, so much of the land adjoining the armory, extending from the canal to the river, as the said R. Archer and Company are now in possession of, or entitled to occupy under their present lease, on such terms and conditions as may be agreed upon by the governor and the said lessees.

Commencement 2. This act shall be in force from its passage.

CHAP. 51.—An ACT to amend the 3d section of an act for the relief of Indigent Soldiers and Sailors, &c., passed October 31st, 1863.

Passed February 24, 1864.

Act amended 1. Be it enacted by the general assembly, that the third section of an act for the relief of the indigent soldiers and sailors of the state of Virginia, who have been or may be disabled in the military service, and the widows and minor children of soldiers and sailors who have died or may hereafter die in said service, and of the indigent families of those now in the service, passed October thirty-first, eighteen hundred and sixty-three, be amended and re-enacted so as to read as follows:

Sojourners and refugee soldiers, &c. "§ 3. Whenever any county or corporation court shall be satisfied that any such soldiers and sailors were, at the date of their enlistment, residents of any county or corporation of the commonwealth, and whose families may have been or may hereafter be driven from their homes by fear of the public enemy, and are residing in such county or corporation, it shall be the duty of such court to enroll such soldiers and sailors and their families, according to the provisions of the first section of this act, and to make the same provision for their support as for those soldiers and sailors and their families described in said section. The said county or corporation court shall state and certify their accounts for the support of such refugee soldiers and sailors and their families, and forward the same to the auditor of public accounts; and it shall be the duty of said auditor to pay said accounts by warrants upon the treasurer of the commonwealth."

Accounts how paid

Commencement 2. This act shall be in force from its passage.

CHAP. 52.—An ACT authorizing Banks or Branch Banks in certain cases to receive payment of Debts payable at Branch or Mother Banks within the enemy's lines.

Passed March 3, 1864.

When debts due to banks may be paid 1. Be it enacted by the general assembly, that it shall be lawful for any person, body politic or corporate, who may be indebted to any of the branch banks of this state, and unable, because of the presence of the public enemy, to discharge said indebtedness at the office of said branch bank, to deposit in the mother bank thereof, if within the lines of the confederate armies, the amount represented to be due said branch bank; and the said mother bank is hereby authorized to receive, at its discretion, said amount, and give a receipt to the party paying the same; and such payment shall be held as a discharge, to the extent thereof, of said indebtedness: provided, that such payment shall operate as a discharge in no case in which such debt has been bona fide transferred for value to any loyal citizen of any one of the Confederate States, at any time prior to the date of such payment: and provided further, that the provisions of this act shall be applicable in case of any mother bank within the enemy's lines; in which case, such payment may be made to any branch thereof within our lines, in like manner and with like effect and limitations as are above provided. Proviso

2. This act shall be in force from its passage, and continue in force during the existing war. Commencement

---

CHAP. 53.—An ACT to amend and re-enact the 2d section of an act passed October 9th, 1863, entitled an act to amend the act passed February 13th, 1863, entitled an act amending and re-enacting the 1st and 2d sections of an act entitled an act to repeal the Fence Law of Virginia as to certain Counties, and to authorize the County Courts to dispense with Enclosures in other Counties, passed October 3d, 1862, and to legalize the action of County Courts held under said law.

Passed March 3, 1864.

1. Be it enacted by the general assembly, that the second section of an act passed October ninth, eighteen hundred and sixty-three, entitled an act to amend the act passed February thirteenth, eighteen hundred and sixty-three, entitled an act amending and re-enacting the first and second sections of an act entitled an act to repeal the fence law of Virginia as to certain counties, and to authorize the county courts to dispense with enclosures in other counties, passed October third, eighteen hundred and sixty-two, and to legalize the action of county courts held under said law, be amended and re-enacted so as to read as follows: Act amended

"§ 2. Be it further enacted, that the county courts of the counties of Augusta, Frederick, Clarke, Warren, Culpeper, Rappahannock, Norfolk, Princess Anne, Mercer, Shenandoah, Page, Prince William, Spotsylvania, Hampshire, Berkeley, Caroline, Rockingham, Richmond, Westmoreland, Loudoun, Jefferson, Orange, Essex, King & Queen, Goochland, Giles, Bland, Fairfax, Greenbrier, New Kent, Charles City, James City, Prince George, Nansemond, Highland, Hardy, King William and Madison shall have power, all the justices having been summoned, and a majority thereof being present, to dispense with the existing laws in regard to enclosures, so far as their respective counties may be concerned, or such part thereof, to be described by metes and bounds, as in their discretion they may deem it expedient to exempt from the operation of such law." Counties included

2. This act shall be in force from its passage. Commencement

CHAP. 54.—An ACT for the protection of Sheep, and to increase the growth of Wool.

Passed February 10, 1864.

Whereas an increase of the growth of wool in this commonwealth is at all times important, but more especially so in the struggle the Southern Confederacy is maintaining for her independence: Therefore, Preamble

Sheep not to be sold to be slaughtered

1. Be it enacted by the general assembly, that from and after the passage of this act it shall not be lawful for any person whatever to buy or sell, within the limits of Virginia, any sheep for the purpose of being butchered, or to slaughter the same at home with a view of sending the meat to market, during the continuance of the present war, under a penalty, for every sheep so slaughtered, of fifty dollars. But this section shall not apply to the purchase or sale of mutton or lamb, upon the certificate of a physician or surgeon that it is needed, and in good faith intended for any sick or wounded person under his care.

Duty of justices

2. It shall be the duty of all magistrates, sheriffs and constables to see that this law is executed; and upon information given or complaint made by any person of a violation thereof, to a justice of the peace, he shall issue his warrant against the party charged; and if satisfied of the guilt of the party so charged, shall cause the collection and payment of the above penalty, by execution as in cases of judgments on warrants.

Proceedings in case of complaint

3. Upon complaint before a justice, by any inhabitant of a county, that sheep owned by him have been destroyed or injured by dogs within his county, the justice shall, by warrant under his hand, appoint not less than two nor more than three discreet freeholders of the county, residing near the place where the injury is alleged to be committed, whose duty it shall be to proceed forthwith, upon actual view, and such other information as may be accessible, to ascertain the truth of the complaint, and the value of the injury, if any, which has been sustained, and make return thereof, in writing, under their hands, together with the warrant of the justice, to him; and upon proper information so obtained, he shall issue his warrant against the owner whose dog or dogs may have done the injury, and shall assess him with the amount of damage, and cause execution to be issued against him; and upon collection thereof, with the costs incurred, shall pay to the party sustaining the loss: and where the dog belongs to a slave, the master shall in all cases be responsible for the loss sustained, together with the costs; but either party shall have the right to appeal from the decision of such justice, according to the provision of section seven of chapter one hundred and fifty of the Code.

Remedy against owner

Proviso

4. Provided, that the execution authorized to be issued under the third section of this act shall be directed to the sheriff of the county, and levied and returned by him according to law, should the amount of damages assessed exceed fifty dollars.

Commencement

5. This act shall be in force from its passage.

CHAP. 55.—An ACT authorizing the collection of Dividends due by the Raleigh and Gaston Rail Road Company to the City of Norfolk.

Passed February 10, 1864.

Agent appointed

1. Be it enacted by the general assembly, that Thomas J. Corprew, sergeant of the city of Norfolk, be and he is hereby authorized and empowered to collect and receive from the Raleigh and Gaston rail road company all uncollected dividends now due, or which may hereafter become due, during the existing war, by the said rail road company to the said city of Norfolk, upon the stock owned by the said city in the said company.

Duties of agent

How one-third of dividends to be distributed

2. Upon the collection and receipt of the said dividends the said Thomas J. Corprew is directed to appropriate one-third part of the amount so received by him to the relief and support of the indigent families of persons from said city now in the military or naval service or employment of the Confederate States, who are outside of the lines of the enemy and accessible to him, and who may be personally known to him, or satisfactorily shown to be in need of such

aid; the distribution among said families to be in money, and in proportion to the number of persons in each.

3. The other two-thirds of the said dividends the said Corprew is directed to expend in the purchase of articles of clothing, shoes, blankets and other necessaries for the soldiers and sailors from the said city in the service of the Confederate States; to be supplied to them by him, upon the requisition of the commanding officer of their respective companies, preferring, however, when all cannot be supplied, those who, from the character of service in which they are engaged, and other causes, are most exposed, and most in need of relief. How remaining portion to be expended

4. The said Thomas J. Corprew is required to make a report to the auditor of public accounts, semi-annually, of his receipts and disbursements under this act, with his vouchers for the same. Report to be made

5. The commonwealth of Virginia hereby guarantees the said Raleigh and Gaston rail road company against any future claim of the city of Norfolk for all dividends that may be paid by said company under the authority and provisions of this act. Guarantee of the commonwealth

6. Before receiving any money authorized to be received by this act, the said Corprew shall file in the office of the auditor of public accounts a bond in the penalty of thirty-five thousand dollars, with sufficient security, to be approved by the auditor of public accounts, payable to the commonwealth of Virginia, conditioned for the faithful performance of the duties of the office hereby created. Bond to be given

7. This act shall be in force from its passage. Commencement

CHAP. 56.—An ACT to amend and re-enact the 2d section of chapter 7 of the Code of Virginia, relating to the election of Judges.

Passed March 9, 1864.

1. Be it enacted by the general assembly, that the second section of chapter seven of the Code of Virginia (edition of eighteen hundred and sixty) be amended and re-enacted so as to read as follows: Code amended

"§ 2. Every election of judge, other than such election as is provided for in the twentieth section of chapter seven of the Code of Virginia (edition of eighteen hundred and sixty), shall be held, if it be for a circuit, at the end of eight years, and if it be for a section, at the end of twelve years next succeeding the preceding election in such circuit or section, and on the same day of the month on which the said preceding election was held, unless that day would come within the thirty days mentioned in the sixteenth section of the sixth article of the constitution; in which case, the election shall be held on the first day afterwards that may be consistent with the said sixteenth section: provided, however, that no election for a judge shall be held under this section during the existing war between the Confederate States and the United States, unless otherwise provided by law." Election of Judges Proviso

2. This act shall be in force from its passage. Commencement

CHAP. 57.—An ACT to amend and re-enact the 11th section of the 208th chapter of the Code of Virginia (edition of 1860), as amended and re-enacted by an act entitled an act to amend and re-enact section 11 of chapter 208 of the Code of Virginia, passed October 30th, 1863, concerning Jurors in Criminal Cases.

Passed March 10, 1864.

1. Be it enacted by the general assembly, that the eleventh section of chapter two hundred and eight of the Code of Virginia, as amended by the act passed October thirtieth, eighteen hundred and sixty-three, entitled an act to amend and re-enact section eleven of Code amended

chapter two hundred and eight of the Code of Virginia, be amended and re-enacted so as to read as follows:

Lodging and board, how furnished

"§ 11. When in a case of felony the jury are kept together during or beyond the day on which they are impanneled, the court shall direct its officer to furnish them with suitable board and lodging while so confined. The expense thereof, not exceeding three dollars per day for each juror, shall be paid out of the treasury, when allowed by the court: provided, that in the cities of Richmond, Petersburg and Lynchburg, the court may allow not exceeding six dollars a day for each juror."

Allowance

Commencement

2. This act shall be in force from its passage, and continue in force until the expiration of six months after the ratification of a treaty of peace between the Confederate States and the United States

CHAP. 58.—An ACT amending and re-enacting the 10th section of chapter 170 of the Code of Virginia (edition of 1860), concerning the Service of Process.

Passed February 24, 1864.

Code amended

1. Be it enacted by the general assembly, that the tenth section of chapter one hundred and seventy of the Code of Virginia (edition of eighteen hundred and sixty), be amended and re-enacted so as to read as follows:

Process

"§ 10. On affidavit that a defendant is not a resident of this state, or that diligence has been used by or on behalf of the plaintiff to ascertain in what county or corporation he is, without effect, or that process, directed to the officer of the county or corporation in which he resides or is, has been twice delivered to such officer more than ten days before the return day, and been returned without being executed, or that the defendant resides within a portion of the state occupied by the public enemy, so that process from the courts of this commonwealth cannot be served upon him, an order of publication may be entered against such defendant. And in any suit in equity, where the bill states that the names of any persons interested in the subject to be divided or disposed of, are unknown, and makes such persons defendants, by the general description of parties unknown, on affidavit of the fact that the said names are unknown, an order of publication may be entered against such unknown parties. Any order under this section may be entered either in court or at the rules. In a proceeding by petition there may be an order of publication in like manner as in a suit in equity."

Order of publication

Parties unknown

Commencement

2. This act shall be in force from its passage.

CHAP. 59.—An ACT amending and re-enacting the 5th section of chapter 184 of the Code of Virginia (edition of 1860), concerning Fees of Commissioners in Chancery.

Passed February 24, 1864.

Code amended

1. Be it enacted by the general assembly, that the fifth section of chapter one hundred and eighty-four of the Code (edition of eighteen hundred and sixty) be amended and re-enacted so as to read as follows:

Fees of commissioner

"§ 5. A commissioner in chancery, for services which might be performed by notaries, the like fees for like services. For any other service, such fees as the court by which the commissioner is appointed, or the judge of such court in vacation, may from time to time prescribe, not exceeding two dollars, where less than an hour is employed, and if more than an hour be employed, not exceeding the rate of two dollars for each hour."

2. This act shall be in force from its passage, and continue in force during the present war; whereupon the laws in force immediately before the passage of this act, regulating the fees of commissioners in chancery, shall be deemed to be in force. Commencement

CHAP. 60.—An ACT to amend the 6th section of chapter 98 of the Code of Virginia (edition of 1860), concerning Patrols.

Passed March 10, 1864.

1. Be it enacted by the general assembly, that the sixth section of chapter ninety-eight of the Code of Virginia (edition of eighteen hundred and sixty) be amended and re-enacted so as to read as follows: Code amended

"§ 6. For every twelve hours' service each captain of a patrol shall be entitled to compensation not exceeding five dollars, and every other man of the patrol not exceeding four dollars, at the discretion of the court of the county or corporation where, the service is rendered; which shall be chargeable to the county or corporation to which such patrol may belong." Compensation of patrols

2. This act shall be in force from its passage. Commencement

CHAP. 61.—An ACT amending and re-enacting section 2 of chapter 12 of the Code of Virginia, so as to authorize the employment by the Confederate Government of the Collectors of Taxes and Commissioners of the Revenue.

Passed March 10, 1864.

1. Be it enacted by the general assembly, that section second of chapter twelve of the Code of Virginia (edition of eighteen hundred and sixty) be amended and re-enacted so as to read as follows: Code amended

"§ 2. No person shall be capable of holding any such post who holds any post of profit, trust or emolument, civil or military, legislative, executive or judicial, under the government of the Confederate States, or who receives in any way from the Confederate States any emolument whatever: provided, that nothing in this section shall, until six months after the ratification of a treaty of peace between the Confederate States and the United States, be so construed as to prevent any of the several officers of this state, whose duty it may be to list, assess and collect the public revenue, from being employed by the Confederate States, within their respective counties and corporations, in the listing, assessment and collection of the public revenue of the Confederate States: and provided further, that this act shall not be construed to repeal or alter any ordinance of the late convention of Virginia, enabling persons in the service of the Confederate States to accept or act in any civil capacity in the service of this state during the existing war." Who not to hold office; Proviso; Ordinance not repealed or altered

2. This act shall be in force from its passage. Commencement

CHAP. 62.—An ACT repealing all laws authorizing Insurance of Tobacco by the State, and amending the 59th section of chapter 87 of the Code (edition of 1860), so as to render the Inspector liable to the owners of Tobacco in certain cases.

Passed March 10, 1864.

1. Be it enacted by the general assembly, that the fifty-fifth, fifty-sixth and fifty-seventh sections of chapter eighty-seven of the Code of Virginia (edition of eighteen hundred and sixty), and all acts amendatory thereof, are hereby repealed. Sections repealed

2. The fifty-ninth section of chapter eighty-seven of the Code (edition of eighteen hundred and sixty), shall be amended and re-enacted so as to read as follows: Code amended

Liability of inspector "§ 59. If the fire from which any such damage occurred was caused by an inspector permitting any other person to use or occupy the warehouse, or any part of it, or by the neglect or voluntary act of said inspector, he and his sureties shall be liable to the owners of any tobacco damaged by such fire for the amount of their damages."

Commencement 3. This act shall be in force from and on the first day of April eighteen hundred and sixty-four.

CHAP. 63.—An ACT to authorize the sale of certain Slaves now in the Penitentiary.

Passed February 10, 1864.

Code amended 1. Be it enacted by the general assembly, that the twentieth section of the seventeenth chapter of the Code of Virginia (edition of eighteen hundred and sixty) be amended and re-enacted so as to read as follows:

Slave, how sold "§ 20. In the case of a slave condemned to death, the governor may order a commutation of the punishment, by directing that such slave be sold at public auction, to be transported beyond the limits of the Confederate States. The governor shall cause him to be sold, and the purchaser, before delivery to him of the slave, shall pay into the treasury the price agreed, and enter into bond, approved by the governor, in the penalty of one thousand dollars, conditioned that the slave shall within three months be transported beyond the limits of the Confederate States, and shall never afterwards return into this state: provided, however, that in the case of any female slave heretofore or hereafter convicted of any offence other than arson or a crime against a white person, which in the case of a free negro would have been punishable with death, such female slave, and the children of any female slave convict born after conviction, may be caused by the governor to be sold at public auction unconditionally, and without requiring bond as aforesaid."

Commencement 2. This act shall be in force from its passage.

CHAP. 64.—An ACT amending and re-enacting the 1st section of chapter 214 (Code of 1860), so as to provide for the punishment of Free Negro Convicts in certain cases.

Passed February 23, 1864.

Code amended 1. Be it enacted by the general assembly, that section first, chapter two hundred and fourteen of the Code (edition of eighteen hundred and sixty) be amended and re-enacted so as to read as follows:

What deemed felony "§ 1. A convict confined in the penitentiary, or in custody of an officer thereof, shall be deemed guilty of felony, if he shall kill, wound, or inflict other bodily injury upon an officer or guard of the penitentiary, or shall escape from the penitentiary or such custody; or who shall escape from the custody of any party who may have hired said convict, when a free negro, or from the agent of such party; or shall break, cut or injure any building, fixture or fastening of the penitentiary, or any part thereof, for the purpose of escaping, or aiding any other convict to escape therefrom, or rendering the penitentiary less secure as a place of confinement; or shall make, procure, secrete, or have in his possession any instrument, tool or thing for the said purpose, or with intent to kill, wound or inflict bodily injury as aforesaid; or shall resist the lawful authority of an officer or guard of the penitentiary, for the said purpose or with such intent."

Commencement 2. This act shall be in force from its passage.

CHAP. 65.—An ACT amending the 9th section of chapter 104 of the Code of Virginia, in relation to Harboring or Employing Slaves

Passed January 23, 1864.

1. Be it enacted by the general assembly, that the ninth section of chapter one hundred and four of the Code of Virginia be amended and re-enacted so as to read as follows: Code amended

"§ 9. Any person harboring or employing a slave without the consent of his master, shall forfeit to the master not less than ten nor more than fifty dollars for every day of such harboring or employment; but this section shall not apply to any person within the lines of the public enemy, who shall so harbor or employ any slave, unless it shall appear that the same was done with the intent and purpose to defraud the owner of the services of such slave, or to deprive the owner of his right of property in such slave." Harboring slaves Proviso

2. This act shall be in force from its passage. Commencement

CHAP. 66.—An ACT to amend the 21st section of chapter 66 of the Code, in regard to Appointments of Directors and Proxies by the Board of Public Works.

Passed March 10, 1864.

1. Be it enacted by the general assembly, that the twenty-first section of the sixty-sixth chapter of the Code of Virginia (edition of eighteen hundred and sixty) be amended and re-enacted so as to read as follows: Code amended

"§ 21. The appointment of directors and proxies in a company, according to the preceding and seventeenth section, shall be made by the board at the time it first subscribes to the capital stock of such company, and afterwards before each annual meeting therein: but at least one of the directors and one of the proxies in office at the time of an annual appointment, shall not be reappointed for the ensuing year." Directors and proxies, how appointed Proviso

2. This act shall be in force from its passage. Commencement

CHAP. 67.—An ACT to amend and re-enact the 5th section of chapter 53 of the Code (edition of 1860) in relation to County Levies.

Passed March 4, 1864.

1. Be it enacted by the general assembly, that the fifth section of chapter fifty-three of the Code (edition of eighteen hundred and sixty) be amended and re-enacted so as to read as follows: Code amended

"§ 5. After an order shall have been made by the court of any county at one term, for the justices to meet at the next term and consider the expediency of levying upon lands and other property, if, at such next term a majority of the acting justices be actually present and concur therein, the court may order the levy on free male persons over the age of sixteen years, and on all slaves, land and other property assessed with state tax within the county, and without the limits of a town that provides for its poor and keeps its streets in order, and on the interest and profits mentioned in the forty-ninth, the yearly income in the fifty-first, and the fees in the fifty-seventh sections of the thirty-fifth chapter, on which taxes are assessed against persons residing in the said county, and without the limits of such town. The order of levy under this section shall be for a certain sum on each free male person over the age of sixteen years, and on other subjects, including slaves, for a certain per centum upon the amount of taxes thereon. If the state shall not by law impose taxes upon land, slaves and other property for the year in which the court may make such levy, the court may adopt the assessment of state taxes for any previous year, as a basis for the levy, under this section, on land, slaves and other property." How assessment made Basis for levy

2. This act shall be in force from its passage. Commencement

CHAP. 68.—An ACT to amend and re-enact section 48 of chapter 85 of the Code of Virginia, to increase the Allowance for Clothing of Lunatics in Jail.

Passed March 10, 1864.

Code amended

1. Be it enacted by the general assembly, that the forty-eighth section of chapter eighty-five of the Code of Virginia be amended and re-enacted so as to read as follows:

Allowance for clothing

"§ 48. The allowance to the jailor for the maintenance and care of a lunatic shall be fixed by the court in whose jail he is confined. No more shall be allowed for his clothing than two hundred dollars a year. No such allowance shall be audited and paid, unless it appears in the certificate of it that the jailor proved to the court that immediately after the commitment of the lunatic, and at least once every two months thereafter, application was made to the board of directors of the Central lunatic asylum for admission, and that such application was refused for want of room, or that such applications were not continued, because the admission of the lunatic had been refused for some other cause than the want of room."

Application to lunatic asylum

Commencement

2. This act shall be in force from its passage, and continue in force until the expiration of six months after the ratification of a treaty of peace between the Confederate States and the United States.

CHAP. 69.—An ACT to repeal section 8, and to amend and re-enact section 9, of chapter 85 of the Code of Virginia (edition of 1860), so as to dispense with the office of Treasurer of the Central Lunatic Asylum, and to direct the Funds of said Asylum to be kept in either of the Banks in Staunton.

Passed March 2, 1864.

Section repealed

1. Be it enacted by the general assembly, that the eighth section of chapter eighty-five of the Code of Virginia (edition of eighteen hundred and sixty), so far as it relates to the Central lunatic asylum at Staunton, be and the same is hereby repealed.

Section amended

2. Be it further enacted, that section ninth of chapter eighty-five of the Code (edition of eighteen hundred and sixty) be amended and re-enacted so as to read as follows:

Deposits, where made, &c.

"§ 2. The directors of the said Central asylum, upon the receipt of money, whether by appropriation of the general assembly, or from any other source, shall immediately deposit the same in the office of discount and deposit of either of the banks at Staunton, to their credit; and it shall not be lawful for the cashier or other officer of either of the said banks to pay out said money so deposited, upon the order, draft or check of the said directors, except it be in such form as shall be prescribed to said bank by the board of directors of said asylum."

Commencement

3. This act shall be in force from its passage.

CHAP. 70.—An ACT to amend the 13th section of chapter 34 of the Code of Virginia, concerning the Virginia Military Institute.

Passed January 11, 1864.

Code amended

1. Be it enacted by the general assembly, that the thirteenth section of the thirty-fourth chapter of the Code of Virginia (edition of eighteen hundred and sixty) be amended and re-enacted so as to read as follows:

How cadets may be admitted

"§ 13. The board of visitors shall admit as state cadets, free of charge for board and tuition, upon evidence of fair moral character, and of inability on the part of the applicant and of his parent or guardian to defray charges, fifty young men, in lieu of the number now required, who shall be not less than fourteen nor more than eighteen years of age; one of whom shall be selected from each of the senatorial districts as at present constituted. Whenever a vacancy has occurred, or is likely to occur, due notice of the time and place of making the appointment to supply the vacancy shall be given. If, after such notice, no suitable person shall apply from any district, the vacancy may be supplied from the state at large. And for the purpose of providing a fund for the support of the state cadets herein required to be admitted, the additional sum of five thousand seven hundred and ninety dollars is hereby appropriated annually; and the auditor of public accounts is hereby authorized and required to issue his warrant or warrants on the treasury for the same, in the manner that other warrants to the said institution have been heretofore issued." When no application made from a district

2. This act shall be in force from its passage. Commencement

CHAP. 71.—An ACT to amend and re-enact the 12th section of the 77th chapter of the Code of Virginia.

Passed March 10, 1864.

1. Be it enacted by the general assembly, that the twelfth section of the seventy-seventh chapter of the Code of Virginia (edition of eighteen hundred and sixty) be amended and re-enacted so as to read as follows: Code amended

"§ 12. Such trustees shall not take or hold at any time more than two acres of land in an incorporated town, nor more than two hundred acres out of such a town: provided, however, that it shall at all times be in the power of the legislature to reduce the amount of real estate authorized to be held under this section, and upon such reduction to require sale to be made of so much of any such real estate as may be held in excess of the quantity that may thenceforward be lawfully held." Amount of land to be held

2. This act shall be in force from its passage. Commencement

CHAP. 72.—An ACT to prevent the destruction of Enclosures and Private Property on Public Highways.

Passed March 9, 1864.

1. Be it enacted by the general assembly, that if any person shall willfully injure, burn or destroy any enclosure not his own, he shall be guilty of a misdemeanor. What to constitute misdemeanor

2. If any slave or free negro in charge of a white person, shall commit the offence specified in the first section, by the direction or with the knowledge of such white person, the latter shall be deemed guilty to the same extent as if he had committed it in person.

3. Upon complaint made before any justice of the peace, verified by affidavit of the complainant, that any person has been guilty of said offence, the justice shall issue his warrant for the arrest of the person accused, and require him to be brought before him, or some other justice of the county, who, if there be probable cause to believe him guilty, shall commit him to jail to answer the said charge at the next term of the circuit or county court for the county in which the offence was committed, if a white person, unless he shall give bail as in other cases of misdemeanors; and if a free negro or slave, shall be tried by the justice before whom he may be brought, and if found guilty, shall be punished by stripes, at the discretion of the justice, not exceeding nine and thirty at any one time. Justice to issue warrant; If free negro or slave, to receive stripes

4. This act shall be in force from its passage. Commencement

PRIVATE OR LOCAL ACTS.

CHAP. 73.—An ACT to incorporate the Stonewall Insurance Company.

Passed February 18, 1864.

1. Be it enacted by the general assembly of Virginia, that J. S. Davis, N. H. Massie, E. R. Watson, B. C. Flannagan, R. W. N. Noland, A. P. Abell, R. Colston, J. B. Minor, C. T. Antrim, M. Schele De Vere, T. L. Preston, J. H. Bibb and W. B. Mallory, together with such other persons as they may associate with them hereafter, are hereby created and declared to be a body politic and corporate, by the name and style of The Stonewall Insurance Company; and by that name may sue and be sued, plead and be impleaded; make and have a common seal, and alter and renew the same at pleasure; contract and be contracted with; and make by-laws and regulations not inconsistent with the laws of this state or of the Confederate States; and generally may do every thing necessary to promote the object of this corporation, which is not contrary to the laws of the land. Company incorporated

2. The said company shall have power to make insurance upon dwellings, houses, stores, and all other kinds of buildings, either in town or country, and upon household furniture, merchandise or other property; against loss or damage by fire, or by any other liability, casualty or hazard; to make insurance upon lives, and upon boats and vessels of all kinds, freights, goods, wares, merchandise, bullion, coin, bank notes, mercantile and other securities, profits, commissions, bottomry and respondentia interests, and upon all risks of navigation and of transportation by land or water; to cause themselves to be reinsured upon all risks upon which they may have made insurance, and to insure any interest belonging to the company; to grant annuities; to receive endowments; to contract for reversionary payments; to guarantee the payment of bonds, promissory notes, bills of exchange, and all debts, however evidenced; and to receive money on deposit, and grant certificates therefor, in accordance with sections four and five, chapter fifty-nine of the Code of Virginia; but in no case shall such deposit be liable to make good any policy or liability entered into by the company. Insurance, how and upon what made. Money received on deposit

3. The company shall have power to invest its capital stock, deposits and other funds, in bank, state or other stocks; in bonds of this or any other state, or of the Confederate States, or of any incorporated company, and in any other personal property; to lend money upon personal or real security, and to take the interest; and to purchase, hold, sell and convey any real estate for the purpose of securing any debt due the company, or for their own use and convenience; but nothing herein contained shall be construed to authorize the said company to issue or put in circulation any notes of their own in the nature of bank notes. How funds invested

4. The capital of said company shall not be less than one hundred thousand nor more than eight hundred thousand dollars, divided into shares of fifty dollars each. The subscribers shall respectively pay for the shares subscribed for by them, at such times and in such proportions as the president and directors shall prescribe; and if any subscriber shall fail to pay the sum or sums so called for on any share held by him, within twenty days after the same has been so called for, then the amount for which he is delinquent may be reco- Capital. How payable

vered by motion, on twenty days' notice in writing, in any court of record for the county or corporation where such subscriber may reside: provided, however, that said company shall not commence its business until at least fifty thousand dollars of its capital stock have been actually paid in; and that from time to time, when any increase of capital stock is ordered, one-half thereof shall be actually paid in, and the balance well secured, before such increase shall be deemed valid.

Affairs, how managed

5. The affairs of the said company shall be managed by a president and board of directors, five in number, including the president, of whom three shall constitute a quorum. The directors shall be elected by ballot, from among the stockholders in general meeting assembled, by a majority of the votes of the stockholders present in person or by proxy; and the directors thus chosen shall choose a president from among themselves. The said president and directors shall continue in office one year and until their successors are appointed; and in the case of a vacancy in the office of president or director from any cause, it shall be filled by the remaining directors, or a legal quorum thereof, for the remainder of the term of the said president or director.

Officers

Clerks, &c. how appointed

6. The president and directors may appoint, and at their pleasure remove, a secretary and such clerks and other officers as they may deem expedient for the proper conduct of the company's business, taking bond, in their discretion, with good security, from any or all of them, conditioned for the faithful performance of their respective duties, and shall prescribe the compensation and duties of them and of the president.

Agents

7. The president and directors shall have power to appoint and at pleasure to remove agents in this state or elsewhere; and it shall be their duty to appoint them in any county or corporation in this state, when requested so to do by not less than ten stockholders resident in such county or corporation, and holding not less than one hundred shares of stock.

Dividends

8. The president and directors shall have power from time to time to declare, out of the profits of the company, such dividends as they shall deem proper, so as in no case to impair the capital stock of the company thereby. They shall also make and publish, at the end of every year, except that in which the company goes into operation, a statement showing the condition of the company for the current year.

Transfers

9. Any member may transfer one or more of his shares of stock in the manner prescribed by the by-laws, and the president and directors may sell as many shares in addition to those first taken as the stockholders in general meeting shall direct, so as that the capital stock shall in no case exceed the maximum amount of eight hundred thousand dollars herein before prescribed: provided, however, that no stockholder indebted to the company as principal, endorser, guarantor, or otherwise, on paper due or yet to mature, or in any other form of liability, shall be permitted to transfer his stock, or any part thereof, or to receive a dividend, until such debt or liability is paid or secured to the satisfaction of the board of directors.

Proviso

Stockholders, how liable

10. No stockholder shall be liable for any loss, damage or responsibility, otherwise than to the extent of the shares held by him in the capital stock, and any profits arising thereupon not divided.

General meeting

11. General meetings of the stockholders shall be held annually, at such time and place as the by-laws shall prescribe; and such meetings shall be called specially by the president and directors whenever five stockholders, having in the aggregate as many as four hundred shares, shall in writing require, or the president and directors shall themselves deem it proper. And in all meetings of the stockholders, a majority of all the shares shall be a quorum for the transaction of business, but a less proportion may adjourn from time

Quorum

to time. At any meeting of the stockholders each stockholder shall be entitled to as many votes as he may own shares.

12. The persons named in the first section, or a majority of them, shall fix upon some suitable place, and shall give five days' notice for a meeting of the stockholders to choose directors, and shall supervise the election. Directors, how chosen

13. This act shall be in force from its passage, and shall be subject to be altered, amended or repealed, at the pleasure of the general assembly. Commencement

CHAP. 74.—An ACT to incorporate the Richmond City Insurance Company.

Passed February 13, 1864.

1. Be it enacted by the general assembly of Virginia, that William B. Jones, John T. Butler, A. A. Hutcheson, T. H. Wynne, William S. Morris, and all others who may be associated with them under this act, be and they are hereby created and declared to be a body politic and corporate, by the name and style of The Richmond City Insurance Company; and by that name and style shall be invested with all the rights, powers and privileges conferred, and made subject to all the rules, regulations and restrictions imposed by the Code of Virginia, applicable to such corporations, and to all other acts amendatory thereof, which have heretofore or may hereafter be passed, so far as the same are not inconsistent with this act. Company incorporated

2. This company shall have authority and power to make insurance upon dwellings, houses, stores, and all other kind of buildings, either in town or country, and upon household furniture, merchandise and other property, against loss or damage by fire; to make insurance upon lives; to cause themselves to be reinsured, when deemed expedient, against any risk or risks upon which they have made or may make insurance; to grant annuities; to receive endowments; to contract for reversionary payments; to guarantee the payment of promissory notes, bills of exchange, or other evidences of debt; to make insurance upon vessels, freights, goods, wares, merchandise, specie, bullion, profits, commissions, bank notes, bottomry and respondentia interests; and to make all and every insurance connected with marine risks of transportation and navigation; and to receive money on deposit, and pay interest thereon, as may be advantageous to the stockholders; to invest the funds of the company in any stocks of any kind, or loans, as may be judged best for the interests of the company: provided, that in no event shall the deposits be liable for the satisfaction of any policy. Power to make insurance, &c.

3. The capital stock of the company shall be one hundred thousand dollars, divided into shares of the par value of ten dollars. The said capital stock shall be payable by each subscriber, at such time or times as it may be called for by the president and directors, and in such proportion as they may deem necessary: provided, however, that said company shall not commence its business until at least fifty thousand dollars of the capital stock has been actually paid in. Capital; Proviso

4. The affairs of said company shall be managed by a president and board of directors, seven in number, four of whom shall constitute a quorum. Affairs, how managed

5. No stockholder indebted to the company shall be permitted to make a transfer or receive a dividend until such debt is paid or secured to the satisfaction of the board; and if such debt shall remain unpaid for three months after it has become due and payable, the directors may sell such portion or all of the stock belonging to the stockholder in default, as may be necessary to satisfy the debt. Transfers

6. The persons named in the first section shall be commissioners, any three of whom may act, to open books to receive subscriptions to the capital stock of said company; and three days' notice shall be Commissioners

given by said commissioners of the time and place of opening such books, in a newspaper published in the city of Richmond; which books shall not be closed in less than five days from the time of opening.

Capital, how increased

7. Whenever, in the opinion of a majority of the stockholders, it may be deemed expedient, the capital stock of the company may be increased in such amounts as they may direct, not exceeding five hundred thousand dollars.

Commencement

8. This act shall be in force from its passage, and shall be subject to amendment, modification or repeal, at the pleasure of the general assembly.

CHAP. 75.—An ACT to amend the Charter of the Farmers and Mechanics Insurance Company of the City of Richmond.

Passed February 29, 1864.

Act amended

1. Be it enacted by the general assembly, that the second section of the act passed March twenty-eighth, eighteen hundred and sixty-one, to incorporate the Farmers and Mechanics insurance company of the city of Richmond, be amended and re-enacted so as to read as follows:

Capital

"§ 2. The capital stock of said corporation shall not be less than one hundred thousand dollars nor more than one million dollars, divided into shares of the par value of twenty dollars each; but said company shall not commence business until at least fifty thousand dollars of said capital be paid in."

Commencement

2. This act shall be in force from its passage.

CHAP. 76.—An ACT amending the 2d section of an act amending the Charter of the Virginia Fire and Marine Insurance Company, passed January 4th, 1858.

Passed February 25, 1864.

Act amended

1. Be it enacted by the general assembly, that the second section of the act amending the charter of the Virginia fire and marine insurance company, passed January fourth, eighteen hundred and fifty-eight, be and the same is hereby amended and re-enacted so as to read as follows:

Capital, how increased

"§ 2. The capital stock of the said corporation shall not be less than two hundred thousand dollars; and they shall have authority to increase the same from time to time as they may find it necessary and expedient, so as not to exceed two millions of dollars; and the par value of the shares in the said capital stock shall be twenty-five dollars each: provided, however, that upon any increase of the capital stock of said company, in pursuance of this act, at least one-half of such increase shall be paid in by the subscribers, and the balance well secured."

Proviso

Commencement

2. This act shall be in force from its passage.

CHAP. 77.—An ACT to amend and re-enact an act entitled an act to incorporate the Richmond Importing and Exporting Company, passed February 21st, 1863.

Passed February 29, 1864.

Company incorporated

1. Be it enacted by the general assembly of Virginia, that Thomas W. McCance, John D. Harvey, Emanuel Miller, T. Edward Hambleton, junior, Andrew L. Ellett, Alfred Moses, W. M. Barrett, James L. Apperson, R. H. Maury, William Boulware, William Allen, William G. Payne and Samuel J. Harrison, together with such other persons and firms as are now connected with them, under the name

and style of the Richmond importing and exporting company, be and the same are, together with their successors and assigns, hereby made and constituted a body corporate, under the said name and style of The Richmond Importing and Exporting Company, for the purpose of owning, navigating and freighting ships and other vessels engaged in foreign and domestic commerce, and of buying and selling the products and commodities so freighted or intended to be freighted. The capital of the said company shall not be less than five hundred thousand dollars nor more than five millions of dollars, and shall be held in shares of five hundred dollars each. The affairs of the company shall be managed by a president and board of directors, whose term of office and their number shall be determined and elected by the stockholders; and the said board of directors shall possess all the corporate powers of the company: provided, however, that nothing in this act shall change or affect the rights, obligations, exemptions and immunities of the said company, under the provisions of the laws of the Confederate States applicable to owners of vessels: and provided, that the said company shall be subject to such general laws as may affect corporations of this character. This act shall be in force from its passage, and be subject to repeal, modification or amendment, at the pleasure of the general assembly. Corporate name. Powers. Capital. Affairs, how managed.

2. This act shall be in force from its passage. Commencement.

CHAP. 78.—An ACT confirming and amending the Charter of the Richmond Glass Manufacturing Company.

Passed March 10, 1864.

Whereas, by an order of the circuit court for the county of Henrico and state of Virginia, dated the thirtieth day of October eighteen hundred and sixty-three, and the certificate of G. W. Munford, secretary of the commonwealth, dated November twenty-seventh, eighteen hundred and sixty-three, it appears that a company by the name and style of the Richmond glass manufacturing company, was duly incorporated and declared to be a body politic and corporate, under authority of chapter sixty-fifth of the Code of Virginia: And whereas it is deemed advisable to have said charter confirmed and amended by an act of the general assembly: Preamble.

1. Be it therefore enacted by the general assembly of Virginia, that the said charter is hereby sanctioned and confirmed, and that William S. Morris, as president and ex-officio member of the board, and J. H. Montague, Samuel J. Harrison, M. Jones and Robert A. Lancaster, as directors, as a body politic and corporate, by the name and style of The Richmond Glass Manufacturing Company, are hereby invested with all the rights, powers and privileges, and subject to all the rules, regulations and restrictions provided and prescribed in the Code of Virginia, applicable to such corporate bodies, and any laws amendatory thereof, not inconsistent with the charter granted in manner aforesaid, and with the provisions of this act. Charter confirmed. Company incorporated.

2. That the capital of said company shall not be less than one hundred and fifty thousand dollars, and not more than one million dollars, with power to manufacture glass, glass ware, tile and crockery ware, and to purchase, lease, take and hold, sell and convey real estate, not exceeding two thousand acres. Capital.

3. This act shall be in force from its passage. Commencement.

CHAP. 79.—An ACT to incorporate the Henrico Manufacturing Company.

Passed March 4, 1864.

1. Be it enacted by the general assembly, that William S. Morris, Thomas H. Wynne and P. M. Thompson, and such other persons as Company incorporated.

may be hereafter associated with them, not less than five, shall be and are hereby incorporated and made a body politic and corporate, by the name and style of The Henrico Manufacturing Company, for the purpose of mining iron, copper or lead ore or coal, and also for the purpose of manufacturing paper, cotton and woolen, iron and other metals, in the county of Henrico, and counties adjoining thereto, and of transacting the usual business of companies engaged in mining, manufacturing, and of transporting to market and selling the products of their mines and manufactory.

Powers

Delegated powers

2. The said company is hereby invested with all the rights, privileges and powers, and made subject to the restrictions and regulations now provided by law for the general regulation of bodies politic and corporate, and of the mining and manufacturing companies of this commonwealth, so far as the same may apply, and are not inconsistent with the provisions of this act: provided, however, that said company shall not commence business until at least twenty-five thousand dollars of the capital stock has been actually paid in.

Proviso

Capital

3. The capital stock of said company shall consist of not less than fifty thousand dollars nor more than five hundred thousand dollars, to be divided into shares of one thousand dollars; and the said company shall have the right to purchase and to hold land not exceeding one thousand acres.

Commencement

4. This act shall be in force from its passage, and shall be subject to amendment, alteration or repeal, at the pleasure of the general assembly.

CHAP 80.—An ACT to amend and re-enact the 2d section of an act to incorporate the Union Manufacturing Company.

Passed February 27, 1864.

Act amended

1. Be it enacted by the general assembly, that the second section of the act passed September thirtieth, eighteen hundred and sixty-two, entitled an act to incorporate the Union manufacturing company in the county of Fluvanna, be amended and re-enacted so as to read as follows:

Capital

"§ 2. The capital stock shall be not less than fifty thousand dollars nor more than four hundred thousand dollars, to be divided into shares of one hundred dollars each, four-fifths of which shall never be owned by less than four shareholders; and it shall be lawful for the commissioners herein after named or referred to, to open books of subscription for raising the said capital stock, at such times and places as they may designate."

Commencement

2. This act shall be in force from its passage.

CHAP. 81.—An ACT incorporating the Virginia Porcelain and Earthenware Company in the County of Augusta.

Passed January 22, 1864.

Company incorporated

1. Be it enacted by the general assembly, that Martin Coiner, William W. Withrow, Dr. T. W. Shelton, Gerard B. Stuart, Alexander H. H. Stuart, of the county of Augusta, and such others as may be hereafter associated with them, shall be and are hereby incorporated a body corporate and politic, under the name and style of The Virginia Porcelain and Earthenware Company, for the purpose of mining kaolin and manufacturing porcelain, china and other earthenware and fire-bricks, and such like articles, and disposing of their products in market; and as such incorporation, shall have all the powers and privileges conferred, and be subject to all restrictions imposed on corporations by the fifty-sixth and fifty-seventh chapters of

Delegated powers

the Code of Virginia, so far as the same are not inconsistent with the purposes of this act.

2. That the capital stock of the corporation shall be not less than fifteen thousand nor exceed two hundred and fifty thousand dollars, to be divided into shares of fifty dollars each: and the said corporation may hold land for their purposes, not exceeding three thousand acres. Capital

3. This act shall be in force from its passage, and be subject to modification at any time by the general assembly. Commencement

CHAP. 82.—An ACT to incorporate the Confederate States Porcelain Company.

Passed March 3, 1864.

1. Be it enacted by the general assembly, that F. J. Barnes of the county of Charlotte, and such other persons as may be hereafter associated with him, shall be and are hereby made a body corporate and politic, under the name and style of The Confederate States Porcelain Company, for the purpose of mining kaolin and fire clay, and manufacturing porcelain, china and other earthenware and fire bricks and other articles, and disposing of their products in the markets; and as such incorporation, shall have all the powers and privileges conferred, and be subject to all restrictions imposed on corporations by the fifty-sixth and fifty-seventh chapters of the Code of Virginia, so far as the same are not inconsistent with the purposes of this act. Company incorporated Powers

2. That the capital stock of the corporation shall not be less than one hundred thousand nor more than five hundred thousand dollars, to be divided into shares of one hundred dollars each; and the said corporation may hold land for their purposes, not exceeding five thousand acres. Capital

3. This act shall be in force from its passage, and be subject to modification at any time by the general assembly. Commencement

CHAP. 83.—An ACT to incorporate the Hardy Coal Mining Company.

Passed March 4, 1864.

1. Be it enacted by the general assembly of Virginia, that George Lee, George Arents, Charles Hartwell, John Fisher, G. W. Jones and W. Peterson, and such other persons as may be hereafter associated with them, and their successors, shall be and are hereby incorporated and made a body politic and corporate, under the name and style of The Hardy Coal Mining Company, for the purpose of mining for coal and other minerals in the county of Hardy, and for transporting and selling the same; and by that name and style may have a common seal, and be invested with all the rights, privileges and powers, and made subject to all the limitations and restrictions contained in the Code of Virginia for the management and control of such bodies politic and corporate, so far as the same may be applicable, and not inconsistent with the provisions of this act. Company incorporated Powers

2. The said company may purchase and hold real estate in the county of Hardy, not exceeding six thousand five hundred acres, and such other property as they may deem necessary for the purposes of this incorporation. Lands

3. The capital stock of said company shall be not less than sixty thousand dollars nor more than five hundred thousand dollars, and shall be divided into shares of one hundred dollars each; which shall be transferable agreeably to the laws of said company. Capital

4. This act shall be in force from its passage, and shall be subject to any amendment, alteration or modification at the pleasure of the general assembly. Commencement

CHAP. 84.—An ACT to incorporate the Catawba Rail Road Company.

Passed March 9, 1864.

Company incorporated

1. Be it enacted by the general assembly, that Joseph R. Anderson, Francis B. Deane, junior, Thomas H. Ellis, Francis T. Glasgow, John T. Anderson, and such other persons as they may associate with them, be and they are hereby incorporated, under the name and style of The Catawba Rail Road Company; for the purpose of constructing a rail road from some point at or near the Catawba furnace, in the county of Botetourt, to some point on the James river and Kanawha canal, between the town of Buchanan and the mouth of Catawba creek.

Corporate name

Capital

2. The capital stock of the said company shall not exceed one million of dollars, and it shall be organized in conformity with the fifty-seventh chapter of the Code, and have all the rights and privileges, and be subject to all the restrictions contained in the fifty-sixth and sixty-first chapters of the Code.

Commencement

3. This act shall be in force from its passage, and shall be subject to modification or repeal, at the pleasure of the general assembly.

CHAP. 85.—An ACT amending and re-enacting an act entitled an act to amend the Charter and extend the Corporate Limits of the Town of Charlottesville, passed March 14th, 1860.

Passed February 23, 1864.

Act amended

1. Be it enacted by the general assembly, that the fifth section of the act passed March fourteenth, eighteen hundred and sixty, entitled an act to amend the charter and extend the corporate limits of the town of Charlottesville, be amended and re-enacted so as to read as follows:

Powers of council

"§ 5. For the purpose of improving the streets, maintaining a sufficient police, and providing for the support of the poor of the town, the council may levy and collect annually a tax on the tithables and taxable subjects within the limits of the corporation, not exceeding six thousand dollars; and for the erection of any building or purchase of any property, real or personal, which they may deem necessary for the use of the town, they may levy such additional tax as may be sufficient therefor: provided, that no additional tax for any such special purpose shall be levied unless by consent of two-thirds of the freeholders qualified to vote for members of the council; which consent shall be ascertained by holding a poll at such place as may be prescribed by ordinance, after giving not less than two weeks' notice thereof in one or more newspapers published in the town of Charlottesville. The result shall be determined by the face of the poll book; reserving, however, the right to the council to examine and purge the poll of all illegal votes. Upon the consent of two-thirds of the freeholders, indicated in the same manner, the mayor and council of the said town of Charlottesville shall have power to borrow money, not exceeding five thousand dollars at any one time, and shall have power to issue therefor coupon or other bonds."

Commencement

2. This act shall be in force from and after the passage thereof.

CHAP. 86.—An ACT to amend the Charter of the City of Petersburg.

Passed February 17, 1864.

Act amended

1. Be it enacted by the general assembly, that the fifth section of the act entitled an act providing for the election of certain state and municipal officers in the city of Petersburg, passed April twentieth, eighteen hundred and fifty-two, be amended and re-enacted so as to read as follows:

"§ 5. For superintending said elections the common council shall, previous thereto, appoint five persons in each ward as commissioners, any two or more of whom may act, to superintend the election in such ward; and the said commissioners shall have such powers and perform such duties as are prescribed by the sixth section of the seventh chapter of the Code of Virginia, after taking such oath as is prescribed in the seventh section of the same chapter; a certificate of which oath shall be returned to the clerk of the council, to be preserved in his office. The polls at such election shall be opened and closed in the manner directed in the second section of the said seventh chapter. An officer to conduct the election in each ward shall be appointed by the council; or if the council fail to do so, or the officer appointed fail to attend, by the commissioners. Under the superintendence of the commissioners, it shall be the duty of said officer (after taking the oath prescribed by the tenth section of said chapter, a certificate whereof shall be returned to the clerk of the council) to cause the polls to be opened publicly in the ward for which he is appointed; to proclaim and see recorded the votes admitted by the commissioners; to preserve order and remove force. The said officer shall employ writers and furnish poll books, for which the council shall allow compensation out of the city treasury. Each writer shall take an oath, to be administered by said officer, faithfully to record the votes, and shall enter the name of each voter in a column to be headed with the words 'Names of voters;' and opposite the name of the voter, a mark under the name of each person for whom he votes. The said votes shall be given as prescribed by the fourth section of the third article of the constitution; but at the time a vote is given, the officer shall receive of each voter a paper or ticket (with his name written on it), which shall specify the names of the persons for whom he votes, and for what office." Election, how conducted; Officers, how appointed; Writers; Polls, how kept; Tickets

2. This act shall be in force from its passage. Commencement

CHAP. 87.—An ACT to amend the Charter of the Town of Ashland, in Hanover County.

Passed January 11, 1864.

1. Be it enacted by the general assembly of Virginia, that the third section of the act passed February nineteenth, eighteen hundred and fifty-eight, entitled an act to incorporate the town of Ashland, in the county of Hanover, be amended and re-enacted so as to read as follows: Act amended

"§ 3. The council shall elect from their own number a president, who shall preside at all the meetings of the council, and when they are equally divided, shall, in addition to his individual vote, give the casting vote; and he shall be invested with all the powers of a justice of the peace within the precincts of said town, for one mile around the corporate limits thereof, and shall have like power with a justice of the peace to commit any person, charged with an offence before him, to the county jail, or let to bail on recognizance to appear before the county court; and the sergeant of said corporation shall have the like power with the constable of said county, to pursue and arrest all offenders for offences within said corporate limits, and to convey any one so ordered to be committed to the county jail, there to be dealt with as if committed by warrant of a justice of the peace." Powers of president of council; Of sergeant

2. This act shall be in force from its passage. Commencement

CHAP. 88.—An ACT to amend the Charter of the Town of Bridgewater, in the County of Rockingham.

Passed March 3, 1864.

Act amended

1. Be it enacted by the general assembly of Virginia, that the seventh section of an act passed February seventh, eighteen hundred and thirty-five, entitled an act to establish the town of Bridgewater, in the county of Rockingham, be amended and re-enacted so as to read as follows:

Corporate limits extended

"§ 7. For the purpose of maintaining the police of said town, the jurisdiction of the trustees shall be extended to the southwest shore of North river: and Liberty street shall be laid off and established twenty feet wide; Main street, fifty-five feet wide; Grove street, twenty feet wide, and Centre alley, twelve feet wide: and the said trustees shall elect from their own number a mayor, who shall pre-

Powers of mayor

side at all the meetings of the trustees; and he shall be invested with all the powers of a justice of the peace within the precincts of said town, and for one mile around the corporate limits thereof, and shall have like power with a justice of the peace to commit any person charged with an offence before him, to the county jail, or let to

Of sergeant

bail on recognizance to appear before the county court; and the sergeant of said corporation shall have the like power with the constable of said county, to pursue and arrest all offenders for offences committed within the last aforementioned corporate limits, and to convey any one so ordered to be committed to the county jail, there to be dealt with as if committed by warrant of a justice of the peace."

Commencement

2. This act shall be in force from its passage

CHAP. 89.—An ACT to authorize the Common Council of Danville to acquire Lands in the County of Pittsylvania, for certain public uses.

Passed February 17, 1864.

Quantity of land

1. Be it enacted by the general assembly, that the common council of the town of Danville be and they are hereby authorized to purchase and hold such quantity of land in the county of Pittsylvania, not exceeding seventy-five acres, as may be necessary for the use,

Purposes

convenience and comfort of the people of said town, as a public cemetery, a public park and poor house. Any land so acquired and bona fide used for such purposes, shall be subject to the jurisdiction of said common council and the court of hustings of said town, in like manner as if the same were within the corporate limits of said town.

Commencement

2. This act shall be in force from its passage.

CHAP. 90.—An ACT to amend and re-enact the Charter of the Union Female College.

Passed February 13, 1864.

Act amended

Be it enacted by the general assembly, that the act passed twenty-second of December eighteen hundred and fifty-nine, entitled an act to incorporate the Union female college, be amended and re-enacted so as to read as follows:

Preamble

Whereas it is represented to the general assembly of Virginia, that sundry citizens of Danville and the vicinity have united and contributed a considerable sum of money, in shares of fifty dollars, for the purpose of establishing in the said town of Danville, Virginia, an institution of learning, as a joint stock institution, to be called the Roanoke female college: And whereas the said contributors desire, as the best means of carrying out their purpose, that J. J. Crews, J. W. Pace, William Wilson, J. R. Lipscomb, William Robinson, T. D. Neal, P. W. Ferrell, T. H. Stumps, C. C. Chapline, J. W. McCraw,

J. T. Averett, W. A. Tyrer, W. P. Graves, W. S. Penick, Jere White, James B. Miller and John A. McCown, be appointed trustees of said institution, and as such incorporated and constituted a body politic and corporate: Therefore,

1. Be it enacted by the general assembly, that the said J. J. Crews, J. W. Pace, William Wilson, J. R. Lipscomb, William Robinson, T. D. Neal, P. W. Ferrell, T. H. Stumps, C. C. Chapline, J. W. McCraw, J. T. Averett, W. A. Tyrer, W. P. Graves, W. S. Penick, Jere White, James B. Miller, John A. McCraw, and their successors in office, be and they are hereby constituted a body politic and corporate, under the name and style of The Trustees of the Roanoke Female College; and by that name shall have perpetual succession and a common seal, and may sue and be sued, implead and be impleaded in any court of law or equity, with power to purchase, receive and hold, to them and their successors forever, any lands, tenements, money, goods or chattels which shall be purchased by, or devised or given to them, or contributed and paid to them for the use of said institution, and to lease, rent, sell or otherwise dispose of the same, in such manner as shall be most conducive to the interest and advantage of said institution: provided, that the property acquired by the said trustees, for the use of the said institution, shall not exceed in value, at any one time, the sum of fifty thousand dollars. College incorporated

2. It shall be the duty of the said trustees and their successors to call a general meeting of the stockholders of said college, at some convenient period, biennially or oftener, when a majority of the board of trustees for the time being, or at least twelve of the said stockholders, not members of the board of trustees, shall deem such general meeting necessary, and shall request the same to be called. At such general meetings of the stockholders a majority of the stock of said college shall be necessary to constitute a quorum for the transaction of business; and any person holding shares of said stock may vote in such general meetings, either in person or by proxy, made in writing, according to such regulations as shall be prescribed in relation thereto by the board of trustees. The said general meeting shall have power to revise, alter and modify the rules, regulations and by-laws prescribed by the board of trustees for the government of said college, and to control and correct, through the board of trustees, the acquisition and disposition of all property held for the use of said college, as well as the general economy and management of said college. They shall also have power to elect a new board of trustees, to succeed those herein appointed, whose terms of office expire on the first day of September eighteen hundred and sixty-one, and to elect in like manner succeeding boards of trustees for said college biennially thereafter, and to add to the number of said trustees, so that the same shall not exceed twenty. But any number of the present and succeeding boards of trustees shall be eligible. Duty of trustees

3. The said Roanoke female college shall be under the immediate control and management of the said board of trustees and their successors, subject to the revisory control of the stockholders in a general meeting, as herein above expressed. The said trustees shall remain in office until the first day of September eighteen hundred and sixty-one, and until their successors are elected at a general meeting of the said stockholders. They shall appoint a treasurer and all necessary officers and professors of said college, and make such rules, regulations and by-laws for the government of the institution as to them may seem fit, not inconsistent with the laws of this state or the Confederate States. Seven of the said trustees shall constitute a quorum for the transaction of business; and any vacancy in said board of trustees, occasioned by death, resignation or otherwise, shall be filled by appointment of the surviving trustees, until the vacancy is filled, or a new election held by a general meeting of the stockholders; and they may remove any member of their board, two-thirds of the whole number being present and concurring.. Powers of trustees

Duty of treasurer

4. The treasurer shall receive all moneys accruing to the college, and property delivered to his care, and shall pay or deliver the same to the order of the board of trustees. Before entering upon the discharge of his duties, he shall give bond with such security, and in such penalty as the board may direct, made payable to the trustees for the time being, and their successors, and conditioned for the faithful performance of the duties of his office, under such rules and regulations as the board may adopt; and for any delinquency on the part of said treasurer and his securities, his or their executors or administrators, the said board of trustees may recover judgment, by motion on ten days' notice, in any court of record in the commonwealth.

Capital, how raised

5. The board of trustees are hereby authorized to raise, by joint stock subscription, a sum not less than three thousand dollars nor more than fifty thousand dollars, to be divided into shares of fifty dollars each, and shall from time to time declare such dividend on the same as the net profits of the institution may justify; and shall also have power to collect the subscription to said stock in the manner now provided by law for collection of subscription to joint stock companies. No person shall sell or transfer his stock in said college to any person not already a stockholder, without first offering the same to the stockholders, through the board of trustees; and all undivided stock in said college shall be deemed personal estate, and as such shall pass to purchasers, executors and administrators.

Stockholders not liable

6. The stockholders of said college shall not be liable pecuniarily for any debt, contract or agreement made and entered into by the said trustees or stockholders, other than the property they have in the capital stock thereof, to the amount of their respective share or shares.

Diplomas

7. The board of trustees, in connection with the president and professors of the college, shall have power to confer such diplomas and literary titles as they may think best calculated to promote the cause of female education.

Commencement

8. This act shall be in force from its passage.

CHAP. 91.—An ACT to amend an act entitled an act to regulate the Tolls for passing Mayo's Bridge, passed March 12th, 1835.

Passed February 20, 1864.

Act amended

1. Be it enacted by the general assembly, that the first section of the act entitled an act to regulate the tolls for passing Mayo's bridge at Richmond, passed March the twelfth, eighteen hundred and thirty-five, be amended and re-enacted, so as to read as follows:

Rates of toll

"§ 1. That hereafter, instead of the tolls now allowed by law to be charged and received for the passage of persons and things over the bridge called and known as Mayo's bridge, across James river, at the city of Richmond, the property of Edward Mayo and others, it shall be lawful to demand and receive, for passing the same, the following increased tolls and rates of toll, and no more: For a person on foot, one cent; for every horse, mule, ass, ox or other cattle, ten cents; for every score of sheep or hogs, twenty-five cents; for every vehicle with one horse, twenty-five cents; for every vehicle with two horses, thirty-five cents; for every vehicle with three horses, fifty cents; for every vehicle with four horses, sixty cents."

Penalties

2. Be it further enacted, that the same penalties imposed by the third section of an act entitled an act to regulate the tolls for passing Mayo's bridge, passed March the twelfth, eighteen hundred and thirty-five, upon such persons as evade the law by taking two or more horses out of a four-horse wagon, shall be and are hereby imposed upon any person who shall take one horse out of a three-horse wagon, and pass over the bridge with two horses.

Commencement

3. This act shall be in force from its passage, and shall continue

in force until the expiration of twelve months after the ratification of a treaty of peace between the Confederate States and the United States, and shall be subject to amendment, modification or repeal, at the pleasure of the general assembly.

CHAP. 92.—An ACT amending and re-enacting sections 2d and 7th of an act for improving the Navigation of Willis' River, passed January 28th, 1817.

Passed March 4, 1864.

1. Be it enacted by the general assembly, that sections second and seventh of an act entitled an act for improving the navigation of Willis' river, passed the twenty-eighth January eighteen hundred and seventeen, be amended and re-enacted so as to read as follows: Act amended

"§ 2. The said trustees and their successors shall be and they are hereby declared to be incorporated, by the name and title of The Trustees of Willis' River; and may sue and be sued as such. The said trustees, or a majority of them, may from time to time appoint any five of their own body to superintend the clearing of the said river; a majority of which five shall have full power to do all things necessary for the purpose of carrying this act into effect; and the said five trustees so appointed as aforesaid shall, at the expiration of the term during which they may be so authorized to act, well and truly report to the said board of trustees all things which may by them, or a majority of them, be ordered or done by virtue of this act and of their said appointment. The said trustees shall remain in office for the term of two years only from the time the subscription hereafter mentioned shall be completed; and that an election of trustees shall be held once in every two years by the subscribers holding a majority of shares, each subscriber giving one vote for every share he possesses, in voting either in person or by proxy: provided always, that until an election shall be made from time to time by those holding said shares, or a majority thereof, the former trustees shall continue to act, although the two years for which they were elected may have expired; and in case of the death, removal to the distance of twenty miles from the said river, resignation or incapacity of the said trustees, it shall be lawful for the remaining trustees, or a majority of the whole number of them, to appoint other trustees to fill such vacancies; which trustees so appointed shall continue to act until the next general election: and provided further, that in the biennial election of trustees herein before required, only nine trustees shall hereafter be elected; and no vacancy in the office of trustee shall hereafter be filled so long as there remain nine trustees qualified to act." Powers of trustees Term of service Proviso Vacancies, how filled

"§ 7. That after the said river shall be made navigable for the passage of boats, agreeably to the provisions of this act, the same shall be deemed and taken to be a public highway; and for and in consideration of the expense the subscribers will be at, not only in cutting canals, erecting locks and other labor, for opening and extending the navigation of the said river, but in maintaining and keeping the same in repair, it shall and may be lawful for the said trustees and their successors, at all times after the said river shall be made navigable, agreeably to this act, to demand and receive at such place or places upon the said river, and at such place or places on James river, and on the James river and Kanawha canal, as they may think most convenient, for all commodities transported up or down the same, tolls according to the following rates: On every pipe or hogshead of wine, containing more than sixty-five gallons, sixty-five cents; on every hogshead of rum or other spirits, fifty cents; on every hogshead of tobacco, forty-two cents; on every cask between sixty-five and thirty-five gallons, half a pipe or hogshead; barrels, one-fourth part; and smaller casks or kegs in proportion, according When river a public highway Rates of toll to the quality and quantity of their contents of wine or spirits; for casks of linseed oil, the same as spirits; on every bushel of wheat, peas, beans or flax seed, two cents; on every bushel of Indian corn or other grain, or salt, one and a half cent; on every barrel of pork, twenty-one cents; on every barrel of beef, fifteen cents; on every barrel of flour, ten cents; on every ton of hemp, flax, potash, bar or manufactured iron, one hundred and five cents; on every ton of pig iron or castings, thirty-five cents; on every ton of copper, lead or other ore, other than iron ore, eighty-three cents; on every ton of stone or iron ore, seventeen cents; on every hundred bushels of lime, eighty cents; on every chaldron of coal, seventeen cents; on every hundred pipe staves, eight cents; on every hundred hogshead staves or pipe or hogshead heading, five cents; on every hundred barrel staves or barrel heading, four cents; on every hundred cubic feet of plank or scantling, thirty-five cents; on every hundred cubic feet of other timber, twenty cents; on every ton of hay or fodder (of two thousand pounds), eighty-three cents; on every bushel of potatoes, two cents; on every cord of wood, twenty-five cents; on every ton (of two thousand pounds) of guano or other manures, eighty-three cents; on every gross hundred weight of all other commodities or packages, five cents; on every boat or vessel which has not commodities on board to yield so much (provided that an empty boat or vessel returning, whose load has already paid at the respective places, the sums fixed at each, shall repass toll free), one hundred cents. One-half toll to be charged on all articles above enumerated, from Walton's mill or from any point below. And in case any person shall refuse or neglect to pay the tolls at the time of offering to pass the place appointed for the payment thereof, and previous to the vessel's passing the same, the collector of the said tolls may lawfully refuse passage to such vessel; and if any vessel shall pass without paying toll, then the said collector may seize such vessel wherever found, and sell the same at auction for ready money: which so far as is necessary, shall be applied towards paying the said tolls and all expenses of seizure and sale; and the balance, if any, shall be paid to the owner; and the person owning or having the direction of such vessel shall be liable for such toll, if the same is not paid by the sale of such vessel."

Duty of collector

Commencement

2. This act shall be in force from its passage.

CHAP. 93.—An ACT to provide for the Preservation of the Records of the Counties of Warwick, Elizabeth City and James City, and of the City of Williamsburg.

Passed February 4, 1864.

Preamble

Whereas it has been represented to the general assembly, that the clerk of the county and circuit courts of the county of Warwick is now in the army of the Confederate States, and the clerk of the county and circuit courts of Elizabeth City county is within the lines of the public enemy, and that the records of said counties are now in the city of Richmond, and are in a confused state, and not under the care of any one:

Records of Warwick and Elizabeth City

1. Be it enacted by the general assembly, that it shall be the duty of the commonwealth's attorney for said county of Warwick, with his consent, to take said records in charge, and to arrange them in such manner that said records may be duly preserved and readily referred to by the citizens of said counties, and that he deposit them in some safe and convenient place.

Compensation

2. Be it further enacted, that the said attorney shall for his services receive such compensation out of the public treasury as to the auditor of public accounts may seem fit and reasonable, and shall also be paid in like manner any necessary expenses incurred in pro-

viding suitable boxes for the storing and preservation of said records and papers. But the amount so paid shall be refunded to the public treasury by the said counties, in equal proportions.

3. Be it further enacted, that the clerk of the circuit court for the county of James City and city of Williamsburg, having now in his charge the records and papers of his said court, which have been removed to the city of Richmond for the safe-keeping thereof, shall, for services rendered by him in the arrangement and preservation of the same, be compensated in the same manner provided in the preceding section, and shall also be repaid any necessary expenses incurred in providing suitable boxes for the safe-keeping of said records and papers; which amounts so paid shall be refunded to the public treasury by the county and city aforesaid, in equal proportions. James City and Williamsburg

4. This act shall be in force from its passage. Commencement

CHAP. 94.—An ACT increasing the Capital Stock of the Bank of the City of Petersburg.

Passed February 27, 1864

1. Be it enacted by the general assembly of Virginia, that the first section of the act entitled an act incorporating The Bank of the City of Petersburg, passed March twenty-ninth, eighteen hundred and sixty, be and the same is hereby amended and re-enacted so as to read as follows: Act amended

"§ 1. That it shall be lawful to organize and establish in the city of Petersburg a bank, authorized to carry on business as a bank of circulation, deposit and discount, the capital stock of which shall not be less than one hundred and fifty thousand dollars nor more than two millions of dollars, to be raised by subscription, in shares of one hundred dollars each." Capital increased

2. This act shall be in force from its passage. Commencement

CHAP. 95.—An ACT to make Clinch River a Lawful Fence through the County of Scott.

Passed March 4, 1864.

1. Be it enacted by the general assembly, that Clinch river is hereby declared a lawful fence, so far as it runs through the county of Scott. Clinch river lawful fence

2. This act shall be in force from its passage, and continue in force until six months after the close of the present war. Commencement

---

CHAP. 96.—An ACT to authorize the Charlottesville Savings Bank to reduce the Number of its Directors.

Passed December 19, 1863.

1. Be it enacted by the general assembly of Virginia, that it shall be lawful for the stockholders of the Charlottesville savings bank, by vote in annual meeting, to reduce the number of directors in the same to five or three, as they may prefer; and such directors shall exercise the same powers, perform the same duties, and be subject to the same obligations in all respects as now pertain to the present directors. Number of directors, how reduced

2. This act shall be in force from its passage. Commencement

CHAP. 97.—An ACT refunding to Peter Engleman part of a License Tax paid by him.

Passed March 9, 1864.

Auditor to issue warrant

1. Be it enacted by the general assembly, that the auditor of public accounts be and he is hereby authorized and required to issue his warrant on the treasury, payable out of any money therein not otherwise appropriated, in favor of Peter Engleman, or his legal representatives, for the sum of sixty-six dollars and sixty-six cents, being a portion of the tax paid by him for a license to operate a distillery in the county of Augusta, for the year eighteen hundred and sixty-two, and which said license was revoked by act of the general assembly, passed seventeenth March eighteen hundred and sixty-two.

Amount

Commencement

2. This act shall be in force from its passage.

CHAP. 98.—An ACT authorizing the payment of a sum of money to William J. Morgan, for a Slave condemned to be hung.

Passed March 9, 1864.

Auditor to issue warrant

1. Be it enacted by the general assembly, that the auditor of public accounts be and he is hereby authorized and required to issue his warrant on the treasury, payable out of any money therein not otherwise appropriated, in favor of William J. Morgan of the county of Fauquier, or his legal representatives, for the sum of one thousand three hundred and twenty-five dollars, being the amount fixed by the county court of Smyth county as the value of a slave named Beverly, the property of said Morgan; which said slave was condemned to be hung by said county court, at its March term eighteen hundred and sixty-three, and committed suicide by hanging prior to the day fixed for his execution.

Amount

Commencement

2. This act shall be in force from its passage.

CHAP. 99.—An ACT for the relief of the Securities of R. P. Baker, late Sheriff of Grayson County.

Passed February 22, 1864.

Securities released

1. Be it enacted by the general assembly, that the securities of R. P. Baker, late sheriff of Grayson county, are hereby released from the payment of damages, and the excess of interest over six per centum, on judgments in favor of the commonwealth against them as such securities, rendered by the circuit court of the city of Richmond. But the said securities shall not have the benefit of this act, unless within ninety days from the passage hereof they pay into the treasury all that remains of the principal unpaid, interest, costs and actual expenses of collection: provided, that this act shall not be construed as releasing said R. P. Baker, late sheriff of Grayson county, from the payment of any damages adjudged against him.

R. P. Baker not released

Commencement

2. This act shall be in force from its passage.

CHAP. 100.—An ACT releasing R. F. and D. G. Bibb from liability under a Contract for the Hire of Negro Convicts.

Passed February 18, 1864.

Preamble

Whereas a contract was entered into on the thirty-first day of December eighteen hundred and sixty, between the governor of this commonwealth and Robert F. and D. G. Bibb, for the hire, for the term of twelve months, of a large number of negro convicts, who had been condemned to sale and transportation, and their punishment commuted to labor on the public works: And whereas it appears that these convicts were hired for the purpose of executing a contract with the board of public works for constructing three sections of the Covington and Ohio rail road: And whereas, in consequence of the secession of the state, and the war consequent thereon, the board of public works made an order to stay any further execution of the said contract in the construction of said road: And whereas an order was also made by the governor requiring the parties hiring said convicts to redeliver them to the keeper of the penitentiary; which was accordingly done about the twenty-eighth day of May eighteen hundred and sixty-one, whereby much loss and damage was sustained by said R. F. and D. G. Bibb; and it appearing to the general assembly just and proper to release the said parties from the payment of the amount stipulated to be paid for the hire of said convicts: Therefore,

1. Be it enacted by the general assembly, that the said R. F. and D. G. Bibb shall be and they are hereby released from all liability, under the said contract, for any hires stipulated to be paid by them for said convicts; and the said contract, and all obligations executed therefor, shall be null and void: provided, however, that the release hereby granted shall be upon the express condition that all claim for damages sustained by said parties by the abrogation of any contract made by them with the board of public works for the construction of the said work, or by the order of the governor for the return of said convicts to the penitentiary, shall be abandoned and released by said parties. Parties released. Proviso

2. This act shall be in force from its passage. Commencement

CHAP. 101.—An ACT for the relief of William R. C. Douglas, late Steward of the Eastern Lunatic Asylum.

Passed January 22, 1864.

1. Be it enacted by the general assembly, that the auditor of public accounts be and he is hereby authorized and required to draw his warrant upon the treasury, payable out of any money therein not otherwise appropriated, in favor of William R. C. Douglas, for the sum of three hundred and thirty-three dollars and fifty cents, that being the amount of his salary as the late steward of the Eastern lunatic asylum from the first day of January eighteen hundred and sixty-three to the thirteenth of May following, at the rate of nine hundred dollars per annum. Auditor to issue warrant. Amount

2. This act shall be in force from its passage. Commencement

CHAP. 102.—An ACT authorizing the payment of a Sum of Money to Lee A. Dunn of King William County, for Extra Copies of his Land and Property Books.

Passed January 21, 1864.

1. Be it enacted by the general assembly, that the auditor of public accounts be and he is hereby authorized and directed to issue his warrant on the treasury, payable out of any money therein not otherwise appropriated, in favor of Lee A. Dunn of King William county, or his legal representatives, for the sum of one hundred dollars, the same being the amount paid by said Dunn to William D. Pollard, for making out two extra copies of the property book and two extra copies of the land book for the year eighteen hundred and sixty-three, for the said county of King William. Auditor to issue warrant. Amount

2. This act shall be in force from its passage. Commencement

CHAP. 103.—An ACT for the relief of A. G. Ingraham.

Passed March 1, 1864

Auditor to issue warrant

1. Be it enacted by the general assembly, that the auditor of public accounts be and he is hereby authorized and required to issue his warrant on the treasury of the commonwealth, payable out of any money therein not otherwise appropriated, in favor of A. G. Ingraham, for the sum of three hundred and twenty-six dollars and eighty-eight cents, being the amount of damages erroneously awarded against him, in addition to principal, interest and costs on two judgments recovered against him in favor of the commonwealth.

Amount

Commencement

2. This act shall be in force from its passage.

CHAP. 104.—An ACT releasing William B. Ball from the payment of a certain sum of money.

Passed March 1, 1864.

Claim released

1. Be it enacted by the general assembly, that the claim of the commonwealth against William B. Ball for one hundred and twenty-two dollars and fifty cents, as of the twenty-seventh of May eighteen hundred and sixty-one, for forty-nine pair of shoes furnished by R. M. Nimmo, agent, for a cavalry company commanded by said Ball, be and the same is hereby released; and the same shall be allowed as an offset in favor of the said Nimmo against the debt asserted in the suit of the commonwealth against him in the circuit court of the city of Richmond.

Commencement

2. This act shall be in force from its passage.

CHAP. 105.—An ACT for the relief of John C. Heiskell, Sheriff of Hampshire County.

Passed March 4, 1864.

Damages released

1. Be it enacted by the general assembly, that John C. Heiskell, sheriff of Hampshire county, be and he is hereby released from the payment of the damages and interest on a judgment obtained against him for failure to pay the license tax due May eighteen hundred and sixty-one, said Heiskell having paid into the treasury the amount of the principal of said judgment.

Commencement

2. This act shall be in force from its passage.

CHAP. 106.—An ACT for the relief of William E. Prince of Sussex County.

Passed January 23, 1864.

Auditor to issue warrant

1. Be it enacted by the general assembly, that the auditor of public accounts be authorized to issue his warrant on the treasury, payable out of any money therein not otherwise appropriated, in favor of William E. Prince of Sussex county, or his legal representatives, for the sum of two hundred and eighty-five dollars, the same having been paid by said Prince into the treasury, in pursuance of an order entered by the judge of the circuit court of Sussex county, under a misapprehension of the law, for the purchase of a free negro named Billy Barlow, allowed to enslave himself by order of the said circuit court of Sussex county at the October term of said court in eighteen hundred and sixty-three.

Amount

Commencement

2. This act shall be in force from its passage.

CHAP. 107.—An ACT for the relief of Thomas M. Hundley, Commissioner of the Revenue for the County of Matthews.

Passed March 10, 1864.

1 Be it enacted by the general assembly, that the auditor of public accounts be and he is hereby authorized and required to issue his warrant upon the treasury in favor of Thomas M. Hundley of the county of Matthews, for such sum as may be the value of his services in making out his property book and records of births and deaths for said county for the year eighteen hundred and sixty-three, not exceeding the sum of two hundred and twenty dollars; which property book and records were not returned, because it is alleged they fell into the hands of the public enemy; but such payment shall not be made until the said Thomas M. Hundley shall furnish to said auditor satisfactory proof that the said property book and records of births and deaths for the county of Matthews were completed, and not returned in consequence of their having fallen into the hands of the public enemy. Auditor to issue warrant. Proof to be furnished

2. This act shall be in force from its passage. Commencement

CHAP. 108.—An ACT for the relief of the Personal Representatives of A. B. Urquhart, Joseph E. Gillett and Madison J. Davis.

Passed February 20, 1864.

Whereas it is represented that A. B. Urquhart, Joseph E. Gillett and Madison J. Davis of the county of Southampton, have died intestate, leaving respectively large landed estates, together with a number of slaves, to which the children of said decedents (all or most of whom are minors) are entitled: And whereas, in the present state of the country, it is alleged that to hire, sell or divide said slaves would probably cause them to escape to the enemy: Preamble

1. Be it enacted by the general assembly, that it shall be lawful for the county court of said county of Southampton, if it be clearly shown that the interest of those interested in said estates will be promoted, and that the rights of no person will be violated thereby, to authorize, by decree, the personal representatives of said estates respectively, or the guardians of said children, to retain said slaves on said plantations, and to cultivate the same for the benefit of said heirs and distributees respectively, precisely in all respects as if they had been empowered so to do by will duly made by said decedents, subject to any further order and decree of said court, during the existence of the present war, taking bond with satisfactory security from the parties to whom the management of said estates may be entrusted, in such penalty as the court may deem reasonable, and conditioned for the faithful discharge of the duties required of them, and for duly accounting with the parties interested. Powers of court

2. The proceedings under this act, in order to obtain such decree, shall in all respects conform mutatis mutandis to the requirements of the second, third, fourth, fifth, sixth and seventh sections of chapter one hundred and twenty-eight of the Code of Virginia (edition of eighteen hundred and sixty). Proceedings

3. Nothing in this act shall be construed so as to prevent any of said heirs or distributees now of age, or who may become so, or the widow of either of said decedents from proceeding to have his or her share of said estates allowed to him or her, precisely as if this act had not been passed. Limitation

4. This act shall be in force from its passage. Commencement

CHAP. 109.—An ACT authorizing and directing the payment of the Dixie Boys.

Passed March 10, 1864.

Auditing board to settle claim

1. Be it enacted by the general assembly, that the auditing board be and they are hereby authorized and directed to audit and settle, and the auditor of public accounts is hereby directed to pay the claim of an independent company of scouts and rangers, known as the Dixie Boys; which claim the auditing board refused to allow on the twenty-ninth day of May eighteen hundred and sixty-three.

Restriction

2. The said auditing board shall only allow so much of said claim as is for pay for the actual time each member of the said company was in service; and the auditor of public accounts shall issue his warrant upon the treasury, payable out of any money therein not otherwise appropriated, for the said amounts, when so audited and settled.

Auditor to issue warrant

Commencement

3. This act shall be in force from its passage.

CHAP. 110.—An ACT releasing the Commonwealth's Claim to certain Land to Matthew Sylvia.

Passed February 8, 1864.

Claim released

1. Be it enacted by the general assembly of Virginia, that the title and interest of the commonwealth to and in a certain lot in the city of Petersburg, owned jointly by Matthew Sylvia and by Joseph Leonards (alias Leonard) deceased, be and the same is hereby released to said Matthew Sylvia: provided, however, that nothing herein contained shall be construed to impair or affect the rights of any creditor, heir at law or devisee of said Joseph Leonards (alias Leonard), but the same shall remain as if this act had not passed.

Commencement

2. This act shall be in force from its passage.

RESOLUTIONS.

No. 1.—Address of the General Assembly to the Soldiers of Virginia.

Adopted March 9, 1864.

Soldiers of Virginia in the Armies of the Confederate States—It is now nearly three years since you left your homes and firesides, at the call of your state, to repel the invasion of her soil. Before taking up arms, every effort to obtain the peaceful enjoyment of your rights under the constitution had been exhausted, your appeals for justice spurned with contempt, and a war to subjugate our sister states of the south commenced by Abraham Lincoln. Address of general assembly to soldiers of Virginia

By this lawless proceeding, the federal administration threw off the mask it had hitherto worn. In such a contest Virginia could not remain an indifferent spectator. Bound by every tie of blood, sympathy, common interests and common wrongs to the states against whom this hostile preparation was set on foot, she withdrew at once from an association which no longer respected a written constitution, and resolved to receive on her own bosom the threatened shock of invasion. She invoked you to rally to defend your homes, your altars and your honor; and this appeal was not made in vain. Promptly and generously you responded to the call of duty. Most faithfully have you performed it. In your long and arduous service you have shrunk from no toil, no danger and no sacrifice. During your absence in the field, your wives and little ones may have suffered want; your homes been ravaged, and the fruits of industry destroyed by a ruthless and barbarous enemy. But, in despite of every temptation, you have never looked back. Your eye has always been fixed on the foe, and your ear waiting for the summons to battle. Amid the toil of the march, the weary watch, the labor, the hunger, the cold, the privations of the camp, you have never complained, but have always rendered a cheerful obedience to the state which honors and cherishes you with a mother's love.

You have been present in most of the important battles of the war, and in all your valor has been conspicuous. It has made you the theme of praise by your heroic companions from other states, and by the whole civilized world.

Many of your comrades have fallen in battle, or from disease contracted in service, and been transferred from the roll of life to that of immortality. There are many more, whose mutilated forms attest their honorable devotion to their country. In your prolonged absence from home, your sacrifice of personal interests and of all the enjoyments of life, has indeed been great. The war, forced upon us by the malice of a people whom we had not injured, has entailed upon us all deep sorrow and cruel suffering. Its unavoidable calamities have been greatly augmented by the refusal of the enemy to respect the laws of civilized warfare, and by their fiendish attempt to wrest submission from us, by visiting the most relentless barbarities upon women and children, the aged and the helpless. Unbridled license has been given to their cupidity. Untold millions of property have been wantonly destroyed by their malice, or swelled the coffers of the pampered villains, who, unwhipt of justice, have been openly rewarded and promoted for their crimes. Aged and unoffending men have been dragged from their beds to dreary prisons and solitary labor. Refined and virtuous women have been brutally insulted, and, manacled by rude unfeeling soldiery, have been led captive from their homes as hostages for negroes. Farms have been desolated; dwellings laid in ashes; unprotected women and helpless children have been turned out from their homes without bread or shelter. The tombs of the gallant dead have been robbed and desecrated by fiends, who have ruthlessly invaded the sanctity of the grave, and outraged the sensibilities of the living.

Under the hypocritical guise of liberating from slavery a population happier and more virtuous than themselves, they have sought to subject us to a yoke more galling than they have essayed to remove.

Within a few days past an expedition has been projected and an abortive effort made to carry into execution, with minute instructions emanating (as we have reason to believe) from the government at Washington, to sack and fire the city of Richmond, and in the darkness of the night to consign its inhabitants, without a moment's warning, to flames and to death. For this purpose, a special "burning party" was organized, provided with implements of destruction, and orders to carry into execution their fell designs. Amid its blazing ruins the released prisoners from "Belle Isle" and "the Libby" were to unite with the bands of Dahlgren and Kilpatrick in dealing out death and slaughter upon unoffending and peaceful citizens, and inflicting outrages upon pure and unprotected women, more horrible than death.

The heart sickens at the contemplation of the enormities that would have been committed, had this nefarious scheme succeeded. No prayer for mercy would have been heard; no scream for help would have been heeded. Fire, rapine, slaughter and lust would have held undisputed dominion in this fair city.

We forbear to enlarge, but make this recital, that you may know more clearly the character of our foe, and that he may be held up to the odium and execration of mankind.

In shameless disregard of all the rules of civilized warfare, your chief magistrate and his cabinet were, by special directions, to be denied the rights of prisoners of war, and killed in cold blood. Every species of public and private property was to be destroyed, and the entire country within their reach laid waste.

Stimulated and encouraged by the precepts and example of their leaders, this band of robbers and murderers entered private houses; broke open ladies' wardrobes; destroyed of their rich contents what they could not appropriate; carried off jewels and plate; consigned to the flames stores of provisions; burnt mills and other houses; desolated some of the fairest homes of the state, and left whole families without food.

Thanks to the gallantry of a citizen soldiery, they were routed and repulsed, in the midst of this carnival of crime, which must outrage the sensibilities of the civilized world. Many of them, with awakened consciousness of their deserts, now contemplate their doom within the walls of the prison from which they hoped to release their companions.

An avenging God suddenly summoned their atrocious leader from the scene of his wickedness to the bar of judgment, and on his slain body were found his atrocious instructions, stained with his own blood. The name of Dahlgren will be handed down to history as a fit associate in infamy with Butler, and a host of lesser criminals, who have disgraced humanity, and shocked the moral sense of the world.

But in these very atrocities you will discern the motive, if any were needed, for continued services and fresh sacrifices. Virginia takes no step backward. Every consideration of honor, interest, duty and safety demand that we shall go forward in the grand struggle for human rights and human liberty, so bravely begun, and so manfully maintained.

After all that we have suffered and endured, subjugation or submission to the cruel foe would reduce us to a degree of degradation and misery which has no parallel in the history of civilization.

The sacrifices of blood and treasure, that we have expended, the memories of the noble martyrs who have freely given their lives for the achievement of our independence, forbid that we should needlessly throw away what has been already won, in the vain hope of obtaining peace or security.

Nothing but wretchedness and untold misery await us, if we stop short of the unconditional acknowledgment of our independence. This your valor will surely command.

Men of Virginia! you are soldiers of a renowned commonwealth, whose fame you have illustrated and borne aloft on every battle field. We need not unfold to you the muniments of your right to self-government. We are assured that you fully comprehend the necessity of a successful assertion of that right, and that you will never lay down your arms until you have secured it. Born to an inheritance of freedom, you cannot hesitate to choose between slavery or death. Submission to an enemy, who has exhausted every infamy, is not endurable even in thought; but were we base enough to desire peace upon any terms less than the unqualified recognition of our independence, self-interest alone would teach us the folly of relying upon the forbearance of a nation who have shown in every step of the war, that their faith is perfidy, and their only policy is rapine, plunder and oppression. The whole history of our former association with the northern states admonishes us that in a common government they will never fail to employ their power to take away our property. Their present malice springs chiefly from baffled cupidity. But for this master passion of their nature, an honorable and speedy peace would be easy. The war has fully developed all their purposes, and you now know the fate that awaits you in the event of subjugation. Your liberties will utterly perish. Your state organization will be blotted out. All your property of every description will be confiscated, for all of us have participated in the revolution. Your lands will be divided out among the banditti from the north and from Europe, who have invaded our state. A free negro population will be established in your midst, who will be your social equals and military governors. Negro guards will, at their pleasure, give you passes and safe conducts, or arrest you to be tried and punished by negro commandants and magistrates: and to these, yourselves, your wives and children will be menial laborers and slaves, except those of you whom the malice of your enemies shall reserve for the dungeon or the gallows.

Such is the doom denounced for the people of the south by the wicked race now warring upon us. But we know it can never be executed. An army of veterans have resolved that their country *shall not* be enslaved; and while their purpose stands, the enemy's designs will continue to be baffled. Among you there is one spirit—that of eager and resolute determination. The temper of the army has reached the people at home, and inspired them with a fresh courage and a more assured confidence. Every where we see multiplied evidences of energy and enthusiasm. In all the states we find the resolution to endure every extremity rather than submit; and with this spirit our people are invincible. The armies are filling up their ranks, and the legislation of congress has added still further to their numbers and efficiency. Those citizens who remain at home to carry on the industrial pursuits essential to the support of the army, will see to it that you shall not want for food while you are exposing your lives to protect their property and homes from rapine. The defence of the country has become its business, and every citizen is required to contribute to it in his proper sphere. The general assembly of the commonwealth has taken steps to aid those families of her soldiers who may be in want, and it will not fail to do all in its power to provide for and cherish them. They have authorized and directed the purchase or impressment of unlimited supplies for their maintenance; appropriated one million dollars for the relief of such as are within the lines of the enemy, and half a million as a hospital fund for the sick and wounded. An organized agency of the state distributes the voluntary contributions of patriotic citizens. Individually and collectively, in county, city and state organizations, the people with one accord are determined to feed, clothe, sustain and cherish the army.

On the other hand, your enemies are appalled by the magnitude of the task before them. The loud boastings which a few weeks since they so freely uttered, have been silenced by your unanimous re-enlistments, for the war, and the stern and resolute bearing of the south. Dissensions exist among them. Eager to possess the spoils of their corrupt and profligate government, they hate each other nearly as much as they do us. The war is no longer popular. The rich are allowed to buy an exemption, and thus cast all the burden and risk upon the poor. The laboring classes have already revolted against the draft. To escape its odium, enormous bounties have been offered to volunteers; but all these expedients have failed, and again a heavy draft has been ordered. The armies of the enemy are every day diminishing, and it is evident they cannot recruit them to the numbers with which they began the struggle. A large and growing party are for peace. A still larger party have discovered that the war has so far only served to entail upon themselves a despotism which tramples down every public and private right. They feel and acknowledge that they are the slaves of one whose character has made him odious to the world. Torn by party and personal strife, and conscious of the impotence of their scheme of conquest, the ranks of your enemies are already beginning to waver. One more resolute effort, and the day is ours.

God will strengthen your arms in the hour of battle, and give his blessing to a just cause. Independence and peace will be conceded by your enemies, and you, the defenders of the commonwealth, may return to your homes to receive the welcome due to the brave, and to enjoy those honors which will grow brighter as your years shall be prolonged. And when our ears shall be no longer startled by the "clash of resounding arms," and a happy, prosperous and permanent peace shall succeed, returning from the fields of your fame, you will be greeted with tears of joy by the loved ones at home—the heroes of every circle—to receive the smiles of the fair and become the theme of gratitude and praise around every hearthstone, protected by your valor.

Then every heart shall rejoice in that quiet which your courage has secured. Not the quiet of deserted homes and desolated farms; of sacked cities and rifled churches; of villages in ashes and towns in ruins; but the quiet of smiling farms, when the blue smoke shall curl again above the ancestral trees, to welcome back the long exiled refugee to his home. The quiet of thriving villages, when the old man on his crutch and the brave and warnworn veteran with his armless sleeve, shall tell of bloody battles and scenes of privation to smiling children around him. The quiet of prosperous cities, whose wharves shall whiten with an opulent commerce; whose shops shall hum with a busy industry, and whose spires point to that haven of rest which is far away. Then from a thousand happy hearts and happy homes shall arise thanksgiving and praise to the God of battles, as of grace, while tears of gratitude will embalm the memories and bedew the graves of the brave men whose blood has been shed as a libation to liberty.

A. D. DICKINSON, *Chn.*
A. J. MARSHALL,
ANDREW HUNTER,
Senate Committee.
B. H. SHACKELFORD, *Chn.*
R. W. HUNTER,
F. B. DEANE,
A. C. CUMMINGS,
R. H. BAKER,
House Committee.

No. 2.—Joint Resolution authorizing the Publication and Distribution of the Address of the General Assembly to the Soldiers of Virginia.

Adopted March 9, 1864.

Resolved by the general assembly, that the address of the general assembly to the soldiers of Virginia be published in the Richmond newspapers for one week, on alternate days, and that ten thousand extra copies be printed for distribution by the governor among the soldiers of Virginia, in such mode as in his judgment will best attain that object. Address to be published and distributed

---

No. 3.—Joint Resolutions affirming the Right of the State of Virginia to appoint all Officers needful to perform the various functions of her State Government, and declaring certain Officers indispensable to the proper maintenance of the dignity, integrity and efficiency of the Government of the State, &c.

Adopted March 10, 1864.

Resolved by the general assembly of Virginia, that this state claims as an absolute right, not relinquished or compromised in any manner by her adoption of the constitution of the Confederate States, the appointment of all officers deemed needful by her to perform the various functions of her state government, and their total immunity, except with the assent of the legislature, so far as the same might be given consistently with the constitution of the state, from any military service or duty to the confederate government. Claim of state

Resolved, that the following officers of the state of Virginia, elected or appointed under and by virtue of the constitution and laws thereof, to wit:

In the legislative department—The members of both houses of the general assembly, and their officers. Legislative

In the executive department—The governor, the lieutenant governor, the secretary of the commonwealth and his clerks, the treasurer, the two auditors, and the register of the land office, and all their regular clerks provided for by law; the board of public works and their secretary; the public printer and the printer of the senate; the adjutant general and his clerk; the inspector general; the commissioned officers, one clerk and necessary artificers of the ordnance department, certified as such by the colonel of ordnance; the quartermaster general, and the officers and men of the public guard; the commissioners of the revenue, and the superintendent of the salt works and his assistants authorized by law. Executive

In the judiciary department—The judges of the court of appeals and of the circuit courts, and the judge of the hustings court of the city of Richmond; the clerks of said courts, and of the district, county and corporation courts, or a deputy clerk for each of said courts, where the clerk thereof is in the military service of the Confederate States; the justices of the peace, the attorney general and Judiciary attorneys for the commonwealth; the sheriff of each county and corporation, and the sergeant and collector of taxes of each corporation having a hustings court; the high constable of the city of Richmond.

Public establishments

In the public establishments—The professors and officers of the university of Virginia, and the superintendent and professors of the Virginia military institute; the superintendents of the public hospitals and the lunatic asylums, and the physicians and employees employed therein, and the teachers employed in the institution for the deaf, dumb and blind; the superintendent of the penitentiary, his assistants and clerk, are indispensable to the performance of the public functions with which they are charged, and to the proper maintenance of the dignity, integrity and efficiency of the government of this state, and the public institutions thereof, and are not, and of right should not be liable to be called into the military service of the confederate government, by virtue of any law thereof, so long as they hold their respective offices under this state: provided, that all the clerks, assistants and employees between the ages of eighteen and forty-five years, embraced in the foregoing clauses, shall not be entitled to exemption, unless the person authorized by law to employ such clerk, assistant or employee, shall first certify that they are absolutely necessary for the performance of the duties assigned them, and that he does not believe he can procure the services of any person or persons qualified to discharge the duties assigned them respectively, not liable to military service.

Power, &c. of governor

Resolved, that the governor be and he is hereby authorized and directed, in such mode as he may deem best, to apprise the proper confederate authorities that the state of Virginia claims and requires the exclusive service of the above enumerated officers, and their immunity from all military service to the confederate government, by virtue of any law thereof.

Other powers of governor

Resolved, that the governor be further empowered and directed to certify as to such other officers as he may deem necessary for the proper administration of the government, and to bring to the notice of the said authorities the presidents, cashiers, tellers, and such other officers of the banks of discount and deposit of this commonwealth as he may think necessary to the safe conduct of their business; also, any special cases of persons whose services he may consider important to the public interest, to the preservation of order, to the security of our cities, or the efficiency of our public establishments, and request their exemption so long as they may be rendering such services, from the military service of the Confederate States.

No 4.—Joint Resolution in relation to Perpetuating Testimony.

Adopted March 8, 1864.

Duty of attorney general

Resolved by the general assembly, that the attorney general of Virginia be and he is hereby instructed to cause the facts and circumstances of the recent raid upon the city of Richmond by Colonel Dahlgren, to be verified and perpetuated, by making a record of the evidence in relation thereto, and filing the same in the office of the secretary of the commonwealth.

No. 5.—Preamble and Joint Resolution relative to the Arrest and Sentence of Certain Citizens of Portsmouth by the Federal Authorities.

Adopted March 8, 1864.

Preamble

Whereas the general assembly of Virginia have learned that the Reverend George M. Bain, cashier of the Portsmouth savings fund society, and William H. H. Hodges, cashier of the Merchants and Mechanics savings bank, citizens of Portsmouth, Virginia, the first named being over sixty years of age, and the other a cripple, have been arrested and sentenced to hard labor at Hatteras, North Carolina, by order of Major General Butler, or some other officer of the federal government, for alleged fraudulent disposal of the funds of their respective banks; and that the Reverend John H. Wingfield, rector of Trinity Episcopal church, Portsmouth, had been put to hard labor on the public streets of that city, with a ball and chain to his leg, because he refused to renounce his allegiance to this his native state: Therefore,

Attention of confederate authorities to be invited

Be it resolved by the general assembly, that the governor of the commonwealth be and he is hereby requested to invite the attention of the confederate government to the arrest and sentence of those three worthy citizens of this state, and to respectfully ask that the facts may be investigated; and if found as stated and believed, that three citizens of the federal states, if there be such in the hands of the confederate authorities, be held at hard labor as hostages for these three citizens of Virginia; and if none, that three federal officers be placed at hard labor, one with ball and chain, on the public streets, and held as hostages for Messrs. Bain, Hodges and Wingfield.

No. 6.—Joint Resolution in relation to the employment of Free Negroes, &c.

Adopted February 29, 1864.

Preamble

Whereas the congress of the Confederate States of America, by an act passed on the thirteenth of February eighteen hundred and sixty-four, and approved by the president, entitled an act to increase the efficiency of the army, by the employment of free negroes and slaves in certain capacities, have declared that all male free negroes and other free persons of color, &c., shall be held liable to perform such duties with the army, &c. as the secretary of war, &c. may prescribe: And whereas it is provided that the secretary of war, &c., with the approval of the president, may exempt from the operations of this act such free negroes as the interest of the country may require should be exempted, or such as he may think proper to exempt on grounds of justice, equity or necessity: And whereas large districts of this commonwealth have been deprived of a large amount of their labor by the escape of slaves, and are solely dependent upon free negro labor: And whereas it is important and necessary that this class of labor should be permitted to remain in the districts aforesaid for purposes of production: Therefore,

Duty of governor

Be it resolved by the general assembly, that the governor be directed to request the secretary of war to exempt from the operations of this act those counties of this commonwealth in the power or possession of the public enemy, or so threatened that any attempt to remove the free negroes would endanger their escape to the public enemy.

No. 7.—Preamble and Joint Resolution in relation to the death of Dr. D. M. Wright of the City of Norfolk.

Adopted March 10, 1864.

Preamble

Whereas the arrival within confederate lines of the distressed family of the deceased, establishes beyond question the newspaper announcement of the execution by the federal authorities in obedience to the sentence of a military commission, of Dr. David M. Wright in the city of Norfolk, on the twenty-third day of October eighteen hundred and sixty-three: And whereas it is fit and proper that Virginia should place upon permanent record her high appreciation of a son, whose courage, zeal and devotion marked with blood the first effort to establish upon her soil an equality of races, and introduce into our midst the leveling dogmas of a false and pretended civilization:

Recognized as a martyr

1. Be it resolved by the general assembly of Virginia, that in the death of Dr. Wright this commonwealth recognizes another addition to the long and illustrious catalogue of martyrs, whose stern, inflexible devotion to liberty have rendered heroic the history of her people, in the present struggle.

Imitation of his example invoked

2. That as the proudest tribute which Virginia can offer to his memory, she would earnestly invoke her children, whether within or beyond the enemy's lines, to imitate his example and emulate his high resolves.

To be transmitted to family

3. That the governor of the state be requested to transmit a copy of this preamble and these resolutions to the family of Dr. Wright—together with assurances of the sincere sympathy of the general assembly.

No. 8.—Joint Resolution giving certain Instructions to the Board of Public Works.

Adopted February 26, 1864.

Duty of board of public works

Resolved by the general assembly, that the board of public works be instructed to use the power vested in it by law to secure an adequate supply of fuel to and transportation of salt from the salt works, according to the order of priority established by the general assembly, at its late extra session, in connection with the report of the joint committee on salt, in respect to salt for Georgia.

No. 9.—Preamble and Joint Resolution authorizing the Secretary of the Commonwealth to certify the result of the Elections in the second and thirty-first Senatorial Districts, without awaiting the lapse of time required by law.

Adopted February 2, 1864.

Preamble

Whereas elections have been held to supply the vacancies in the second and thirty-first senatorial districts; and it appearing that the senators elect cannot take their seats until the expiration of forty-two days after the day of election, under the act passed March twenty-fourth, eighteen hundred and sixty-three, entitled an act to provide representation for the counties where the courthouses are in the possession of the public enemy; and there appearing to be no good or substantial reason why the senators elect from the said districts should not be declared elected, and admitted to the floor of the senate: Therefore,

Power of secretary of commonwealth

Resolved by the general assembly, that the secretary of the commonwealth be and he is hereby authorized to certify the result of said elections, without waiting for the lapse of said forty-two days, to the end that representation may be secured to said districts as early as possible: provided, that the rights of no contestant shall be prejudiced hereby.

No. 10.—Joint Resolution in relation to the convening of the General Assembly.

Adopted February 27, 1864

Governor requested to convene legislature

Resolved by the general assembly, that the governor be and he is hereby respectfully requested to convene the general assembly on the first Wednesday in December eighteen hundred and sixty-four; but this application is not intended to interfere in any manner with the exercise of the discretion vested in the governor by the constitution, should he think proper for any cause to convene the general assembly at an earlier day.

No. 11.—Resolution concerning the Pay of Soldiers in the Confederate States Army.

Adopted December 18, 1863.

1. Resolved, that in the opinion of the general assembly of Virginia, some provision for the increase of the pay of the soldiers in the army of the Confederate States should at once be made by the congress of the Confederate States; and that the senators from Virginia be instructed and the representatives in congress be requested to take immediate steps to pass a law providing for such increase of pay as will, under the present circumstances, be just and adequate to supply the wants of the soldiers in the army. Increase in soldiers' pay suggested

2. Resolved, that the governor of this commonwealth be requested to communicate the passage of the above resolution to our senators and representatives in congress. To be transmitted to congress

---

No. 12.—Joint Resolution for the appointment of a Committee to enquire into the Treatment of Conscripts at Camp Lee.

Adopted February 25, 1864.

Whereas it has been stated in the public press of this city and elsewhere, that the conscripts at Camp Lee have been subjected to harsh and inhuman treatment, and it is due alike to the officers in charge and to the conscripts, that such a charge should be investigated: Therefore, Preamble

Resolved by the general assembly, that a joint committee of three on the part of the senate and five on the part of the house of delegates be appointed to enquire and report whether any, and if any, what abuses or inhumanity may have been practiced or tolerated at Camp Lee, in the treatment of conscripts, and that they report to the assembly the result of their investigation. Investigating committee

---

No. 13.—Joint Resolution in regard to the requisition for Slaves to work on Fortifications.

Adopted February 19, 1864.

Whereas, in view of the pressing importance of making extraordinary efforts to produce as large crops as possible the present year: And whereas the recent requisition by the confederate authorities for slave labor to work on fortifications will, if carried out, interfere seriously with the farming productions of the state: Therefore, Preamble

Be it resolved by the general assembly, that the governor of this state be respectfully requested to confer with the authorities of the Confederate States, and urge upon them the necessity, in the present emergency, of releasing the slaves from said requisition, if in the judgment of the confederate authorities this release may be granted consistently with the necessities of the military situation. Release of slaves suggested

---

No. 14.—Joint Resolution in relation to B. F. Murray, Sheriff of Shenandoah County.

Adopted February 29, 1864.

Whereas it is represented that B. F. Murray, sheriff of Shenandoah county, transmitted to the seat of government the sum of twelve thousand five hundred dollars, to be placed to his credit on the taxes collected by him for the year eighteen hundred and sixty-two, which, by a misapprehension, was credited against his collections for the year eighteen hundred and sixty-three: Preamble

Be it therefore resolved by the general assembly, that if the auditor of public accounts shall be satisfied that the payment was impro- Auditor authorized to correct error perly credited to the taxes of eighteen hundred and sixty-three, he may correct the credit, by applying the same to the taxes of eighteen hundred and sixty-two.

No. 15.—Joint Resolution instructing the Auditor of Public Accounts to obtain certain information from the Commissioners of the Revenue, and to communicate the same to the General Assembly, at its next Session.

Adopted March 10, 1864.

Losses of slaves, &c. to be reported to auditor

Resolved by the general assembly, that the auditor of public accounts give instructions to the commissioners of the revenue in the several counties of the commonwealth, to make out and return to his office detailed statements, in such statistical form as he shall prescribe, of the losses of slaves and other property, personal and real; also churches, courthouses, records and other public property, sustained by the citizens thereof, with a list of the owners thereof, from the commencement of the existing war to the first day of July eighteen hundred and sixty-four, specifying the losses in each fiscal year, and the value thereof at the prevailing prices of eighteen hundred and sixty; and showing the productions of agriculture in those fiscal years, compared with the said products in the year preceding the existing war; and that the auditor lay the details so obtained before the general assembly at its next session.

Auditor to report to legislature

No. 16.—Joint Resolution authorizing the Keeper of the Rolls to correct a Clerical Error.

Adopted March 10, 1864.

Keeper of rolls to correct error

Resolved by the general assembly, that the keeper of the rolls of Virginia be directed to correct a clerical error in an act passed January twenty-ninth, eighteen hundred and sixty-four, entitled an act extending the jurisdiction of the circuit court of the town of Danville, so as to insert "county" instead of "circuit" court.

SEPARATE ELECTION PRECINCTS.

Accomack—Court-house; Chingoteague; New Church; Corbin and Fletcher's; Mapp's, Guilford; Newstown; Onancock; Pungoteague.

Albemarle—Court-house; Lindsay's Turnout; Everettsville; Stony Point; Earleysville; Blackwell's; Free Union; Whitehall; Woodville; Batesville; Hillsborough; Crossroads; Covesville; Porter's; Warren; Wingfield's; Milton; Scottsville; Monticello House; Howardsville.

Alexandria—Five districts—Identical with magisterial districts.

Alleghany—Court-house; Robert Skeen's Hotel; John O. Taylor's; George Stull's; Clifton Forge; Jabez Johnston's; Griffith's Mill; Fork Run.

Amelia—At the same place as magisterial elections.

Amherst—New Glasgow; New Hope; Orouoco; Chestnut Grove; Folly; Temperance; Pedlar Mills; Elon; Court-house; Buffalo Springs.

Appomattox—Court-house; Union Academy; Wesley Chapel; Hamner's; Spout Spring; Oakville.

Augusta—Court-house; Waynesborough; Middlebrook; Spring Hill; Mt. Meridian; Greenesville; District No. 2, Staunton; Mt. Sidney; Stuart's Draft; Fishersville; Churchville; New Hope; Craigsville; Deerfield; Mt. Solon; Swoop's Mill; Midway; Newport.

Barbour—Court-house; Burner's; Nutter's; Bartlett's; Mitchell's; Yeager's; Glady Creek; Holtsberry's; Coal Precinct.

Bath—Court-house; Cedar Creek; Hamilton's; Cleek's Mill; Williamsville; Milton; Green Valley.

Berkeley—Court-house; Billingre's Hotel; Mill Creek; Hedgesville; Falling Waters; Robinson's Mill; Gerrardstown; Oak Grove; Glen Spring; Crossroads.

Boone—Court-house; Adkins' on Mud river; Adkins' on Big Coal; Lawrence's; Curtiss'; Daniel Laurel's; Thompson's Mill; Miller's.

Botetourt—Court house; Mountain Union; Carver's; Buchanan; Rocky Point Mills; Jackson; Junction Store; Dibrell's Spring; Amsterdam.

Braxton—Court-house; Triplett's; Rilney's; Cool's; John Crite's former Residence; Christian Moda's former Residence; Haymond's Mill; Cunningham's; Saulsberry; Stene-street; Jacob P. Conrad's.

Brooke—At same place as magisterial elections; Goodwill School-house.

Brunswick—Court-house; Benton Precinct; Trotty's Store; Oak Grove; Lucy's Store; Smoky Ordinary; Nicholson's Precinct.

Buckingham—Court-house; Stanton's Shop; New Store; Wright's; Curdsville; Allen's.

Cabell—Court-house; Guyandotte; Laidley's Store; Spurlock's; Doolittle's Mill; Barrett's Precinct; McComas'; Falls of Guyandotte; Killgore's Precinct; Peter Buffington's.

Campbell—Places the same as for magisterial elections.

Caroline—Court-house; Reedy Church; Oakley's; Needwood; Sparta; Pitts'; Port Royal; Sycamore; Golansville; Madison's.

Carroll—Court-house; Polly Quesenberry's; Thomas Quesenberry's; Laurel Fork; Kinney's; Easter's; Newman's; Sulphur Springs; Richard Haynes'; Nathaniel Haynes'.

Charles City—Court-house; Delarue's; Ladd's; Waddell's; Apperson's; Vaiden's.

Charlotte—Court-house; Keysville; Smith's Tavern; Clement's; Wyliesburg; Roby's Shop; Hawrey's Store; Matthews & Smith's Store.

Chesterfield—Court-house; Britton's Shop; Shell's Tavern; Manchester; Robinson's Store; Clover Hill.

Clarke—Court-house; Russell's Tavern; White Post; Millwood; Royston's Tavern; Collier's Toll-gate.

Craig—Court-house; Carper's Tavern; Walker's Store; Scott's Tavern; Martin Huffman's; George Sarver's.

Culpeper—Court-house; Rixyville; Colvin's; Stevensburg; Pottsville; Gathright's; Wellsborough; Griffinsburg.

Cumberland—Court-house; Tavern Precinct; Oak Forest; Irwin's.

Dinwiddie—Court-house; Billups'; Goodwynsville; Williams' Shop; Darvill's; Williams'; Sutherland's.

Doddridge—Court-house; Allen's; Bond's; Key's; Davis'.

Elizabeth City—Court-house; Liveley's Ordinary; Fox Hill.

Essex—Court-house; Occupacion; Lloyd's; Miller's; Bestland; Centre Cross.

Fairfax—Court-house; Crossroads; Arundel's; Sangster; Ross'; Dranesville; Ananale; West End; Accotink; Centreville; Falls Church; Fars; Bayless; Pulman's.

Fauquier—Court-house; Plains; Salem; White Ridge; Farrowsville; Orleans; Liberty; Morrisville; Paris; New Baltimore; Rectortown; Weaversville; Upperville.

Fayette—Court-house; Blake's; Gauley Bridge; Fleshman's; Lewis'; Keeney's; Terry's; Coleman's.

Fluvanna—Court-house; Howard's Store; Columbia; Morris' Store; Kent's Store; Haden's Store; Bashan and Snead's; Bledsoe's; Union Grove.

Franklin—Court-house; Allen's; Union Hall; Booth's Store; McVey's Tanyard; Helm's; Dickerson's; Kinsey's; Richland Grove; Bush's Store; Sydnorsville; Snow Creek; Aldridge's Store.

Frederick—Court-house; Engine-house; Gwinn's Tavern; Hoover's Tavern; Newtown; Middletown; Russell's; Anderson's; Brucetown; Swhier's; Cole's School-house; Pughtown.

Giles—At the same places as magisterial elections; Howe's Hotel.

Gilmer—Court-house; Jerkland; Burke's; Widow Stump's; De Kalb's; Peregrine Hays'; Knott's; Hewett's; Troy.

Goochland—Court-house; Little Store; Perkinsville; Smith's Shop; Mills'; Holland's; Poor's; Jennings'.

Gloucester—Places the same as for magisterial elections.

Greenbrier—Court-house; Blue Sulphur Springs; Lick Creek; Anthony's Creek; Spring Creek; Southside; Lewisburg; White Sulphur; Miller's; Irish Corner; Williamsburg; Frankfort.

Greene—Court-house; Ruckersville; Terill Shiflett's; McMullansville.

Greensville—Court-house; Ryland's Depot; Blunt's Mill; Poplar Mount.

Halifax—Court-house; Meadesville; Mount Carmel; Halifax Springs; High Hill; Hudson's; Garrett's Store; Whiteville; Republican Grove; Brooklyn.

Hampshire—Court-house; John Liller's; Miers'; Burlington; Taylor's; Doyles'; Thompson's; Lupton's; Kisner's; Lovett's; Mrs. Offutt's; Stump's; Fority; Sherrard's School-house; Hash's; Blair's; Arnold's; Piedmont.

Hancock—Court-house; Holliday's Cove; New Manchester; Aton's School-house.

Hanover—Court-house; Hughes'; Jones' Crossroads; Negrofoot; Dentonsville; Cold Harbor; Ashland.

Harrison—Court-house; Shinnston; Union Meeting-house; West Milford; Lumberport; Bridgeport; Davis'; Lynch's; Sardis; Swisher's Mills.

Henrico—Court-house; Kidd's; Sweeney's; Alley's; Lovingsteine's; Dickman's; Hughes'; Walkerton; Hungary.

Henry—Court-house; Rough and Ready; Irisburg; Oak Level; Leatherwood; Ridgway; Horse Pasture.

Highland—Monterey; Ruckmansville; Wiley's; Crab Bottom; Doe Hill; McDowell; Pullins' School house; Gwin's.

Jackson—Ripley; Click's; Jones'; Range's; California; Depue's; Three forks of Reedy; Trunamsville; Ravenswood; Squire Slaven's; Murrayville; Moor's Mill; McGrew's Mill.

James City—Court-house; Burnt Ordinary; York River.

Jefferson—Eight districts—Places the same as for magisterial elections.

Kanawha—Court-house; Fleetwood's; Richards'; Bradley Low's; Atkinson's Mill; Alizs'; Couts' Mouth; Dog Creek; Givens'; Malden; Fork Coal; Harper's; Gatewood's; Mouth Sandy; Brooks' Store.

King George—Court-house; Hampstead; Clifton; Shiloh.

King & Queen—Court-house; Clark's Store; Stevensville; Newtown; Centreville.

King William—Court-house; Plain Dealing; Aylett's; Lanesville.

Lancaster—Court-house; Litwalton; Kilmanock; White Stone.

Lewis—Court house; McLaughlin's Store; Jane Lew; Freeman's Creek; Skin Creek; Hall's Store; Leading Creek; Collins' Settlement.

Logan—Same places as for magisterial elections.

Loudoun—Court-house; Waterford; Lovetsville; Hillsborough; Waters'; Purcell's Store; Snickersville; Union; Middleburg; Mt. Gilead; Gum Spring; Whaley's; Goresville.

Louisa—Court-house; Free Union; Hopkins' Mill; Trevilian's; Bell's Crossroads; Walton's Tavern; Terrell's Store; Parrish's Store; Fredericksball; Bunpass' Turnout; Thompson's Crossroads; Isbell's Store; Hope's Tavern; Gentry's Store; Cosby's Tavern.

Lunenburg—Court-house; Brown's Store; Pleasant Grove; Knight and Oliver's Mill; Lochlomond; Bagley's Store; Jordan's Store.

Madison—Court-house; Stony Hill; Criglersville; Huffman's Mill; Graves' Mill; Rapidan Meeting house; Fleshman's Shop; Locust Dale.

Marion—Places the same as those for magisterial elections, and at Glover's Gap.

Marshall—Court-house; Pleasant Hill; Jones' Hotel; Bleak's School-house; Parsons' Precinct; Mouth of Fish Creek; Sand Hill; Crossroads; Smart's School house; Burley's; Terrill's School-house; Big Run; Fair View; Linn Camp.

Mason—Court-house; Berringe Precinct; Love Precinct; Barnett Precinct; West Columbia; Neaso Precinct; Eighteen Mile Precinct; Grigg's; Sixteen Mile Precinct; Thirteen Mile Precinct.

Matthews—Same places as for magisterial elections.

Mecklenburg—Court-house; Jones'; Edmundson's; Clarkesville; Recke's; Overby's; Wright's; Harwell's; Christiansville: Gillespie's.

Middlesex—Jamaica; Saludo; Sandy Bottom.

Monongalia—Court-house; Guseman's; Jones'; Osburn's; Ross'; Lefter's; Cassville; Cristman's; Laurel Point; Cox's; Moore's River; Tenant's; Dowall's; Warren.

Monroe—Court-house; Dickson's; Miller's Store; Rollingsburg; Mrs. Peck's; Red Sulphur; Haynes'; Centreville.

Montgomery—Court house; Guerrant's; Peterman's; Price's Forks; Keister's; Crumpacker's; Lafayette; Kent and McConkey's; Rough and Ready; Lovely Mount.

Morgan—Court-house; Lowe's; Baker's; Unger's; Hume's; Swann's; Miller's.

Nansemond—Court-house; Hargrove's Tavern; Harrison's Shop; Holyneck; Chuckatuck; Somerton; Darden's Store; Cypress Chapel.

Nelson—Fortune's; New Market; Faber's Mill; Greenfield; Massie's Mill; Roberts'.

New Kent—Court house; Barhamsville; Chandler's Store; Ratcliff's Tavern.

Nicholas—Court-house; Taylor's; Brown's; Neil's; Dunbar's; Nutter's; Sawyer's; Pierson's.

Norfolk City—Four Wards.

Norfolk County—Court-house; Glebe School-house; Sycamore's; Deep Creek; School-house, District No. 2; School-house in Providence; Pleasant Grove School-house; Butts' Road School-house.

Northampton—Court-house; Bay View; Franktown; Johnsontown; Capeville.

Northumberland—Court-house: Lottsburg; Burgess' Store; Wicomico.

Nottoway—Court-house; Jennings' Ordinary; Wilson and Jones'; Blackfare.

Orange—Court-house; Barboursville; Thomas' Smith's; Thomas Rhoade's; Locust Grove.

Page—Court house; Honeyville; Oakham; George Price's Mill; Springfield; Mohler's Mill; Rileysville; Prunty's Mill.

Patrick—Court-house; Robertson's; Aldridge's and Lee's; Penn's Store; Carter's Store; Hancock's; Elamsville; Slusher's; Conner's; Shilor's; Gates'; Mankin's.

Pendleton—Franklin; Harper's; Kiser's; Vint's; Cowyer's Mill; Mallow's; Seneca; Circleville.

Petersburg—Centre Ward; East Ward; South Ward; West Ward.

Pittsylvania—Court-house; Danville; Spring Garden; Whitmell; Cascade; Smith's; Beaver's; Riceville; Rorer's; Strail's Store; White's; Laurel Grove; Chalk Level; Mooman's.

Pleasants—Court-house; Spring Run; Sugar Creek; Pine Grove; Hale's Mill.

Pocahontas—Four districts—Places of election the same as for magistrates.

Powhatan—Court-house; Clarke's Mill; Macon; Sublett's.

Preston—Brandonville; Miller's; Burner's; Feather's; Summit School house; Germany; Graham's; Huddleson's; Kingwood; Martin's; Independence; Evansville; Nine's; Funk's.

Princess Anne—Court house; Kempsville; London Bridge; Capp's Shop; Creed's Bridge; Blackwater.

Prince Edward—Court-house; Marble Hill; Spring Creek; Prospect; Farmville; Sandy River.

Prince George—Court-house; City Point; Lilley's School-house; Tuttle's Precinct; Harrison's Store; Templeton.

Prince William—Dumfries; Cole's; Occoquan; Reeve's; Brentsville; Kincheloe's; Haymarket; Ludley.

Pulaski—Court-house; Brown's; Galbreath's; Raper's; Thorn Spring Camp.

Putnam—Court-house; Bailey's; Pocataico; Alexander's; Red House; Jones'; Hurricane Bridge; Wheeler's; Buffalo; Eighteen Mile Precinct.

Raleigh—Same places as magisterial elections.

Randolph—Court-house; Pennington's; Minear's; Tayler's; Kemp's; Lee.

Rappahannock—Washington; Sperryville; Yates'; Amissville; Catherine Deatheridge.

Richmond City—Jefferson Ward; Madison Ward; Monroe Ward.

Richmond County—Court house; Stony Hill; Tavern House; Farnham Church; Lyell's Store.

Ritchie—Harrisville; Skelton's; Leedan's; Ireland's; Deems'; Rawson's; Tebbs', Murphy's.

Roanoke—Court house; Big Lick; Cave Spring; Barnett's.

Rockbridge—Court-house; Brownsburg; Fairfield; Natural Bridge; Collierstown; Kerr's Creek; Trevey's; Hamilton's School-house; Paxton's School house; Wilson's Shop; Broad Creek; Goshen.

Rockingham—Harrisonburg; Keezletown; McGaheysville; Conrad's Store; Spartapolis; Henton's Mills; Gordon's Store; Bowman's Mill; Timberville; Menonite School-house; Bridgewater; Ottobine; Wittig's Store; Sprinkle's Store; Taliaferro's Store; Port Republic; Mount Crawford; Samuel Coots'.

Russell—Court-house; Grizle's; Pound; Holly Creek; Guest's Mountain; Castlewood's;

Fugate's; Hanson's; Aston's Store; Cook's Mills; Dorton's; Baylor's Store; Gibson's; Hendrick's Store.

Scott—Court-house; Wineger's; Hart's; Smith's; Puilleng's; Nickelsville; Alley's; Osborne's Ford; Stony Creek; Peters'; Rye Cove; Carter's; Neil's; Roller's.

Shenandoah—Court-house; Strasburg; Crossroads Meeting-house; Conner's Church; Town Hall; Keller's School-house; Edinburg; Columbia Furnace; Mount Jackson; Crossroads School-house; New Market; Forrestville.

Smyth—Court-house; Broad Ford; Hays'; Sanders'; St. Clair's Bottom; Burton's Store; Ashlin's; Atkins'.

Spotsylvania—Court house; Fredericksburg; Mount Pleasant; Andrews'; Chancellor's.

Stafford—Court-house; White Oak; Master's; Tackett's Mill; Falmouth; Coakley's; Harwood's; Acquia.

Southampton—Court-house; Drewrysville; Crosskeys; Joyner's; Murfee's; Black Creek Church; Berlin; Faison's Store.

Surry—Four districts—At the same places as for election of magistrates.

Sussex—Court-house; Comann's Mill; Henry; Stony Creek; Newville; Owen's Store.

Taylor—Court-house; Mahaney; Reed's; Claysville; Knottsville; Haymond's; Fetterman; Grafton.

Tazewell—Court-house; Repass; Tiffany's; Mouth of Slate; Gibson's; Crabtree's; Litzeville; Liberty Hill; Tugg.

Tyler—Court-house; Centreville; David John's; Hammond's; Underwood's; Dancer's; Sistersville; Pleasant Mills.

Upshur—Court-house; Reedy Mills; Simpson's Mill; Posty; Marples; Marshall's; Chesney's.

Warren—Court-house; Boyd's Mill; Bentonville; Leary's School-house; Cedarville; Howellsville.

Warwick—Three precincts—The same as for election of magistrates.

Washington—Court-house; Clark's; Davis'; Waterman's; Merchant's; Gobble's; Mills'; Worley's; Williams'; Morell's; Fullen's School-house; Clark's; Kelly's School house; Delusko Mills; Ons'; Miller's; Good Hope; Green Spring.

Wayne—William Crum's. (No other returned.)

Westmoreland—Court-house; Hague; Warrensville; Oak Grove.

Wetzel—Court-house; Forks of Proctor; Knob Fork; Church's; Cohorn's; Ice's; Willey's School-house.

Williamsburg—Court-house.

Wirt—Court-house; Foster's; Petty's.

Wood—Precincts at the same places as election for magistrates.

Wyoming—Court-house; Cad's; Rhineheart's; McKinney's; Bailey's; Lester's.

Wythe—Eight districts—Precincts at same places as for election of magistrates.

York—Three districts—Precincts at the same places as for election of magistrates

TABLE

Showing the Times for the Commencement of the Regular Terms of each Circuit, County and Corporation Court.

Counties and corporations.	Circuit courts. When terms commence.	County and corporation courts. Monthly terms.	County and corporation courts. Quarterly terms.
	Circuits.		
Accomack,	5. 1st Monday in May and 1st day of November,	Last Monday,	March, May, August, Novem.
Albemarle,	10. 2d Monday in May and Oct.	First Monday,	Do. June, do. do.
Alexandria,	9. 3d Monday in May and 2d Monday in November,	Fourth Monday,	Feb'y, May, do. do.
Alleghany,	14. 13th April and September.	Third Monday,	March, June, do. do.
Amelia,	2. 25th April and 20th Oct'r,	Fourth Thursday,	Do. May, do. do.
Amherst,	10. 22d March and August,	Third Monday,	Do. June, do. do.
Appomattox,	3. 21st April and September,	Thursday after 1st Monday,	Do. May, do. do.
Augusta,	11. 1st June and November,	Fourth Monday,	Do. do do. Octo'r.
Barbour,	21. 8th May and October,	First Monday,	Do. June, do. Novem.
Bath,	11. 15th May and October,	Second Monday,	Do. do. do do.
Bedford,	4. 25th April and September,	Fourth Monday,	Feb'y, May, July, do.
Berkeley,	13. 24th April and September,	Second Monday,	March, June, August, do.
Boone,	15. 2d Monday after 4th Monday in April and Sep'r,	Wednesday after 2d Monday,	Do. do. do. do.
Botetourt,	14. 1st April and September,	Second Monday,	Do. do. do. do.
Braxton,	19. 27th April and September,	First Tuesday,	Do. do. do. do.
Brooke,	20. 18th March and August,	Last Monday,	Feb'y, May, July, do.
Brunswick,	2. 27th March and 2d Oct'r,	Fourth Monday,	March, do. August, do.
Buckingham,	3. 5th April and September,	Second Monday,	Do. do. do. do.
Cabell,	18. 27th March and August,	Fourth Monday,	Do. June, do. do.
Calhoun,	19. 19th April and September,	First Tuesday after 4th Monday,	Do. do. do. do.
Campbell,	3. 18th May and October,	Second Monday,	Do. do. do. do.
Caroline,	8. 1st March and 18th Sept'r,	Second Monday,	Feb'y, May, do. do.
Carroll,	16. Monday before last Monday in March and August,	First Monday,	March, June, do. do.
Charles City,	6. 18th May and November,	Third Thursday,	Do. May, do. do.
Charlotte,	3. 25th March and August,	First Monday,	Do. June, do. do.
Chesterfield,	2. 7th May and 12th Nov'r,	Second Monday,	Do. do. do. do.
Clarke,	13. 12th May and October,	Second Monday in June and 4th in other months,	Feb'y, May, July, Octo'r.
Clay,	15. 1st April and September,	Second Monday,	March, June, August, Novem.
Craig,	14. 15th March and August,	Fourth Monday,	Do. do. do. do.
Culpeper,	10. 1st Monday June and Nov.	Third Monday,	Do. May, do. do.
Cumberland,	3. 5th March and August,	Fourth Monday.	Feb'y, do. July, Octo'r.
Danville,	3. 22d March and August,	Thursday after 2d Monday,	March, June, August, Novem.
Dinwiddie,	2. 20th March and 26th Sept.	Third Monday,	Do. May, do. do
Doddridge,	19. 22d May and October,	Fourth Monday,	Do June, do. do.
Elizabeth City,	6. 15th March and September,	Fourth Thursday,	Do. May, do. do.
Essex,	8. 25th April and 12th Nov'r,	Third Monday,	Do. do. do. do.
Fairfax,	9. 1st Monday June and Nov.	Third Monday,	Do. June, do. do.
Fauquier,	9. Tuesday after 1st Monday in April and September,	Fourth Monday,	Do. May, do. do.
Fayette,	15. 7th June and November,	Thursday after 2d Tuesday,	Do. June, do. do.
Floyd,	16. 1st Monday April and Sept.	Thursday after 3d Monday,	Do. do. do. do.
Fluvanna,	10. 10th April and September,	Fourth Monday,	Do. May, do. do.
Franklin,	4. 15th May and October,	First Monday,	Do. June, do. do.
Frederick,	13. 10th June and November,	Monday before 1st Tuesday,	Do. do. do. do.
Fredericksburg,	— — —	Second Thursday,	Do. do. Octo'r, Decem.
Giles,	15. 20th May and October,	Second Monday,	Do. do. August, Novem.
Gilmer,	19. 19th April and September,	Tuesday after 3d Monday,	Feb'y, do. do. do.
Gloucester,	6. 13th April and October,	First Monday,	March, May, do. do.
Goochland,	10. 1st April and September,	Third Monday,	Do. do. do. do.
Grayson,	16. 4th Monday April and Sept.	Fourth Monday,	Feb'y, do. July, do.
Greenbrier,	14. 1st May and October,	Fourth Monday,	March, June, August, do.
Greene,	10. 3d Monday June and Nov.	Wednesday after 2d Monday,	Do. do. do. do.
Greenesville,	1. 28th April and 2d Nov'r,	First Monday,	Do. May, do. Octo'r.

Counties and corporations.	Circuit courts. When terms commence.	County and corporation courts. Monthly terms.	County and corporation courts. Quarterly terms.
	Circuits		
Halifax,	3. 1st May and October,	Fourth Monday,	March, June, Aug't, Novem.
Hampshire,	13. 1st April and September,	Fourth Monday,	Do. do. do. do.
Hancock,	20. 10th March and August,	Tuesday after 2d Monday,	Jan'y, April, June, October.
Hanover,	8. 10th March and 26th Sept.	Fourth Tuesday,	Feb'y, April, July, Novem'r.
Harrison,	21. 15th April and September,	First Monday,	March, June, August, do.
Hardy,	12. 20th April and September,	Monday before 1st Tuesday,	Do. do. do. do
Henrico,	6. 23d April and 18th October,	First Monday,	Do. May, do. do.
Henry,	4. 1st April and September,	Second Monday,	Do. June, do. do.
Highland,	12. 2d May and October,	Thursday after 3d Monday,	Do. May, do. Octo'r.
Isle of Wight,	1. 16th May and 18th October,	First Monday,	Do. June, do. Novem.
Jackson,	18 2d May and October,	Second Monday,	Feb'y, do. do. do.
James City and Williamsburg,	6. 25th May and November,	Second Monday,	March, do. do. Octo'r.
Jefferson,	13. 20th May and October,	Second Monday in June and October, 3d in other months,	Do. do. do. do.
Kanawha,	18. 27th May and October.	Third Monday,	Feb'y, do. do. Novem.
King George,	8. 23d March and 12th Sept.	First Thursday,	March, do. do. do.
King & Queen,	8. 2d May and 19th Nov'r,	First Thursday,	Do. May, do. do.
King William,	8 13th May and 25th Nov'r,	Fourth Monday,	Do. do. do. do.
Lancaster,	8. 15th April and 2d Nov'r,	Third Monday,	Do. do. do. do.
Lee,	17. 2d Monday after 4th Monday in April and Sept'r,	– –	Do. June, do. do.
Lewis,	19. 8th May and October,	Second Monday,	April, do. do. Septem.
Logan,	15. 1st Monday after 4th Monday in April and Sept'r,	Third Monday,	March, do. do. Novem.
Loudoun,	9. 4th Monday in April and 3d Monday in October,	Second Monday,	Do. do. do. do.
Louisa,	10. 20th April and September,	Second Monday,	Do. do. do. do.
Lunenburg,	2. 13th April and 8th Oct'r,	Second Monday,	Do. May, do. do.
Lynchburg,	3. 3d June and November,	First Monday,	Do. June, do. Octo'r.
Madison,	10. 1st Monday Mar. and Aug.	Fourth Thursday,	Feb'y. do. do. do.
Marion,	21. 10th June and November,	First Monday,	March, do. do. Novem.
Marshall,	20. 1st May and October,	Third Monday,	Do do. do. do.
Matthews,	6. 6th April and September,	Second Monday,	Do. May, do. do.
Mason,	18. 18th April and September,	First Monday,	Feb'y, June, do. do.
Mecklenburg,	2. 2d April and 15th Sept'r,	Third Monday,	Do. May, do. do.
Mercer.	15. 27th May and October,	Thursday after 2d Monday,	March, June, do. do.
McDowell.	17 1st Monday Mar. and Aug.	Second Monday,	Do. do. do. do.
Middlesex,	6. 1st April and October,	Fourth Wednesday,	Do. May, do. do.
Monongalia,	20. 1st April and September,	Fourth Monday,	Do. June, do. do.
Monroe,	14. 12th May and October,	Third Monday,	Do. do. do. do.
Montgomery,	16 2d Monday in Ap'l and Sep.	First Monday,	Do. do. do. do.
Morgan,	13 6th May and October,	Fourth Monday,	Do. do. Sept. do.
Nansemond,	15. 16th April and 12th Oct'r,	Second Monday,	Do. do. Aug. do.
Nelson,	10. 27th April and September,	Fourth Monday,	Feb'y, May, July, do.
New Kent,	6. 10th May and November,	Second Thursday,	March, do. Aug. do.
Nicholas,	15. 6th April and September,	Monday before 2d Tuesday,	Do. June, do. do.
Norfolk city,	1. 1st June and 15th Nov'r,	Fourth Monday,	Feb'y, April, July, October.
Norfolk county,	1. 1st April and 28th Sept'r,	Third Monday,	March, June, Aug't, Novem'r.
Northampton,	5. 3d Monday in Ap'l and Sep.	Second Monday,	Do. do. Sept. do.
Northumberland,	8. 9th April and 28th Oct'r,	Second Monday,	Do. May, Aug. do.
Nottoway,	2. 20th April and 15th Oct'r,	First Thursday,	Do. do. do. do.
Ohio,	20. 10th May and October,	First Monday,	Feb'y, July, Sept'r, Decem
Orange,	10. 1st May and October,	Fourth Monday,	March, May, Aug't, Novem'r.
Page,	12. 11th April and September,	Fourth Monday,	Feb'y, do. July, do.
Patrick,	4. 12th April and September,	Fourth Monday,	Do. do. do. do.
Pendleton,	12. 27th April and September,	Thursday after 1st Tuesday,	March, June, Sept'r, do.
Petersburg,	2. 22d May, 16th November,	Third Thursday,	Do. do. do. Decem.
Pittsylvania,	4. 28th May and October,	Third Monday,	Do. do. August, Novem.
Pleasants,	19. 30th May and October,	Thursday after 2d Monday,	Feb'y, May, July, October.
Pocahontas,	14. 23d April and September,	First Tuesday,	March, June, Aug't, Novem.
Powhatan,	2. 2d May and 27th October,	First Wednesday,	Do. do. do. Octo'r.
Preston,	21. 18th March and August,	Second Monday,	Feb'y, May, July, November.
Princess Anne,	1. 25th May and 22d Sept'r,	First Monday,	March, June, Aug. do.
Prince Edward,	3. 15th March and August.	Third Monday,	Feb'y, May, July. do.
Prince George,	2. 17th May and 12th Nov'r,	Second Thursday,	March, do. Aug't, do.
Prince William,	9. 2d Monday in May and Oct.	First Monday,	Do. June, do. do.
Pulaski,	16 3d Monday April and Sep	Thursday after 1st Monday,	Do. do. do. do.
Putnam,	18. 8th April and September,	Fourth Monday,	Do. do. do. do.
Raleigh,	15. 3d Monday April and Sep.	First Monday,	Do. do. do. do.
Randolph,	21. 26th May and October,	Fourth Monday,	Do. do. do. do.

Counties and corporations.	Circuit courts. When terms commence.	County and corporation courts. Monthly terms.	County and corporation courts. Quarterly terms.
	Circuits.		
Rappahannock,	9. 3d Monday in March and 1st Monday in October,	Second Monday,	March, May, August, Novem.
Richmond city,	7. 1st May and November,	Second Monday,	Jan'y, April, July, October.
Richmond co.	8. 3d April and 23d October,	First Monday,	March, May, August, Novem.
Ritchie,	19. 15th April and September,	Tuesday after 1st Monday,	Feb'y, June, do. do.
Roane,	18. 17th May and October,	First Monday,	Jan'y, April, July, Septem.
Roanoke,	14. 22d March and August,	Third Monday,	March June, Aug't, Novem.
Rockbridge,	11. 12th April and September,	Monday before 1st Tuesday,	Do. do. do. do.
Rockingham,	12. 11th May and October,	Third Monday,	Feb'y, May, do. do.
Russell,	17. 4th Monday April and Sep.	Tuesday after 1st Monday,	March, June, do. do.
Scott,	17. 3d Monday after 4th Monday April and September,	Tuesday after 2d Monday,	Do. do. do. do.
Shenandoah,	19. 30th March and August,	Monday before 2d Tuesday,	Do. do. do. do,
Smyth,	17. 1st Monday April and Sep.	Tuesday after 1st Monday,	Do. do. do. do.
Southampton,	1. 2d May and 7th October,	Third Monday,	Do. do. do. do.
Spotsylvania,	8. 20th May and 6th October,	First Monday,	Do. do. do. do.
Stafford,	9. 4th Monday Mar. and Sept.	Third Wednesday,	Do. do. do. do.
Staunton,	– – –	Wednesday after 1st Monday,	Feb'y, May, July, October.
Surry,	1. 10th May and 25th Oct'r,	Fourth Monday,	March, do. August, Novem.
Sussex,	1. 24th April and 29th Oct'r,	First Thursday,	Do. do. do. Octo'r.
Taylor,	21. 4th March and August,	Fourth Monday,	Do. June, do. Novem.
Tazewell,	17. Last Monday Mar. and Aug.	Wednesday after 1st Monday,	Feb'y, May, July, October.
Tucker,	21. 22d May and October,	Third Monday;	March, June, Aug't, Novem.
Tyler,	20. 22d April and September,	Second Monday,	Do. do. do. do
Upshur,	21. 4th April and September,	Third Monday,	Do. do. do. do.
Warren,	12. 25th March and August.	Third Monday.	Do. May, do. do.
Warwick,	6. 21st March and September,	Second Monday,	Do. June, do. Decem.
Washington,	17. 2d Monday April and Sep.	Fourth Monday,	Do. do. do. Novem.
Wayne,	18. 20th March and August,	Tuesday after 1st Monday,	Do. do. do. do.
Webster,	15. 14th April and September,	Fourth Tuesday,	Do. do. do. do.
Westmoreland,	8. 28th March and 18th Oct'r,	Fourth Monday,	April, May, do. do.
Wetzel,	20. 12th April and September,	Tuesday after 1st Monday,	Feb'y, do. July, October.
Williamsburg,	6. 25th May and November,	Fourth Monday,	March, June, Aug't, Novem.
Winchester,	– – –	First Saturday,	Do. May. do. do.
Wirt,	19. 3d April and September,	Tuesday after 4th Monday,	Feb'y, June, do. do.
Wise,	17. 1st Monday after 4th Monday in April and Sept'r,	Fourth Monday,	March, do. do. do.
Wood,	19. 5th June and November,	Third Monday.	Feb'y, do. do. do.
Wyoming,	15 4th Monday April and Sep.	Friday after 3d Monday,	March, do. do. do.
Wythe,	16. 1st Monday May and Oct'r,	Second Monday,	Do. do. do. do.
York.	6. 26th March and September.	Third Monday,	Do May. do. Octo'r.

RECEIPTS.

1862.			
Oct.	1,	To balance, per last annual report,	434,778 96
		To receipts in October 1862,	2,576,089 71
Nov.		To do. in November 1862,	1,092,624 27
Dec.		To do. in December 1862,	2,355,626 82
			$ 6,459,119 76
1863.			
Jan.	1,	To balance brought down,	1,910,236 74
		To receipts in January 1863,	3,262,429 27
Feb.		To do. in February 1863,	567,734 23
March		To do. in March 1863,	778,340 27
			$ 6,518,740 51
April	1,	To balance brought down,	606,139 84
		To receipts in April 1863,	435,234 35
May		To do. in May 1863,	1,273,203 05
June		To do. in June 1863,	1,668,108 23
			$ 3,982,685 47
July	1,	To balance brought down,	2,287,223 35
		To receipts in July 1863,	959,846 71
Aug.		To do. in August 1863,	580,616 68
Sept.		To do. in September 1863,	825,141 92
			$ 4,652,828 66
Oct.	1,	To balance against the treasurer this day, exclusive of the funds under the direction of the second auditor,	$1,377,868 95

DISBURSEMENTS.

By amount of warrants paid in October 1862,	- -	2,739,186 65
By do. do. in November 1862,	- -	700,911 93
By do. do. in December 1862,	- -	1,108,784 44
Balance December 1862,	- -	1,910,236 74
		$ 6,459,119 76
By amount of warrants paid in January 1863,	- -	4,950,341 49
By do. do. in February 1863,	- -	708,168 04
By do. do. in March 1863,	- -	254,091 14
Balance March 1863,	- -	606,139 84
		$ 6,518,740 51
By amount of warrants paid in April 1863,	- -	382,775 37
By do. do. in May 1863,	- -	130,501 77
By do. do. in June 1863,	- -	1,182,184 98
Balance June 1863,	- -	2,287,223 35
		$ 3,982,685 47
By amount of warrants paid in July 1863,	- -	3,051,739 21
By do. do. in August 1863,	- -	77,717 33
By do. do. in September 1863,	- -	145,503 17
Balance September 1863,	- -	1,377,868 95
		$ 4,652,828 66

Total amount of warrants issued by the auditor from the 1st October 1862 to the 30th September 1863, inclusive, - - -				15,434,770 25
Add warrants Nos.	5073,	766 00	Issued prior to the 1st Oct. 1862, and paid since that day, -	
	6625,	520 99		
	6638,	21 00		
	6687,	25 00		
	6752,	15 96		737 61
	6791,	100 00		
	6847,	28 00		
	6559,	19 00		
				15,435,507 86
Deduct warrants Nos.	2907,	25 00	Issued prior to the 1st Oct. 1863, and unpaid on the morning of that day, - -	
	5405,	108 80		
	5450,	131 04		
	5576,	75 00		
	5579,	2,678 05		3,602 34
	5580,	515 95		
	5581,	68 50		
Paid by the treasurer in the fiscal year 1862–3,				$15,431,905 52

Auditor's Office, October 1863.

INDEX.

www.ingramcontent.com/pod-product-compliance
Lightning Source LLC
Chambersburg PA
CBHW020545270326
41927CB00006B/731
* 9 7 8 3 3 3 7 8 1 1 0 1 3 *